W9-BMT-847

THE WORLD BETWEEN TWO COVERS

The World Between Two Covers

Reading the Globe

ANN MORGAN

LIVERIGHT PUBLISHING CORPORATION
A Division of W. W. Norton & Company
New York • *London*

For Steve, who was there every step of the way

Reading is a solitary act, but one that
demands connection to the world.

(*The Yellow-Lighted Bookshop: A Memoir, A History*
BY LEWIS BUZBEE)

You would think differently if this land was
your land and if these people were your people.

(*The Corsair*
BY ABULAZIZ AL MAHMOUD,
TRANSLATED FROM THE ARABIC
BY AMIRA NOWAIRA)

Contents

1

Deciding to travel

the impulse to read the world

As you drive up the M11 in Cambridgeshire, a junction or two before the motorway fizzles out into the A14, a view opens up to the right of the car. Across the flat fields, you see an expanse of rooftops glistening, and amid them a dark, rectangular tower reaching for the sky. You might not be able to make it out from the motorway with the lorries rattling past, but if you take a detour and drive along Cambridge's West Road, the building may well start to look strangely familiar, even if you've never seen it before. Looming above you, the brown-brick giant bears more than a passing resemblance to the red K2 telephone box that its creator, architect Giles Gilbert Scott, also designed. To my mind, though, this tower has another doppelgänger: with its rectangular windows at the top and blind, enclosed sides, it seems to recall the 1960s police box that stamped itself on British popular culture as the Tardis in *Doctor Who* nearly thirty years after this building welcomed the first visitors through its doors. The anachronistic parallel with the Time Lord's vehicle is oddly fitting, because in many ways that's what this strange creation, with its flanking courtyards and cluster of later wings, really is: a time machine. Step inside and you can travel almost anywhere in the world and back as far as 3,000 years.

Throughout my time as an undergraduate student in Cambridge, the University Library dominated not just the skyline but also my thoughts. Repository of priceless marvels – sketchbooks from Darwin's voyage on the *Beagle*, Newton's papers, ancient Chinese oracle bones, the astonishing Hebrew Genizah Collection, illuminated manuscripts, and some 4,700 fifteenth-century books produced during the first fifty years of printing – it seemed a magical, almost mythical place. Glancing through the revolving doors as I wobbled past on my bicycle, scarfed up against the fenland wind, was like peering through a portal into another world, a Narnia of reading.

The UL didn't just contain stories; it produced them too. There were tales of people camping out on obscure floors of the North Front overnight, as well as rumours of intrepid third-years having sex in obscure corners of the South Wing. People said that the library was so efficient that Oxford professors would forsake the dreaming spires to come and read there, sometimes in disguise. And then, of course, there was the omnivisible, seventeen-storey tower – 'this magnificent erection', as Neville Chamberlain is said to have dubbed it – which, as far as any hormone-riddled undergraduate could see, just had to be stuffed chock-full of outrageous Victorian porn deemed too extreme by the building's soberly dressed guardians to be made openly available.

Whether or not these stories were true hardly mattered. The place seemed to demand them. It was as though the books on the shelves got together after hours and spawned a new generation of tales, as if the library were so packed with plot that it couldn't help but spill over and dribble out of the doors in streams of rumour, speculation and intrigue.

The stories were only the half of it. A number of the authors of the volumes contained in the library had been known to put in an appearance now and then, popping up between the book stacks to the delight and occasional terror of awestruck undergraduates. You might bump into Robert Macfarlane in the Map Room or see Helen Oyeyemi taking a break from her next novel in the Tea Room. Ali Smith could pass you in the entrance hall on her way to talk to the creative writing society and Patricia Duncker could appear at any moment from behind an apocryphal early Bible translation, perhaps plotting another adventure for her elusive Germanist. I'll never forget the day an English student in the year above me arrived in the college bar to announce, with a

2

tremor in his voice, that he had spent the afternoon in the UL working at the same table as – whisper it – Germaine Greer.

For me, however, the single most striking thing about the library was not its extraordinary contents or the people who frequented it, but the fact that it was growing before my eyes. As one of six legal deposit libraries (or copyright libraries, as they used to be known before the Legal Deposit Libraries Act 2003 extended their remit to include electronic publications and other non-print material), the UL keeps a copy of each edition published in the UK and Ireland. For ever. That means that, on an average day, around 500 books and 500 journal issues arrive and have to be found room for. Each year, nearly two miles of bookshelves are added to the more than 100 miles' worth already contained in the library in an effort to accommodate a collection that is growing at a rate of a million publications every eight to ten years. As a result, the UL has little choice but to grow too.

To my eighteen-year-old self, the idea of a perpetually growing library was enthralling, marvellous and faintly monstrous. There was a touch of the grotesque about it, as though a Roald Dahl book and a Kafka novel had been left too close to each other on one of the tables. I loved it, but it also made me afraid. I imagined a day when the UL sprawled to such an extent that its furthest reaches butted up against the extremes of the other copyright libraries – the Bodleian to the west and the British Library to the south. Would we all live among the bookshelves, I wondered, weaving roads, hospitals, schools and other amenities in as best we could? I pictured my street at home in north London overrun with shelves of books; my mother trying to reverse her car out of the driveway around a stack of rare Chinese translations. I wasn't convinced it could work.

When I unravelled the implications of the UL's growth for my own career as a literature student, things didn't look too promising either. Given 500 new British and Irish books to contend with every day (I reckoned I could probably let myself off the journals), my chances of keeping pace with publication rates looked pretty slim, and that was without factoring in the roughly eight million books already tucked snugly within the library's walls. Even just scanning the titles of all the new works that appeared every day would be a mammoth task, let alone having to hunt them down through the facility's labyrinthine vaults and passages. And every minute – well, every 2.88 minutes, to be exact, given the number of texts arriving each day – I was falling further and further behind: another book was being added to the stacks behind the forbidding brown façade, another volume interposed between me and omnilexience. The awful truth hit me: I was never going to read every-thing in the UL. It was an impossible task. Even if I spent every hour of every day of my three years in Cambridge there – even if I cancelled my future, devoted my whole life to the project, and became a creature from the far reaches of the South Front, another legend to add to the UL's mythology – I would never manage it. The whole enterprise was doomed before it had even begun. I might as well give up and go home.

So hopeless did the prospect of trying to get to grips with the contents of the UL seem that, I'm ashamed to say, for the whole of my first year in Cambridge I didn't cross its threshold once. I preferred to stick to the more manageable environs of my college and faculty librar-ies – places in which I felt I might have a chance of making a dent in at least a wall or two of books, institutions where tracking down a title didn't involve walking half a mile and scribbling catalogue numbers of more than a dozen characters. Giles Gilbert Scott's tower loomed at me as I scurried about the city, raised like a warning finger, reminding me at odd moments that I was on a fool's errand, that I would never succeed in knowing it all. But for the most part, I put it out of my mind. The books on my reading lists cropped up regularly enough in Heffers and Waterstones and in the faculty and college collections and when they didn't – well, what was a girl to do?

It wasn't until my second year, when I was looking for some outland-ish critics to pick a fight with over Thomas Hardy, that I ventured through the doors and up into the great active silence beyond. That autumn, I discovered Cambridge and reading anew, huddled cosily at

4

a table on the second floor of the North Wing, in the rusty glow of shelving lights on timers that every so often would click off and have to be reset by turning a dial on the end of one of the bookcases. I sat there, engrossed, as the evenings drew in and the November wind chased another batch of freshers on bicycles along the road outside.

*

Eleven years later, when I first started thinking about reading the world, that same old UL paralysis returned to haunt me. I was roughly halfway through a project that involved me spending 2011 reading books by women when a blogger from a website called 'Commonwealth Cartographies' stopped by my website to add his two penn'orth – or two cents, to be more precise, he being American. He had a book to recommend by an Australian writer: Tim Winton's *Cloudstreet*.

Restraining my inner pedant from pointing out that my blog's name was 'A Year of Reading Women' – which, in the great, grand Ronseal tradition of names, meant that I was spending a year reading only women writers and that there was no point recommending books by men, sheep, goats or any other sentient beings, as I wouldn't be able to read them for at least another six months – by which stage I'd more than likely be up to my eyeballs in a backlog of recommendations from friends, regular visitors and people who actually bothered to read the name of my blog – I wrote an enthusiastic response saying that I would add the title to my list for the following year.

I expected that would be that. Commonwealth Cartographies, I thought, would go jogging off into the virtual sunset, leaving me to tend my reviews of Murdoch, Moran and Delafield in peace.

Not so. Within a few days he was back. Was I going to do another blog next year? He asked because he was anxious to be privy to my love of *Cloudstreet* as, at the risk of sounding presumptuous, he couldn't imagine anyone not liking it.

I was somewhat taken aback. Who was this person trampling all over my delicately cultivated comments section with his great, male doorstoppers? And what was this book that he seemed to like so much anyway? If it was so good, how come I had never heard of it before?

I kept my reply friendly but non-committal. No, I hadn't thought as far as next year, I wrote, but if I were going to continue, the new blog would have to have some kind of angle. Not for me the chance choices of the casual book blogger. I needed a goal.

The next day, the unusually persistent commenter, or Jason Cooper as I later came to know him, returned with a concept designed around the idea of my reading *Cloudstreet*. What about tackling books from different countries? he suggested. Around the world in 365 days?

There were actually 366 days in the upcoming year, it being of the leap variety, but I didn't bother to point this out, so amused was I by the suggestion. What sort of a philistine did Cooper take me for? Did he seriously think that I didn't already read lots of books from around the world?

Why, my year of reading women had already featured a whole load of them. There were books by writers from the US, and South Africa, and India . . . and the US . . . Huh.

I glanced up at my bookshelves, the proud record of more than twenty years of reading, and found a host of British and North American greats staring down at me: the Hardys and the Austens, the Orwells and the Greenes, the Steinbecks, Highsmiths, Hellers, Christies, Tremains, McEwans, Fieldings (both of them), Smiths (hundreds of them) and Shields. They were great friends, all of them, and I loved them dearly, but now that I came to think about it weren't they all a little, well, Western?

Worse, apart from a dog-eared copy of *Madame Bovary* and a jumbled assortment of Freuds picked up during a student book-buying binge and barely touched since, there seemed to be nothing at all in translation. And not because I had been reading books in their original languages, I hasten to add.

No. I had barely touched a work by a foreign-language author in years. My literary diet consisted largely of highly processed British and

American staples, most of which had to have been sampled by at least two major media outlets and seasoned with an online discount or packaged up in a flashy deal to tempt me to pick them up. I was comparable to one of those people who order chips in Chinese restaurants. Or pack teabags for a weekend away on the Isle of Wight. I was the person who preferred to take a mini-break in Milton Keynes to making the trip across the Channel for fear of squat toilets and menus I didn't understand. The awful truth dawned: I was a literary xenophobe.

Something had to be done. As far as I could see, there was only one course of action. I would have to prescribe myself an intensive course of world literature and spend 2012 trying to read a book from every country in the world. I would set out to devour a book-length prose narrative – written or translated into English – from each state during those twelve months, aiming largely for contemporary novels, story collections or memoirs, but leaving the door open for extraordinary blasts from the past here and there. Part-penance, part-prophylactic, this undertaking would, I hoped, atone for my years of literary insularity and inoculate me against the narrowness of mind that such a restricted diet of reading matter must have predisposed me towards. It would be the corrective treatment that my stunted and anaemic reading needed. (When I declared this to my now-husband Steve, he looked far from convinced that it was the treatment our relationship needed, but, having witnessed me getting embroiled in various bonkers projects over the years, he knew better than to object; instead he threw himself into coming up with ideas for photographs to illustrate the progress of the project on the blog. He was helped, perhaps, by my Christmas gift to him of a PlayStation as a sort of advance apology for the fact that I was likely to be incommunicado for much of the coming year.)

The die was cast, but there was a problem: I didn't know where to start. The world has an awful lot of books in it – 500,000 English-language volumes were published in 2009 alone, according to bibliographic monitor Nielsen Book – and I had no way of knowing what to choose. The sea of titles I could access in English, the language in which more than a quarter of the world's books are currently published, was as good as limitless. And, unlike the Cambridge UL, I didn't have the creaky old Newton computer catalogue to help me narrow down books to subject areas and genres that might appeal. I really was on my own.

As the full implications of what the quest entailed hit me, it seemed for a while that my teenage nightmare vision had come true after all. Without my realising it, I had been living in a global library all along, hemmed in by walls of unknowable books. It was as though someone had flicked a switch to reveal miles and miles of dusty shelves stretching off in all directions where I had blithely assumed walls to be. It was exciting and tempting, but it was daunting too. Having spent my adult life reading books by authors who wrote almost exclusively in my mother tongue, I was painfully aware that I was ill equipped to navigate this newly revealed terrain. I had no way of knowing what I should read or where to find it and there were more international books on offer than I could hope to consume in a lifetime of lifetimes. Amid such a bewildering welter of riches, mediocrity and no doubt downright stinkers, it seemed impossible – absurd, even – to pick out and make a start on one volume. How could I do it when, with every page I turned, I would be shutting the door on reading another possibly more marvellous work?

Such anxiety is a common theme among those contemplating taking on the world's stories. Since Goethe first introduced the term *Weltliteratur* into circulation in the late 1820s (he didn't in fact coin it – August Ludwig von Schlözer and Christoph Martin Wieland got there first, but Goethe gets the credit for bringing it to general attention), numerous would-be world readers have quailed in the face of the enormity and even ludicrousness of the task. 'What can one make of such an idea?' exclaimed the critic Claudio Guillén in 1993. 'The sum total of all national literatures? A wild idea, unattainable in practice, worthy not of an actual reader but of a deluded keeper of archives who is also a multimillionaire. The most harebrained editor has never aspired to such a thing.' Or, as Harvard comparative literature professor David Damrosch put it ten years later, 'How can we have it all?'

Guillén and Damrosch were by no means the first to express such anxieties: back in 1964, the French polyglot René Étiemble, who specialised in Arab and Chinese culture, was thrown into a cold sweat by the notion of trying to tackle all stories written everywhere ever. 'I am immediately seized by a kind of panic terror, which reminds me of the proverb "grasp all, lose all",' he confessed in a speech to the Fourth World Congress of the International Comparative Literature Association. 'What would such theoretical openness of spirit to all literatures, whether present or past, bring us given that any mind, however capacious we may imagine it, is limited by the average length of our lives?' The idea clearly niggled Étiemble, for he gave it some detailed thought:

Do the sum yourself: give yourself fifty years of life without one day of illness or rest, or altogether 18,262 days. Rigorously take into account periods of sleep, meals, the obligations and pleasures of life, and of your profession, estimate the time left to you for reading masterpieces with the sole purpose of finding out what precisely is literature. As I'm extremely generous, I will grant you the privilege of reading every day – good ones as well as bad ones – one very beautiful book of all that are accessible to you in your own language and in the foreign languages you have mastered, in the original, or in translation. You know that it will take you more than one day to read *The Magic Mountain* or the *Arabian Nights*; but I also take into account that with a little bit of luck and zeal you might read in one day the *Hojoki*, the *Romance gitano*, the *Menexenos* and *The Spirit of Conquest* of Benjamin Constant. This will give you the couple of days extra that you will need to read *And Quiet Flows the Don*, which for the longest time was thought to have been written by Sholokhov, but which is not any less good for actually being mostly the work of Krioukov. In any case better than *Cleared Land* by the same

Sholokhov. Now, when measured against the total number of very beautiful books that exist in the world, what are 18,262 titles? Sheer misery.

One wonders what Étiemble would have made of today's rate of publication, which, leaving aside the hundreds of thousands of books published every year, sees around 51 million websites added to the internet annually and 100,000 new tweets going live every minute.

The truth is that the volume of printed words in the world has always been unreadable by a single individual, almost from the word go. By 1500, a mere fifty years after Johann Gensfleisch zur Laden zum Gutenberg's first printing press first rattled into life in Mainz, some 27,000 titles had been churned out across Europe – considerably more than even Étiemble's tyrannical proposed regime could allow for getting through in a single lifetime. Devouring it all, or trying to have, as Marx and Engels put it with typically daunting earnestness, 'intercourse in every direction', has always been an impossible fantasy. Whichever way you look at it, if you're trying to read the world, you're pretty much screwed.

With covering all bases definitively off the menu, some element of choice has to come into the equation and therein lies another rub. Because if no individual can have read all the books in the world how can anyone be in a position to say that one text is more deserving of attention than another?

Staring down at me now from the bookshelf across the room is a fat volume titled *1001 Books You Must Read Before You Die*. Edited by one Dr Peter Boxall, it contains details of a mere eighteenth of the number of titles you might be able to get through if you read your head off until you expire. Inside, the selection certainly looks intriguing – while dominated by US and European writers, it includes a good handful of Asian and South American authors and an African work or three. There's no doubt that Boxall and his extensive team of contributors have done a lot of work to compile their recommendations, and if you google the book you'll find comments from armies of ambitious readers champing at the bit to take the list on. Strangely though, for a man putting the finishing touches to so mammoth an enterprise, Boxall takes a rather apologetic tone in his introductory words and seems at times to be fumbling for a disclaimer to distance himself from the bold assertion of the title. 'The contributors to this book are not interested in producing an exclusive list, a list that can achieve transnational and transcultural consensus about which books we should read before we die,' he writes in the Preface, going on to reinforce his point in the Introduction with the assertion that his list 'does not seek to be a new canon . . . Rather, it is a list that lives in the midst of the contradiction between the comprehensive and the partial.' Far from feeling satisfaction as he comes to the end of the gargantuan task of marshalling this ambitious must-read list, Boxall seems rather uneasy, as though, for all their diligence, he and his team will inevitably fall short.

It's a sentiment familiar to many academics working in this field. As the study of world literature as a separate discipline has come into focus in lecture and seminar rooms – most of them in the United States – over the last four decades or so, numerous experts have expressed concerns about what writer Gerard Holden has called 'the problem of what to include and what to leave out' and about their inability to preside over so vast and varied a field of human endeavour. 'How many of us are linguistically qualified to teach such courses?' asked one-time International Comparative Literature Association president Werner P. Friederich in 1960, when mooting the prospect of expanding academic teaching to include Asian literatures. 'In spite of our desperate need to know far more about Asia than we actually do, we are in a particularly deplorable predicament right now.' In recent times, some universities, such as Yale, have attempted to solve the problem by introducing team-taught world-literature courses, bringing in experts on the literature of specific regions to lead on certain texts, and relying on a generalist lecturer to provide continuity and an overview. But with teaching time in short supply, the challenge of selecting texts remains as fraught as ever.

Even at the highest level, mistakes are sometimes unavoidable. Since 1901, the eighteen members of the Swedish Academy have striven to award the Nobel Prize for Literature to writers who, in the words of Alfred Nobel's will, have 'conferred the greatest benefit to mankind', creating a sort of elite world-literature canon along the way. The 111 writers to have been honoured to date – among them Günter Grass, Gabriel García Márquez, Jean-Paul Sartre, Samuel Beckett and Toni Morrison – make for formidable reading. All the same, there are some key omissions and odd inclusions. Virginia Woolf and James Joyce, for example, do not get a look in because the proposers in their home countries never nominated them, and yet, as Academy member and former permanent secretary Horace Engdahl freely admits, 'not even every second author on the list can be said to have reached something like a canonical status'.

Even with their minds focused on recognising writing that most benefits the human race, the Academy members' decisions are swayed by the fashions and prejudices of their times. Feeling duty-bound to recognise only God-fearing writers, the early Nobel Committee passed over Thomas Hardy because of his immoral heroines and rebellious stance towards religion. It rejected Ibsen as 'negative and bewildering' and threw out Zola for being 'cynical'. And when it came to the year in which the prize went to Eugene O'Neill instead of Sigmund Freud, the Committee's report explaining its reasoning was as unapologetic as it was doomed to crumple under the test of time: 'Freud appears, more than any of his patients, to be possessed of a sick and twisted imagination, which speaks volumes, since he has an abundance of unusually strange patients.'

With the great and the good of the literary establishment committing such pratfalls on occasion, what hope is there for everyone else? How are we to proceed when no one is in a position to explain the comparative merits of each offering to us with objective certainty? Faced with the unknowability of what's out there, it often seems simpler and safer to stick with what we know – the stream of recommendations

12

and endorsements that publishers and retailers have developed to ensure we are never more than a few clicks away from a book that is like a book we like.

From endorsement quotes by comparable writers on the jacket, to taster chapters for similar works at the back, we are constantly encouraged to read things similar to the stories we have already read. If we buy a book on Amazon, we are told what other people who bought that title also went for – and then we get emails about it too. In bookshops, even before we inch close enough to make out the title, we can usually tell from a novel's colour scheme and cover design whether the contents tend more towards the Marian Keyes or Ruth Rendell end of the spectrum: stilettos on a candyfloss-pink background and you've got the story of a touchingly dizzy city girl trying to have it all; drops of blood on a snowy landscape and you know you're in for a rough ride. And without realising it, we can find ourselves co-opted into the like-with-like marketing drive through invitations to tweet that we've finished ebooks, and book-club notes nestling in the closing pages of print editions. And that's even before we've liked the author page on Facebook so that all our friends can be in no doubt of our literary preferences.

All this can be useful and often leads to reliably enjoyable reading experiences, but it has a drawback. Ensconced as we are in our individual hall of mirrors, our literary preferences reflected endlessly back at us in slightly altered form, it can be tricky to see a way out. If your default frame of reference for selecting a book is that it looks like, sounds like or is like something you've read before, or that someone you like likes it, how do you begin to navigate your way through literary terrain that has few familiar landmarks, where book jackets don't give off the signals you're used to and where hardly any of your contemporaries may ever have ventured? It's little help knowing that Yan Lianke's *Dream of Ding Village* has been likened to Albert Camus' *The Plague* if you've never read either and have no foundation on which to construct the comparison.

With familiarity providing the rationale for much of what we buy and read, it's small wonder that the few foreign-language writers to top the UK sales charts in recent years have been those that slot into preordained categories. The Scandi-crime giants fit comfortably into popular conceptions of what a gritty crime novel should be, and have the added advantage that publishers can use them to sell one another through a sort of domino effect: Jo Nesbø, stripped of his slashed 'o' for squeamish British eyes, was marketed as the next Stieg Larsson; then Camilla Läckberg took to the UK shelves without her umlaut, her works bearing stickers that read 'If you like Jo Nesbo you will love this.' Small wonder too that, with our preferences so carefully catered for and pandered to, few of us feel tempted to change our reading habits – with the result that, according to a 2013 survey by Literature Across Frontiers, only 4.37 per cent of literary works published in the UK and Ireland in 2008 were translations (a figure not a million miles away from the controversial 3 per cent statistic thought to have originated from a report on the US publishing industry by bibliographic-data provider Bowker in 2005). With so much well-pitched material on hand, the prospect of seeking out stories from further afield feels a bit like being asked to abandon the bright supermarket aisles where everything is arranged just as we like it to forage for literary sustenance in the local park. It seems more than a touch eccentric, rather a lot of effort and as though it may well yield dubious results.

Luckily, however, readers elsewhere don't share our reluctance. As I found when I launched ayearofreadingtheworld.com with a short appeal for book lovers the world over to suggest titles for me to try, bibliophiles around the planet (including those intrepid anglophone readers who have struck out from the familiar shallows of the US and UK markets) are usually only too pleased to share their views, time and expertise. Sitting in my living room on the dreary evening in October 2011 on which that first post went live, I had prepared myself for the possibility that I might be on my own with my capricious quest. In practice, nothing could have been further from the truth: within hours of sharing the link with friends and colleagues and on Facebook and Twitter, I was getting messages from people I had never met suggesting titles and promising to ask the advice of contacts in far-flung destinations. A Portuguese woman in another department at the newspaper where I was freelancing generously donated a volume of translated short stories by Eça de Queiróz, which she had just bought (I promised to return it, but I'm afraid it's still sitting on my shelf), someone who grew up in Saudi Arabia shared her ideas, and a German-language translator pitched in with recommendations for Austria. Before long, strangers had written far more about my plans than I had and the list of comments below my little 300-word appeal extended far down the page. And then, about four days after my post went live, I found a comment from someone called Rafidah waiting in my inbox. Based in Kuala Lumpur, she liked the sound of my project and was offering to go to her local English-language bookshop, choose a book for me from Malaysia and post it to London. I accepted with alacrity, and a few weeks later a package arrived containing two volumes – one Malaysian and a possible choice for Singapore, both selected after lengthy deliberation with the bookseller – along with a card wishing me luck.

As I discovered later, that package also contained the key to my project. Symbolic of the generosity, enthusiasm and creativity of the many book lovers I encountered on my quest – both during my preliminary explorations in the last months of 2011, when I tried to gather a stock of titles so that I'd be able to hit the ground running on 1 January, and then during the year itself, when reading, blogging and researching often took up as much as eight hours a day, fitted around full-time work – it revealed the thing that would keep me going through the months ahead and would ultimately enable me to achieve my goal. The answer to my dilemma about how to select texts from the mass of reading matter out there was not in chilly canons or definitive must-read lists, but in discovery and openness. It was in accepting the impossibility of the project and yet doing it all the same. And it was in a readiness to trust the words of an unknown person on the other side of the world.

*

Not knowing things often feels rather threatening. It carries with it the connotations of failed homework assignments and being singled out in front of the class. In many areas of anglophone culture, to be ignorant is somehow shameful, and many of us go to great lengths to avoid being exposed as poorly informed. We smile and nod when someone mentions a film or celebrity we've never heard of, we come up with elaborate stealth strategies to get people to reveal their names when we've forgotten them. But most of all, given the choice, we try to avoid situations where we're likely to find ourselves out of our depth.

All of this makes venturing into a story from a part of the world we may never have heard of before more than a little daunting. It seems inevitable that such books will contain references to things, places and practices we know nothing about. Faced with the prospect of reading something from a culture quite different to our own, we can feel clumsy and ill-equipped, liable to take things the wrong way or miss the point. In the worst-case scenario, there's the risk that we end up sitting like an unpopular child at the margins of the text while in-jokes buzz about over our heads, full of secret codes we have no means of understanding.

The question of how we go about bridging these gaps so as to be able to read culturally alien texts is a thorny one. 'What is a non-specialist reader to do?' asks David Damrosch in the Introduction to his confidently titled *How to Read World Literature*. 'If we don't want to confine our reading within the narrow compass of one or two of the world's literatures, we need to develop ways to make the most of works from a range of distinct times and places.' Spending the rest of the book addressing this question, Damrosch takes the reader through a series of great works from around the planet, drawing up a list of mental approaches, ideas and preparations that we might want to consider in order to get the most from forays into foreign texts. These include accepting the importance of reading translations 'in critical awareness of the translators' choices and biases, even if we have no direct knowledge of a text's original language'; being open 'to read[ing] different works with different expectations'; learning enough about each new literary tradition 'to achieve an overall understanding of its patterns of reference and its assumptions about the world, the text and the reader'; and endeavouring to engage with works' 'original social, political and biographical contexts' while maintaining a balance so that we are neither guilty of 'submerging ourselves in antiquarian details nor absorbing the works so fully into our own world that we mistake *The Odyssey* for a modern novel or look to it for the same pleasures we expect from movies and television'. Oh, and if we can – although he realises this is pushing it somewhat – it would be very helpful if we could have command of two foreign languages, 'one from [our] home region and one from a very different part of the world'.

The problem with Damrosch's prescriptions is that they sound like a lot of work. If anyone tried to follow them fully, they would be looking at months, if not years, of preparation simply to be in a position to read a single foreign text. Taken to extremes, they might even be seen as advocating a kind of method reading for which we would each be required to immerse ourselves in the cultural practices of the milieu of a work for a period of time before taking it on – spending a month keeping kosher in order to be worthy of reading Primo Levi, say, or fasting through Ramadan to prepare for tackling *The Reluctant Fundamentalist*. Even people who are emigrating don't put in that much groundwork, so it seems over-egging the pudding to suggest that prospective readers go to such great lengths.

Another issue Damrosch overlooks somewhat is that, for many people, one of the major incentives for reading books from other cultures is discovery itself. Rightly or wrongly, we tend to regard literary works as windows on other worlds. Learning about a different way of life and a different way of looking at things is part of the point of the exercise. If we have to mug up on all that in advance, it defeats the object of reading the book at all. By the time we've made our way through the thicket of well-meaning, schoolmasterly tomes Damrosch seems intent on hedging each literary work in with, that initial spark of curiosity that got us interested in the novel or memoir will have been well and truly stubbed out and we will probably just feel like flopping on the sofa with a comforting P.G. Wodehouse instead.

All this earnestness takes the fun out of the idea of reading such works. While many of us might welcome an element of roughage in our literary diets, it's fair to say that most of us who read purely in our spare time look for at least some enjoyment from books. Kafka might have advocated tackling 'only books that bite or sting us' (or 'wound and stab us', depending on which translation you favour), as he wrote in a letter to his friend Oskar Pollak in 1904, but he didn't have to commute through the rush hour, holding on to a swinging strap with only the words in front of his eyes to take his mind off the armpit of the person standing two inches away. We 'common readers', as Samuel Johnson and Virginia Woolf charmingly dubbed us, aren't, by and large, cowards. We're not afraid of being stretched and shocked and made to work for our payoffs, but we probably all have moments when we feel the truth of Dylan Thomas's statement to writer Joan Wyndham: 'Poetry is not the most important thing in life . . . I'd much rather lie in a hot bath sucking boiled sweets and reading Agatha Christie.'

Dr Johnson might have appreciated the point. Despite being the leading man of letters of his age – or any age, some would argue – he knew that reading can be an effort and that enjoyment has an important part to play in engaging people with books. 'I am always for getting a boy forward in his learning; for that is a sure good,' he wrote. 'I would let him at first read *any* English book which happens to engage his attention; because you have done a great deal when you have brought him to have entertainment from a book. He'll get better books afterwards.' Enjoyment might not have been the end of reading for Britain's most celebrated literary critic, but it was not a dirty word. Nor should it be regarded as such for people trying to expand their horizons by reading beyond their own national and linguistic boundaries. After all, the joy of reading is often what makes books travel in the first place. The crowds that hurried to the New York docks to ask sailors on the incoming ships 'Is Little Nell dead?' in 1841 weren't there for the sake of their intellectual improvement, they were there because they were gripped by Dickens' *The Old Curiosity Shop* and wanted to know what happened next.

Still, it can be hard to hold on to that in the face of the rather snooty pronouncements that the discussion of world literature has prompted from time to time. 'It must not be forgotten that everywhere also the great majority is lethargic, ignorant and of poor judgement,' wrote the Danish literary critic Georg Brandes on the question of sifting world literature in 1899. 'The best is inaccessible to the mob and the finest incomprehensible. The mob chases after the bellowing soap-boxers and the inscrutable crackpots, they follow fashion and worship success. That a writer at one point has pleased everyone is by no means enough that we may include him in world literature forever.'

In the face of such statements, it's tempting to feel that world literature is best left to those in the know while you and I stick to our Jordan memoirs and gossip magazines. The French scholar Albert Guérard saw the problem when in 1940 he wrote: 'There is some danger, however, in claiming Goethe as our master. It might foster the notion that World Literature is a formidable subject, fit only for such a titan of culture as he, or, at second-hand, for his learned disciples . . . World Literature . . . is not reserved for a supercilious elite, doctors of philosophy or cosmopolitan sophisticates.'

Yet, despite Guérard's protestations, there's no question that even today the idea of being cultured and widely read brings out a kind of smug, competitive streak in some people. I've certainly encountered it a few times since I embarked on my world-reading quest. Usually it emerges in the company of people who have amassed a little heap of knowledge that they are anxious to show off. This they brood over jealously, comparing it aggressively with the efforts of those around them. On several occasions I've found myself cornered by flushed and slightly wild-eyed figures, determined to have their say about what should be on my list. They differ from people who genuinely want to help in one key respect: if they name their particular recommendations and I confess that I haven't heard of them, a look of triumph scuds across their faces. To me it's no surprise that among the millions of writers past and present spinning tales around the globe, there should be plenty that I've never come across – my global literary adventure opened my eyes to just how much richness the planet has to offer and how little I have managed to sample – but to them my ignorance of their favourites is significant. It means that they are somehow vindicated as better, more cultured, more knowledgeable than me. They have scored.

The irony is that such literary smugness rarely manifests itself among the people who have most cause to gloat over their expertise – the polyglots and regional-literature aficionados who can recall dates and titles and forge links and parallels as easily as most of us draw breath. In my experience, they are hardly ever anything but helpful, enthusiastic and generous to a fault with their time and talents.

Once you break through such jockeying for position and see it for what it is, it poses no threat. But to those hovering on the fringes of the world-literature scene, such posturing can seem fearsome. It alone has no doubt been enough to head off scores of would-be world readers, cutting them off from many wonders.

*

Fear of not recognising texts that everyone else knows backwards is just the start. For some, the idea that there is a right and a wrong way of reading may be enough to put them off attempting unfamiliar works altogether. '"Weltliteratur" is not for us,' wrote Werner P. Friederich in 1959, because we can perceive 'only a few facets and never the totality of God's creation', as though God were watching and shaking his head at our ham-fisted attempts to get to grips with *The Epic of Gilgamesh*. In recent decades, this has been compounded by the general move away from viewing texts as standalone 'verbal icons' open to interpretation by the reader, as suggested by the critic William Wimsatt in the 1940s and '50s, and towards placing greater emphasis on putting works in their social and political contexts, as David Damrosch encourages us to do. It is as though, unless we are guided carefully and are made aware of all the potential connotations and references that might be relevant to a work, we're at risk of making some terrible faux pas for which God – or some equally formidable, all-knowing alien jury that administrates the cabinet of Platonic ideal readings of all texts written everywhere ever – will never forgive us.

When it comes to translated literature, this sense is often heightened by the awareness of the presence of a third party in the text, crashing the cosy little author–reader tête-à-tête that can make the reading experience so delicious. Usually, to read is to enter into a dialogue with a writer who is no longer there. It is covert, anonymous and, if we want it to be, potentially illicit. Even before the strangulation and burning at the stake in 1536 of William Tyndale – the man who first translated the Bible into English, thereby enabling people to access the scriptures for themselves without a priest or liturgical scholar to manage and guide their interpretations – private reading carried connotations of decadence and danger. So risky did it seem to the instigators of the Spanish Inquisition that they introduced a rigorous censorship programme from 1478 onwards, which lasted for nearly 400 years. Even nowadays, there is something deeply seductive and even subversive about the idea of embarking on a secret, imaginary journey that no one else can control or scrutinise. It's surely no coincidence that one of the most frequently commented upon attributes of e-readers is that they afford book lovers an extra level of privacy, with not even the title of the work on public view.

In the case of literature from other cultures and texts originally written in languages the reader doesn't speak, the story is rather different. That cosy dialogue between reader and writer is simply not possible, at least not in the way we're used to with texts from our own milieu. We can skimp on Damrosch's prescriptions all we like and take the risk of diving straight into a foreign text without doing any preliminary reading, but we will frequently find that we are not left to our own devices. In order to access these tales, we need professional help, usually in the form of translators who can convert the indecipherable original into something we can comprehend. Even for works that were written in English, if they are from other parts of the world, we might need the help of footnotes or a glossary to explain terms, ideas and practices we may not have come across before. In addition, editors may judge that numerous forewords, notes on the text and translator's introductions are necessary to help us get the fullest possible sense from the work.

These attendant bits of material can make texts feel rather crowded and can sometimes get in the way. If you're forever having to flick to page 439 to check out the footnotes for fear of getting the wrong end of the stick, you're likely to become a little frustrated. It hardly makes for a relaxing, immersive read and we may feel self-conscious about trying to make sure we ingest every scrap of extraneous material in order to be capable of doing justice to the words before our eyes.

It's odd because, at least when we're reading for pleasure, we Brits rarely look at getting to grips with our own texts in the same light. I'll warrant that many an English-speaking newcomer to Thomas Hardy's *Jude the Obscure* will not know what 'the characteristic part of a barrow-pig, which the countrymen used for greasing their boots, as it was useless for any other purpose' is, but when Arabella flings one at the ill-starred protagonist, the meaning quickly becomes plain. The context helps us to understand it and the fact that most readers of the novel these days will never have set foot on a pig farm, let alone have any knowledge of the butchering process, is neither here nor there.

That's not to say that there's no value in reading around books from different times and places. There is a great deal, and cultural knowledge will almost always provide fresh insights and unlock new meanings in a text. It's just that in their eagerness to explain everything to us, these texts sometimes risk working our consciousness of the importance of contextual awareness up to such a pitch that it paralyses us and prevents us from reading unfamiliar things for fear of getting it wrong. In the face of a thousand footnotes, it can be difficult to maintain enough confidence in our ability to read a story and get something out of it without someone telling us what to think every second word, even if this means that some of it goes over our heads. And it's important to hold on to this. Otherwise why read at all?

Indeed, there may be times when a foreign perspective – being unfamiliar with the host culture of a text – proves to be an advantage. The Czech writer Milan Kundera thinks so. In fact, he has gone so far as to suggest that readers from other countries have an advantage over readers from the nation where a book originated because 'geographic distance sets the observer back from the local context and allows him to embrace the large context of world literature, the only approach that can bring out a novel's aesthetic value'. 'Do I mean by this that to judge a novel one can do without a knowledge of its original language? I do mean exactly that!' he pronounced in an essay in 2005 with the confidence that perhaps only someone who has written a work as extraordinary as *The Unbearable Lightness of Being* can muster.

I'm not a believer that everyone has won and all must have prizes. I don't mean to imply that one reading is necessarily as valid as the next. For a start, we're not all Milan Kundera. Nevertheless, I would suggest that most – if not all – readings have some value and that this is a place to start when we think about reading the world. Perhaps we could all do with taking a leaf out of the book of the Chinese academic Zhang Longxi, who in 1992 called for a 'spirit of interpretive pluralism' to infuse the way we approach global literature. He pointed out that a sense of the possibility of reading texts in different ways has long been a theme in Chinese literary criticism, citing the sixteenth-century scholar Xie Zhen, who declared: 'Of poems some can be understood, some cannot, and some need not be. They are like the moon in water or flowers in a mirror; so don't trace every line too doggedly.' Zhen's point, says Longxi (or at least his reading of it), is 'not only the realization that nothing should be excluded from understanding and interpretation, that the reader should be free to choose whatever is available to him or her, but more radically that the reader should also be free *not* to choose but to declare his enjoyment without thorough understanding'.

The truth is, we as individuals will never be wise enough or cultured enough or fast enough or long-lived enough to read the world as deeply and thoroughly as it deserves – and we never have been. We can only fail. So we have a choice: we can stick with what we know, or we can embrace the impossibility of reading world literature properly and jump right in – 'feel the fear and do it anyway', as Susan Jeffers' self-help classic has it. 'The shelves of books we haven't written, like those of books we haven't read, stretch out into the darkness of the universal library's farthest space. We are always at the beginning of the beginning of the letter A,' writes the Argentinian author, translator and editor Alberto Manguel in the conclusion to his *A History of Reading*. As I found all those years ago, huddled over piles of books in a dingy corner of the UL as the shelving lights flickered on and off, and later when readers around the world began to share their literary loves with me, that is part of the fun.

2

Plotting the route

the global literature landscape

In most of the classrooms of Chalgrove Primary School in Finchley during the last decades of the twentieth century, there was a map of the world on the wall. Tricked out in colours reminiscent of the Queen Mother's wardrobe – cerulean blues, salmon pinks and pastel greens – it watched over me throughout the first seven years of my academic career and, apart from the odd reference to it by a teacher eager to make a new pupil from a far-flung destination feel welcome, went largely unnoticed.

It also went unchanged. The web of lines marking the country boundaries stayed fixed in their chaotic pattern, with only the border between the US and Canada straighter than anything I could rule under the titles in my exercise book. Throughout the late eighties and early nineties – as the USSR collapsed, Yugoslavia shattered and numerous former colonies declared their independence – the map stood firm and resolute. It had its story and it was sticking to it. It would not be moved.

A memory of that map came back to me when I began to prepare to read a book from every country, twenty years on. Fixed and definite, it had seemed to suggest that the world was an easily measurable and quantifiable place – a belief many of those I encountered during my research seemed to share, as the question 'how many countries are there in the world, then?' was almost always the first thing anyone said when the project came up. It was as if we all believe that there is some globally agreed standard that governs the categorisation of places around the planet, and that calculating the answer must therefore be a simple matter of arithmetic.

In many ways, it's no wonder so many of us hold this view. Far from being unique to my primary school, such maps have dominated our way of looking at the planet on paper for generations. It's only natural, therefore, that most of us should have formed the habit of picturing the world as a stable, changeless thing. Ever since the Flanders-born cartographer Gerardus Mercator published his *Nova et aucta orbis terrae descriptio ad usum navigantium emendate accommodata* ('New and more complete representation of the terrestrial globe properly adapted for use in navigation', or 'World Map', for short) in 1569, this chart – or recognisable versions of it – has adorned walls in many parts of the planet. For more than four centuries, it has been the basis for portraying the globe in two dimensions.

This is not as straightforward as it sounds. As Mercator was all too aware, having spent years trying 'to represent the positions and dimensions of the lands, as well as the distances of places, as much as in conformity with very truth as it is possible so to do', it is mathematically impossible to represent a round thing on a flat thing without serious distortion. Something has got to give. In Mercator's case, the compromise was to treat the globe rather like a balloon inflated inside a cylinder, pressing the sides flat and straightening the meridian lines to present a roughly accurate picture of the central, most populous section of the planet. This is all well and good for those in the middle of things, but it begins to get rather awkward at the extremities. Making the meridian lines parallel means that things become larger and larger the further you move from the equator, and, as much of the land in the northern hemisphere sits closer to the pole, the distortion has the effect of making Europe and North America appear disproportionately big. So it is that, on a common or garden Mercator projection map, Greenland will often appear to have the same land mass as Africa (when it is in fact fourteen times smaller), Europe looks as if it covers twice the area of South America (which is actually nearly double

Europe's size), and Australia seems like a pebble compared to Russia (instead of nearly half as big).

For some, these discrepancies reveal more than mathematical compromise. In 1973, when he launched his rival world map based on what was to become known as the Gall–Peters projection, German filmmaker and historian Arno Peters pulled no punches in attacking the motives behind the prevailing world view. The Mercator projection, he said, 'presents a fully false picture particularly regarding the non-white-peopled lands', and 'over-values the white man and distorts the picture of the world to the advantage of the colonial master of the time'. He claimed that his map, by contrast, offered a full and fair picture of the relative sizes of countries – even if it did so by stretching out all the land masses so that, as reviewer Arthur Robinson put it, they 'are somewhat reminiscent of wet, ragged, long winter underwear hung out to dry on the Arctic Circle'. Seen through Peters' eyes, Mercator was less a trail-blazing technical genius than a blinkered Eurocentric, drawing the things that were important to him big and in the middle of the page – much like those children staring up at the fruits of Mercator's labours four centuries later.

But as Jerry Brotton demonstrates in his *A History of the World in Twelve Maps*, Mercator's creation was arguably no more biased than any other representation of the world because 'throughout most of recorded history, the overwhelming majority of maps put the culture that produced them at their centre'. Nevertheless, in the early 1970s, when the ink was still drying on the constitutions of many newly minted ex-colonial nations, Peters' arguments struck a chord. His map was 'the most honest projection of the world yet devised', according to the *Guardian*, and it was taken up and championed by UNESCO and UNICEF, which issued around 60 million copies with the tagline 'New Dimensions, Fair Conditions'. This, despite several academics pointing out errors in Peters' calculations – Nigeria and Chad appeared twice as long as they really are, for example, while Indonesia was squeezed to half its actual breadth.

Flawed though Peters' map may have been, its launch did reveal a truth, even if it was not quite the one its creator intended: it showed that representations of the world and its regions influence the status and development of the places depicted. For there is no doubt that the widespread pictorial presentation of Europe as the central and dominant land mass over the last four centuries, whether intentionally or not, has insinuated itself into the thinking of many people around the planet. The evidence crops up time and again in studies such as Jeremy Crampton's survey of twentieth-century atlases, which revealed that Africa was typically only represented by three maps in each book, despite covering around a fifth of the planet's land area, to Professor Thomas Saarinen's 1999 *National Geographic*-sponsored research project, for which he collected more than 3,800 sketch maps of the world by children from forty-nine countries, most of which inflated Europe and placed it at the centre – regardless of where the child's home was. And, as Palestinian-American critic Edward Said showed in his landmark essay collection on *Culture and Imperialism*, this way of looking at the world has woven itself into the plots of some of our best-loved novels, with suspicious, two-dimensional characters such as Dickens' Magwitch, who returns from Australia, and the natives of Conrad's *Heart of Darkness* and Evelyn Waugh's *Black Mischief,* left to loiter in the margins of their narratives every bit as much as the places they come from do on the world map. When Jules Verne's Phileas Fogg sets out from Western Europe to undertake his bet that he can circumnavigate the globe in *Around the World in Eighty Days,* he does not merely leave his home, but the centre of the planet, if not the universe.

Taken to extremes, this sort of thinking can have terrible results. It can enshrine entitlement and subjection as the self-image of groups of people, so that, in the words of Guinea-Bissauan political activist Amílcar Cabral, 'as soon as African children enter elementary schools, they develop an inferiority complex. They learn to fear the white man and to feel ashamed of being Africans [and] African geography, history and culture are either ignored or distorted.' At its most damaging, such a skewed perspective can be used in an attempt to justify the control or repression of one group at the hands of another simply by virtue of the fact that they don't seem to matter as much. It may, for example, make it seem entirely reasonable for an administration to send someone who has never visited a region before to carve it up into separate states, as happened in 1947, when the British government commissioned Sir Cyril Radcliffe to produce a report partitioning India along religious lines. After Radcliffe, working from outdated census reports, took just over three months to draw the 6,000-kilometre boundary line demarcating Pakistan, the resulting bloodbath – in which an estimated million people died – was a powerful demonstration of the dangers of mapmaking in the wrong hands. 'As soon as men begin to talk about anything that really matters, someone has to go and get the Atlas,' Rudyard Kipling told the Royal Geographical Society in 1927; after all, there can be few things more calculated to make you feel entitled to meddle in things that really matter than a large and beautiful book illustrating your international influence on every page.

In many ways, however, it wouldn't matter whether Kipling and his cronies were looking at the most meticulous representation of the world or a child's scribble. Because the biggest myth that maps peddle is not the privileging of one portion of the planet over another, but the mistaken belief that it is possible for one person to stand outside the world and survey the planet and its contents objectively. The mere fact of creating what seems like a god's or alien-eye view of the world perpetuates the idea that it is possible for one person to look at the planet as an impartial observer might and that the world will stand still, peacefully and changelessly, while we do it. In Brotton's words, a map 'offers its viewers the chance to look down on the world from above, and a god-like perspective on earthly creation'. Essentially, it allows us to dodge the truth that, as Chinese émigré novelist Gao Xingjian puts it, 'man's cognition of the external world and other people can never be divorced from a subjective viewpoint. The world and human events inherently lack meaning: meaning is conferred by human cognition.'

This may be one of the reasons why the idea that it's possible to observe the world objectively persists. Bolstered by the famous Apollo 17 'Blue Marble' photograph (itself inverted to fit the view people would expect to see), which gave us earthlings our first glimpse of home from space in 1972, our confidence in our ability to take a global view remains largely unshaken. To feel that we can look at things in this way is appealing. If all of reality can be contained and delineated in so orderly a manner, then the world must truly be a manageable place, an entity that we can preside over, get our heads round and master. The act of looking at a map has the power to both play to our vanity and banish our fear of confusion. It makes us feel that we have control.

*

This idea of a single, objective world is not the preserve of maps alone. Just google anything to do with 'number of countries in the world', as I spent many hours doing before the start of 2012, and you'll quickly discover source after source packed with confident assertions about exactly how many states make up the global community. Most of them will tell you, as Wikipedia did until recently, that the world consists of either 195 or 196 countries, usually hinging on whether or not Taiwan is counted. So ubiquitous and persuasive are these claims that, in my eagerness to get started when I prepared for my project, I took them as some sort of objective, universal standard and used the 196 (counting Taiwan) as the basis for my 'world'. It was a decision I would later come to question, but back then, bolstered by a childhood played out alongside Mercator's rendering of the globe, I found the concept of a definitive world order entirely natural. The occasional voice protesting that the number of countries depends what world you come from could not shake my cartographically conjured confidence.

It's a shame, because such dissenters are absolutely right. With at least 270 national flags hoisted around the planet and 280 country-code, top-level domain names registered with the Internet Corporation for Assigned Names and Numbers, there's plenty of wiggle room – or, more often than not, skirmish room – in answering the question of how many independent countries exist in the world. Historically, attempts to clarify what constitutes a sovereign state as a means of defining who is in the club, and who isn't, have done little more than articulate the difficulty of pinning the terms down. Even the most widely cited definitions, such as the one set out in the 1933 Montevideo Convention on the Rights and Duties of States, are far from watertight. According to the terms of that treaty, sovereign statehood essentially boils down to having a permanent population, defined borders, a government, and the ability to have dealings with other states. You're a state if you say you are and if the people in and around you agree. But with so much uncertainty over what precisely defines an independent country and so many news bulletins containing something to do with wrangles over sovereignty – from Britain and Spain's spats over Gibraltar to Israel's stand-off with Palestine – this is usually not as straightforward as it sounds.

Even apparently politically neutral categorisations of sovereignty, such as the United Nations' list of recognised states, can only take you so far. For all its rhetoric of inclusivity and impartiality, the UN is not without bias, as the existence of the five permanent members – originally known as the Great Powers – on its Security Council demonstrates. With right of veto on all non-procedural matters to come before the council, the US, UK, France, Russia and China have the power to derail UN Security Council resolutions even in the face of unanimous agreement from the other (non-permanent) members. This, despite the fact that the major allies of the Second World War – plus China – can hardly be said to represent the realities of global power today. (In fact the notion that the UK could be thought of as a Great Power in the twenty-first century verges on the laughable, as evidenced by Vladimir Putin's spokesman's description of Britain as 'just a small island no one pays any attention to' in September 2013.)

Only a handful of decades after the UN's formation, the world had outgrown it. There was no impartial observer to step in and redistribute roles fairly. Consequently, just as Greenland dwarfs China on Mercator's map and Arno Peters' Chad and Nigeria are stretched out of shape, the UN presents a distorted picture of global dynamics, a fudge between what is accurate and what is practicable. It leaves some things out, it makes others appear more important than they really are and – in some matters – it favours the interests of those who had control of creating it. Still, if the history of mapmaking is anything to go by, this may well be the only world we can grasp.

*

Just like the world itself, the international literary landscape has long been a contested and rather unequally represented domain. Since Goethe focused the attention of the European literati on the concept of reading across national boundaries nearly 200 years ago, various subjective concepts of what this might entail have been batted around between academics, publishers and readers. Helpfully, although he mentioned *Weltliteratur* twenty-one times in his work between 1827 and 1831, Goethe did not provide a precise definition of what he meant by it. Perhaps he didn't need to give it much thought – over the course of a career spanning more than seventy-three years, the polyglot translated work from eighteen languages.

In fact, the most powerful impression that anyone encountering Goethe's comments on reading internationally is likely to take away is his impatience with national divisions and distinctions altogether. Far from developing a concept of reading the world that might involve sampling literature from every country, he was anxious to encourage his contemporaries to work towards 'a common world literature transcending national limits'. This, he thought, could be achieved by and could in turn promote exchanges between 'the living, striving men of letters' of the age (it was mostly men in those days), such that they 'should learn to know each other, and through their own inclination and similarity of tastes, find the motive for corporate action'.

It was a conviction that stayed with him throughout his career. 'I am more and more convinced that poetry is the universal possession of mankind, revealing itself everywhere and at all times in hundreds and hundreds of men,' he said in the final years of his life. 'I therefore like to look about me in foreign nations, and advise everyone to do the same. National literature is now a rather unmeaning term; the epoch of world literature is at hand, and everyone must strive to hasten its approach.'

To Goethe, world literature seems to have been a body of work at least partly curated by people with the insight, knowledge and taste to form judgements about what it should and should not comprise, a dialogue conducted 'so that we can correct one another'. 'I am convinced that a world literature is in process of formation, that the nations are in favour of it and for this reason make friendly overtures,' he wrote to Adolf Friedrich Carl Streckfuss in 1827. 'The German can and should be most active in this respect; he has a fine part to play in this great mutual approach.'

Goethe was right in some ways. Germans and other Western Europeans were to play a pivotal role in shaping the concept known as world literature over the next century and a half – so much so in fact that, just as many of their compatriots were doing physically in far-flung nations, they colonised the literary landscape. Adopting the mapmakers' practice of putting themselves at the centre of things, they downplayed and even in some instances entirely disregarded everything that didn't seem directly relevant to their lives and concerns, to the point where, in 1930, making an appeal for his contemporaries to look further, German scholar Fritz Strich observed, 'If one talks about the world, one usually thinks primarily only of Europe, and world literature stands for European literature.'

Despite the fact that, up until the middle of the eighteenth century, more books are thought to have been published in Chinese than in all other languages put together, the prevailing view of world literature had nothing to do with works penned in Mandarin or Cantonese. Many of the early anthologies barely contained a single sample. *Alden's Cyclopedia of Universal Literature* (1882–91), for example, purported to be 'a complete survey of the literature of all ages and of all peoples', but left out the work of non-Western writers almost entirely. Even some sixty years later, the first two volumes of Frank Magill's *Masterpieces of World Literature in Digest Form*, featuring summaries of 1,010 works between them, contained details of only three non-Western works: *The Thousand and One Nights*, *The Tale of Genji* and *Shakuntala* by Kālidāsa.

It wasn't just editors of anthologies with impossibly lofty ambitions who struggled with a universal representation of literature from around the planet. When, in the 1940s, the French scholar Raymond Querneau conducted an experiment that attempted to assemble a list for the *bibliothèque idéale*, or 'ideal library', his findings were thought-provoking. Having compiled the names of some 3,500 works from various countries, Querneau invited numerous writers to select their 100 favourite titles from it, with a view to comparing their choices and constructing a master register. The answers came back and Querneau set about collating them until he had his final list. Whichever way you look at it, the supposedly ideal library had a distinctly Western bias: nine of the titles on the list were by British or American authors, six came from Germany and three were Spanish, while Hebrew and Arabic literature could boast only one entry apiece. But the country that was far and away the front-runner, with a whopping sixty titles to its name, was none other than France.

So what had happened? Could it be that France truly was the writing Mecca it seemed to be in the early decades of the twentieth century, when any self-respecting and not-so-self-respecting British, Irish or American writer – Ernest Hemingway, James Joyce, Djuna Barnes and Ezra Pound among them – flocked to Paris to soak up the literary ambience? Were books written in the language of Flaubert, Balzac and

Molière really *les meilleurs du monde*? The mystery becomes somewhat less puzzling when we refer to the names of the writers who had taken part in the exercise: of the sixty-one people who agreed to share their choices, fifty-eight were French. When invited to chart the global literary terrain, writers and readers had favoured the things closest to them.

The dominance of Western European writing, and the fact that it remained unchallenged in many circles for so long, led some critics to call for the abandonment of the label 'world literature'. 'It is not only a challenging, but also a presumptuous and arrogant term – and we should refrain from using it,' argued Swiss academic Werner P. Friederich in 1960. 'Asia and Europe and, for good measure, Emerson and Whitman comprise, at best, two-and-a-half continents – and the other two-and-a-half continents of our world are left out, without even a word of apology . . . It is simply bad public relations to use this term and to offend more than half of humanity.' More recently, others, keen to get shot of the decades of cultural baggage packed into the phrase, have suggested finding another handle for writing in a supranational context. Eager to circumvent 'the definitive tendency of the dominant to appropriate the emergent', for example, Indian-American academic Gayatri Chakravorty Spivak argues that we should think in terms of 'planetarity', a word she feels would encourage awareness and appreciation of cultural difference across and within national boundaries.

Awkward though such formulations may be, the problem they seek to address is clear: the partiality that underpins the global publishing scene can be damaging, especially for authors in regions that have historically been excluded from the literary world. After all, if you are trying to get your stories read in a country where your national publishers release 15,000 translations of works by anglophone authors in a year, while only fourteen books by your compatriots make it into English, as happened in Brazil in 1987, the odds of finding a wide readership are stacked against you. Not only are your chances of making a name for yourself in the international arena severely limited by the lack of opportunities to be read in the world's most published language, but you are forced to compete with an influx of works to your home market, many of which may already have something of a global reputation. Milan Kundera gives vent to his frustration on this score in his essay, 'Die Weltliteratur':

> Let's try to imagine that the Icelandic sagas had been written in English. Their heroes' names would be as familiar to us as Tristan or Don Quixote; their singular aesthetic character, oscillating between chronicle and fiction, would have provoked all sorts of theories; people would have argued over whether they should or should not be considered the first European novels. I don't mean to say they have been forgotten; after centuries of indifference they are now being studied in universities throughout the world; but they belong to the 'archaeology of letters', they do not influence living literature.

A literary world defined by the writers and thinkers of a few nations is inevitably a space in which the work and influence of many important authors is diminished comparatively, where they are written out of the vital and invigorating exchange Goethe foresaw when he started banging the drum for world literature all those years ago.

Things have changed since the appeals of Friederich and several of his confrères in the mid-twentieth century. In recent decades, anthologies have expanded their reach and involved a wider spectrum of editors in the selection process, and a range of new regional literary festivals and prizes, such as the DSC Prize for South Asian Literature, the Man Asian Literary Prize and the Caine Prize for African Writing, have sought to raise the profile of non-Western literatures around the world. A resurgence of interest in reading across national boundaries over the last fifteen to twenty years – connected in part, no doubt, to the increased global links made possible by the World Wide Web – has seen a new generation of academics revisit the concept of 'world literature' with fresh eyes and broader ambitions.

These days the international literary landscape looks rather different. The quaint Eurocentrism of previous world literatures has faded and flaked off like gold leaf on an antique frame. Search for #world-literature on Twitter and you will mostly find laments from students obliged to sit through world-literature seminars at American universities in order to make up the required number of credits to pass their courses. This is no coincidence: in contrast to the mid-twentieth century, when European scholars dominated the field, the US is largely where it's at for world literature these days, at least as far as the concept as understood by English-language speakers is concerned, with numerous university presses putting out translations of foreign-language works and a raft of books on the subject published by American academics in recent years. As a result, readers inhabit a literary landscape shaped by American thinking. And while David Damrosch rightly identifies 'a natural intellectual drive towards the margins' in the numerous attempts to involve previously unrepresented voices in the definition of its boundaries, the fact remains that the literary world is still effectively a two-dimensional picture with a centre and extremities. It's simply that the centre has moved. Far from the Nobel Prize constituting a 'Greenwich Meridian of literature' that enables us 'to gauge the distance from the centre of the protagonists within literary space', as French scholar Pascale Casanova suggested in the January-February 2005 edition of the *New Left Review*, it would be more accurate to say that the English-speaking written world's longitude of zero now runs through New York.

The effects of this shift are evident in the prominence accorded less to writers from certain geographical regions than to those from a specific language group. Instead of privileging European works as most of their predecessors did, early twenty-first-century attempts to assemble canonical lists of world literature have favoured books in English. The March 2012 third edition of the *Norton Anthology of World Literature*, for example, featured works by fourteen English-language writers and eleven pieces in translation in its 'Contemporary World Literature' section. A further two pieces in that section, 'Wedding at the Cross' by Kenyan writer Ngũgĩ wa Thiong'o and 'The Old Gun' by Mo Yan, are likely also to have been translated, although their translators aren't credited. Assuming they were, this means that, if you take the collection as an accurate, objective snapshot of world literature today – a perhaps not unreasonable assumption, given its billing as 'the most-trusted anthology of world literature available' – and extrapolate from it, slightly more than half of the best works in the world are written in English. Even allowing for the fact that the Queen's mother tongue is an official language in some fifty countries and territories, this seems rather unlikely.

With the best of intentions, it seems, we can never entirely remove the blinkers and filters put on our reading goggles by virtue of who, where and what we are. As comparative literature professor Sarah N. Lawall – herself a contributor to the compilation of the Norton anthologies for many years – observed in her essay on 'Anthologizing "World Literature"', it is extremely difficult to avoid 'unconsciously reinforcing local habits of mind'. Although I can do my level best to escape from the narrow world view – even literary xenophobia – that my Anglocentric bookshelves proved me to have before my global-reading quest, I will never be able to shrug off my national perspective completely and look at books with neutral eyes. And neither will you.

Yet, for all the protests and for all the partiality and ambiguity surrounding the term, the concept of 'world literature' persists. Go into any bookshop of a certain size and you'll find a section dedicated to it – if you're in luck, it might even contain a nook like Waterstones Gower Street's 'Crime Imports' section, which sounds as though it must be brimming with illicit titles. Wander into most universities and you'll hear some mention of world literature, even if it's just a sliver of a seminar wedged into a general course. Google it and you'll discover reams of articles, texts, blogs and forums curated by hosts of experts and enthusiasts, each engaged in reading his or her own very particular world. 'World literature' seems to be a term that nearly everyone uses, even if it doesn't mean the same thing to all of us.

*

In practice, of course – just as many of us quickly became accustomed to the BBC's weather map of Britain, which made Scotland look disproportionately small by putting England at the centre of the default view – most people don't give the question of what makes up the international literary landscape much thought. For those of us who venture beyond our own national borders in our reading, 'world literature' is whatever we can get our hands on. It's the sum total of all the books from other places that we are able to access by way of publishers, bookshops, recommendations and the Web. It consists of books that travel, in other words – or, perhaps more precisely, books that reach us.

So what is it that makes some stories cross national boundaries, while others remain shut up in their local markets? Some commentators have tried to maintain that quality is the key. Nineteenth-century Danish critic Georg Brandes, for example, claimed that the litmus test for texts of any kind was whether they added value to the global community. 'That which Pasteur, Darwin, Bunsen and Helmholtz have written is unconditionally world literature, in that it addresses and enriches all of humanity,' he wrote.

But when you look at which books actually do travel, the idea that benefit to humanity should be the main criterion when it comes to assessing works from elsewhere is problematic. The issue is that most of what we read does not fit unconditionally into that category of indisputable world greats. There might be good books, indifferent books and even bad books in our literary diet. There might be guilty pleasures and indulgences that we have no intention of expanding our souls or advancing world harmony by reading but enjoy all the same. Indeed, Stanford University professor Franco Moretti goes so far as to assert that 99.5 per cent of all literature is non-canonical. And though books that reach our shores from other places often have to go through more layers of selection and editing than home-grown works, there's no guarantee that they will always be anywhere near as good as your average *Beowulf*. From Tolstoy right through to the seediest specimen lurking in 'Crime Imports', books get to us in many guises, and by no means all of them are outstanding. And while Georg Brandes may protest against using popularity as a yardstick when it comes to defining world literature because the great majority of us are 'lethargic, ignorant and of poor judgement', the truth is that there are many things we want to read for reasons other than their objective excellence. For better or worse, our imaginary worlds are made up of all manner of books.

The other problem with Brandes' prescription is that most authors don't write with the aim of addressing the whole world – and if they do, they usually don't succeed. For most writers, an attempt to address everyone will usually result in reaching no one. As Brandes himself observed, 'that which is written directly for the world will hardly do as a work of art'.

Indeed, it's often the specificity of a book that is the secret of its success. The beauty of Mongolian writer Galsan Tschinag's *The Blue Sky*, for example, lies in the author's ability to inhabit the thoughts of his protagonist, a young shepherd boy in the Altai Mountains, and to thereby bring us into his hopes and dreams. By feeling connected to and invested in Tschinag's very distinctive creation, we can take the imaginative leap needed to recognise truths about the world.

Of course, it's not just works from far away that have the power to transport us in the vehicle of their specificity. Jeanette Winterson describes a similar mechanism in her essay 'A Bed. A Book. A Mountain', in which she explores her reaction to Nan Shepherd's *The Living Mountain*, a personal account of living in and with the Cairngorms in north-east Scotland, written in the 1940s but not published until some thirty years later:

> I found myself wandering the mountain range in the company of Nan Shepherd. She is dead but that doesn't make any

difference. Her voice is as clear and fast-flowing as the streams she follows to their source, only to find that the source always points inwards, further. There is always further to go.

. . .

The reason that *The Living Mountain* is a 'good' book is that it takes a very particular and tiny subject and finds in it, or pulls out of it, a story about how we can understand the world.

The book is a metaphor, yes, but it is also specifically about the Cairngorms. The opening it makes in the mind is its capacity to connect the specific and the local with the universal (and as Robert Macfarlane points out in his lovely introduction, the universal is not the same as the general).

Connection is the key here. It's not enough for a book simply to go into the intricacies of a particular culture or situation in great detail – in order to travel beyond its milieu, it must have the ability to make its specificities meaningful and engaging to people with little knowledge of them. A great writer may, as John Donne wrote in 'The Good Morrow', make 'one little room an everywhere', but he or she has got to get us into the little room first.

Often this might be down to the balance of the foreign and the familiar in a particular work. As Berlin-based translator Katy Derbyshire told me, the balance of distinctiveness and recognisable material can determine whether or not a book is picked up for international publication in the first place. Having run several reading groups – sessions at which literature fans assess prospective titles for publication – for independent British publisher And Other Stories, which sources many of its texts through recommendations from readers of other languages, Derbyshire had repeatedly found herself coming up against the question of what makes books travel. Eager to move beyond the 'Nazis and the Stasi', which they felt were the subject matter for the majority of German works translated into English, the group spent a lot of time discussing what was likely to help stories succeed in the anglophone market. Stumbling blocks to recognition included narratives where authors assumed too much local knowledge, and loose plots because, according to Derbyshire, 'a lot of German fiction is not too bothered about plot, unlike English-language writers, and I think we all agreed that it's important for anglophone readers'. The trick was to find works that were different enough from the anglophone mould to be intriguing and *echt*, and yet familiar enough to allow readers to access their worlds.

Far from being exemplars of the mores and styles of their own regions, then, many of the international books that squeeze through the translation bottleneck to reach us are go-betweens. They speak at once to where they've come from and where they're going to. They meld discovery and recognition – enlightening, flattering, challenging and comforting in varying degrees. They may be different to what we're used to, yes, but for the most part they sit within certain limits on a preordained spectrum of difference. In the same way that nations applying for membership of the UN must satisfy others of their sovereignty by conforming to certain conventions in their structure and practices, so books admitted into the sphere of 'world literature' often earn the accolade by communicating local truths and being distinctive in a recognisable way. And just as most of us cannot cross borders without a passport, so many books travel by proving their identities in line with the requirements of the countries they are visiting.

If we are the welcoming committee waiting to greet stories as they traipse disorientated and travel-weary out through the last of the duty free and into the arrivals hall, perhaps our focus should be first and foremost on how we interact with them. As Swedish Academy member Horace Engdahl observed in 2008, 'a literary oeuvre consists not only in a body of texts but also in the mental preconditions for their reading'. Seen in this light, world literature is as much about an openness of approach, a readiness to engage and a willingness to meet halfway as it is about international value and market forces. It has as much to do with the development of a mindset as the creation of a canon. It is about a stranger wanting to send a story to another stranger on the other side of the planet every bit as much as it is about definition and categorisation. If a book inspires that response in us, whether we read it for relaxation, illumination, edification or titillation, then that has to be worth something, whichever world you're from.

3

Identifying landmarks

cultural identity and the problem of authenticity

In the final weeks of my year of reading the world, I arrived home one evening to find a package waiting in the hall. It was book-shaped and covered with stamps of flowers and exotic birds. Inside, along with several paperbacks, was a stack of postcards showing the vivid artwork of Honduran painter Guillermo Yuscarán. When I opened one of the books, I found a pen-and-ink self-portrait on the flyleaf, showing a bearded figure in a broad-brimmed hat. There was also a letter: two A4 pages of computer-typed prose, stapled together, with corrections written on it by hand. In it, Yuscarán thanked me for my review of *Points of Light*, the early short-story collection he'd written during and after his first trip to Honduras in the 1970s. It was on this trip that the US-born William Lewis, PhD, had discovered the country that would eventually transform him from Californian academic into Central American bohemian. His letter went on to tell me the exact circumstances of how William Lewis became Guillermo Yuscarán:

> Here's an interesting anecdote related to *Points of Light*. I think you'll find it amusing: Years ago, when I wrote 'Lia's Song' [one of the short stories in the collection], I had trouble coming up with an appropriate ending. In fact, after writing the story in Tela, I packed it around with me unfinished for weeks, still trying to come up with an ending. Finally, one morning while sitting in Yuscarán's central plaza (Yuscarán is a spectacular mountain town, some 40 miles east of Tegucigalpa), I suddenly thought of

a simple, straightforward way to end the story. I grabbed my journal, wrote down the ending and turned to a kid sitting next to me who was drinking from a small bottle (*pachita*) of cane liquor known as Yuscarán . . . (named for the town in which it's made). 'Hey,' I said, 'how 'bout a toast to my story!' He grinned; we both took a hit . . . Later, back in California, I was writing up the final draft, thinking I'd send the story to *Ms Magazine*, a feminist publication in New York which I thought might go for it, given that Lia's hope in the story, should she give birth to a girl, which she does, is that the child not suffer, as she had, the harsh indignities of machismo. I typed up the story (pre computer days) on an old Smith Corona, thinking I'd sign it Guillermo Yuscarán, the thought being I'd have a better shot at selling it if they perceived me to be latino. Suddenly [I] thought, better yet, I'll sign a woman's name, believing the gals at *Ms* would be more inclined to accept it . . . So, I signed my name Francisca Luis Yuscarán, and mailed off 'Lia's Song', never really believing they'd go for it . . . Prior to that all my work . . . had been signed by my given name, William Lewis. So two months later, my then 5 yr old son Jeb and I were making breakfast in our kitchen in Calif. when the phone rings and he answers it. His first word is 'Who?'. . . then again 'WHO?' . . . then he turns to me, 'Papa, who is Francisca Luis Yuscarán?' I grab the phone, thinkin', Oh shit, what now? . . . falsetto? . . . But I took it like a man, you might say, said 'Good morning, this is Francisca . . .' To make an already long story short, they bought it, published it under that name, sent me 800 dollars and Guillermo Yuscarán came into being . . . Francisca was a one shot deal.

While most authors don't create their national identities as consciously and deliberately as Yuscarán did, there's no question that cultural affinities and ties often affect their work and how we read them. Writers' relationships with funders and decision-makers in particular regions can influence whether or not they get published in the first place. The recognition they receive from national institutions can shape the trajectory of their careers. Indeed, novelist Anna Kim – the daughter of South Korean parents, who moved to Austria from Germany when she was seven – even sees the espousal or exaggeration of national identity as a calculated ploy on the part of some of her contemporaries:

> These days, it's almost as if writers aspire to becoming state writers (*Staatsdichter*) in order to have a comfortable life, because only as a writer approved by the state, will one be invited to prestigious events.

The idea that many authors covet the role of salaried wordsmiths employed to write favourably about certain places or administrations, particularly in totalitarian regimes, may sound extreme, but there is no doubt that it can pay to win the favour of those who command the purse strings. Catch the imagination of those in power, position yourself in alignment with their views, and rewards await. As a laureate, you might even find yourself hailed as a prophet or priest – a saint in what literature and culture professor Vincent Pecora has called 'the modern secular religion' of national identity.

If national identity equates to a religion, though, it is a very schism-ridden one. More Anglican Communion than orthodox, it exists in very many fractured and often conflicting forms around the planet. Indeed, as Pecora goes on to observe in his book *Nations and Identities: Classic Readings*, 'each nation-state now on earth could supply a slightly different meaning for the word "nation"'. It's tempting to push this further and say that almost every person could do the same. As proved by the oohs, ahs, groans and cheers that flooded social media during the Opening Ceremony of the London 2012 Olympics – when millions of Brits picked over the extravaganza to see what they felt did and did not represent them – few people's conceptions of where they come from and what best expresses it are exactly the same. Identity is a broad church that sometimes has very little to do with national borders.

One of the major complications is that it's possible to be both inside and outside the country club at the same time. Although often used interchangeably, nation and state, nationality and citizenship – and for that matter nation and culture – do not mean the same thing. In fact the gap between them is widening, creating a sizeable ravine into which a growing number of writers and stories fall. For many people, citizenship, for example, may be little more than a practicality – a means to obtain better work or travel opportunities. It's a clinical, technical thing stated on forms and expressed in legalese, and its bureaucratic inflexibility makes for some odd glitches. After all, you can be granted citizenship of a place without having set foot in it. Trinidadian literary luminary V. S. Naipaul, for example, has always been British by law, as his homeland was part of the British Empire when he was born. Similarly, you can start life and grow up in a place without receiving the rubber stamp of citizenship – a situation that forms the backdrop for Bahamian novelist Garth Buckner's *Thine is the Kingdom*, in which his protagonist searches for a sense of belonging in the face of a technicality that means he cannot get legal status in his homeland because his father is from the United States.

Yes, citizenship is a cold, clinical technicality. Nationality . . . well, nationality is something else.

But exactly what nationality amounts to, no one seems quite sure. Or rather, we all think we know until someone presses us to explain. 'A nation is the same people living in the same place,' asserts Leopold Bloom confidently in James Joyce's *Ulysses*, only for Ned Lambert to demolish the statement with the announcement that, by that reckoning, he qualifies as a nation in his own right, as he has lived in the same place for five years.

Five years might be on the brief side in many people's books, but an extended period of residency in a place certainly seems to have some weight where defining the pedigree of writers is concerned. Take Nobel laureate Elias Canetti. Born in Bulgaria in 1905 to parents with Spanish Sephardi Jewish roots, he moved to Britain with his family at the age of six and thence to Vienna on the death of his father a year later. There, he learned German, his fifth language and the language he would write in, before moving to Zurich and then to Frankfurt, where he finished school. After another period studying in Vienna, the writer upped sticks for Britain once again, where he spent the best part of more than two decades, becoming a British citizen and developing a close friendship with Iris Murdoch. He passed most of the last years of his life in Zurich and died there in 1994. Depending on which biography you read, Canetti is described variously as a Swiss, Bulgarian, German and Austrian writer, though by the sounds of it he was within striking distance of a plaque in Poets' Corner too.

For others, language can be the deciding factor when it comes to placing people and books. Indeed, for writers in some parts of the world, it has come to be a vital marker of identity. The Kenyan writer Ngũgĩ wa Thiong'o rejected his baptised name James Ngũgĩ, and switched from writing in English to writing in Gikuyu and Swahili as a means of asserting his cultural identity. Similarly, Nigerian author Wole Soyinka has suggested that Kiswahili should be adopted as a pan-African lingua franca, despite the fact that he does not speak it himself, in order that writers from the continent should be able to communicate across borders without having to put their work through the 'colonial sieve' of English. For many, however, the idea of rejecting the language that is threaded through their thinking and in which they have honed their craft and first framed their imaginary worlds is not conceivable, as the St Lucian poet Derek Walcott depicts in 'A Far Cry from Africa', that lyrical and moving account of being torn between hating the ham-fisted and seemingly thoughtless actions of the British administration and loving the linguistic growth that it seeded. It's a theme that has played out in numerous texts in the decades since many colonies gained independence. 'The empire writes back', as the title of that landmark 1980s work on postcolonial literature has it, and – for now – it does so largely in English.

Other writers adopt a yet more ambivalent approach to the question. Filipino author Miguel Syjuco's novel *Illustrado*, for instance, plays with authenticity in all its forms – its central figure, fictional writer Crispin Salvador, even had his own Wikipedia entry for a while, so convinced of his existence were many readers. Language comes in for plenty of scrutiny along the way. At one point, an indignant Manila-based writer even maintains that for a Filipino author to write in English is 'heinous', even as Syjuco is describing her in that very language. The novel went on to win the Grand Prize for the Novel in English at the 2008 Palanca Awards, a neat irony that seems to encapsulate many of the contradictions and ambiguities that bring it to life.

In reality of course, the correlation between languages, writing and state boundaries is loose. While many countries share a single, widely spoken official tongue – such as English, French, Spanish or Portuguese – others, like South Africa, have numerous languages enshrined in their constitutions, several of which may not be spoken outside the region. Then there are all the unofficial languages: the Aragoneses, Araneses, Falas, Leoneses, Calós, Asturians and Extremadurans of this world (all of which are found in Spain and several of which straddle national borders), or the more than 850 tongues spoken among the different tribes of Papua New Guinea. Many of these do not have written literature or even an orthographical system, and to require it of them may seem as blinkered as the actions of previous generations of anglophone monoglots, who rampaged through nations insisting that the indigenous inhabitants wear wool suits and drink tea, regardless of the climate or their personal preferences. *Gyn chengey, gyn cheer* (no language, no country), claims an old saying – but as that saying is in Manx Gaelic and therefore comes from the Isle of Man, a British Crown Dependency, it also demonstrates that language alone is not enough to establish independent nationhood.

Other factors, such as parental heritage, religion and ethnicity, are similarly insufficient as markers of national or cultural identity. For every corroborating instance, there is a counter-example, along with (most notably in the case of religion and ethnicity) some rather disturb-ing arguments – a case in point being the nineteenth-century French novelist Arthur de Gobineau's *Essay on the Inequality of Human Races*, which sets out its author's grounds for advocating the establishment of an Aryan master race. As the numerous brutal attempts to put such ideas into practice across the centuries demonstrate, categorising people along such lines can have sinister consequences. Small wonder that many commentators have rejected defining groups and individuals by country altogether, echoing Albert Einstein's declaration that national-ism is 'the measles of mankind'.

But turn the telescope around and try to frame cultural identity in terms of people accepted by specific nations or regions and you come unstuck yet again. Indeed, for many celebrated writers, recognition in other parts of the world only serves to underline how unwelcome or mistrusted they are in their home nations. When Chinese-born Gao Xingjian won the Nobel Prize for Literature in 2000, for example, China wrote to congratulate France, where Xingjian has lived since receiving asylum there in the 1980s, on its success. It was Mo Yan, twelve years later, who was hailed as the first Chinese winner of the award. A similar controversy erupted in Turkey the year that Orhan Pamuk received the accolade, with conservative commentators refus-ing to recognise the author as Turkish because they felt he was too influenced by Western values. In fact, even John Steinbeck couldn't be honoured without the *New York Times* asking why the Committee had given the prize to a writer whose 'limited talent is, in his best books, watered down by tenth-rate philosophising' and lamenting that it 'was not awarded to a writer . . . whose significance, influence and sheer body of work had already made a more profound impression on the literature of our age'. Nations, it seems, are chary of celebrating their great artists unreservedly and often prefer to keep them at arm's length. As Swedish Academy member Horace Engdahl puts it, when you examine the reactions to naming of the Nobel laureate, 'the hostile comments usually come from the writer's own country. Great authors are a great annoyance. Nations are happiest with their geniuses when they are dead.'

Given that external yardsticks such as citizenship, birthplace and national recognition often prove inadequate, many would argue that nationality is first and foremost a state of mind. It is a statement of where we feel our allegiances lie. The nineteenth-century philosopher John Stuart Mill, who is widely cited on the question of statehood, championed this idea in his 1843 book *A System of Logic*:

> [We do not mean] nationality in the vulgar sense of the term; a senseless antipathy to foreigners; an indifference to the general welfare of the human race, or an unjust preference of the supposed interests of our own country; a cherishing of bad peculiarities because they are national or a refusal to adopt what has been found good by other countries . . . We mean a principle of sympathy, not of hostility; of union, not of separation. We mean a feeling of common interest among those who live under the same government, and are contained within the same natural or historical boundaries. We mean, that one part of the community shall not consider themselves as foreigners with regard to another part; that they shall cherish the tie which holds them together; shall feel that they are one people, that their lot is cast together.

Idealistic though Mill's vision is, much of it seems to have stuck. Even today, many talk of national identity in terms of shared perspectives, emotions and faith. And in extreme cases, it can become a position we adopt consciously as a way of showing solidarity with a particular cause.

I saw this a few years ago. I was freelancing at a magazine in central London when a noisy protest march went by outside, dragging us all away from our desks to look. It turned out to be a long procession of people filing past the building, holding Palestinian flags and banners aloft and shouting slogans in response to prompting from several leaders with megaphones. At first glance, it seemed no different to the numerous demonstrations happening that year, as Palestine pushed to be recognised as a state by the UN. Looking closely, however, it was clear that many of the people marching were not Palestinians – at least not in the technical sense of the word. There were blond blokes in football shirts carrying signs that read 'Manchester United fans are Palestinians'; Caucasian women marching bareheaded alongside Arab women in hijabs; and, perhaps most striking of all, there was a group of Orthodox Jews walking under the banner 'We are Palestinians'. By demonstrating their differences from the standard conception of 'Palestinian', while at the same time embracing that identity, these diverse peoples were making a powerful statement about the wide-ranging nature of support for the cause. It was *Spartacus*-like solidarity on a national level; it was less an assertion of fact than a statement of belief.

For many people, demonstrating allegiance to a particular nation has moral implications. When Nelson Mandela died, the South African president Jacob Zuma praised him as 'the one person who more than any other came to embody [our] sense of common nationhood'. And on the flip side of the coin, when *Guardian* newspaper editor Alan Rusbridger gave evidence to the Home Affairs Select Committee on the Snowden files in December 2013, Member of Parliament Keith Vaz felt it was appropriate to ask him 'Do you love your country?', as though Rusbridger's actions in publishing and sharing the information leaked by former CIA employee Edward Snowden might be construed as a betrayal of a relationship.

But just as relationships can range from life-enhancing to toxic, so the affiliations between people and the places that have played a role in shaping their identities can vary dramatically from individual to individual. As Montserrat Guibernau puts it in her book *The Identity of Nations*, 'not all citizens feel with the same intensity the emotional bond which connects them to their nation-states'.

Writers are often unusually tricky customers in this respect. Tending to be outsiders and observers by the very nature of their craft, they frequently seem divided when it comes to the question of their own national identities. Familiarity with and the ability to modulate between two or more cultures seem to be an advantage when it comes to story-telling. On close analysis, many wordsmiths turn out to be translators rather than narrators of experience, explaining one part of the world to another. The celebrated Dominican-American writer Junot Díaz, who has lived in the US for most of his life, and is creative writing professor at MIT, uses both his intimacy with and distance from his island birth-place to communicate its richness in his Pulitzer Prize-winning novel *The Brief Wondrous Life of Oscar Wao*. At once versed in and able to remove himself from American and Dominican cultures, he can emphasise and even make comic capital out of the gap between the prevailing attitudes in the two cultures. He can appreciate and celebrate them, while being conscious of the things that will make them curious to readers. Similarly, P. G. Wodehouse – once said to be one of only two writers, along with Agatha Christie, whose work was on sale at every train station in India – capitalised on his transatlantic lifestyle to serve up both British and American characters with the wit that comes from looking at things at one step's remove. More recently, the long-lists of numerous book prizes have bristled with stories that owe much to their writers' mixed cultural heritages and experiences. Charlotte Mendelson's *Almost English* is a prime example. 'What am I? I can't even say I'm half-Hungarian, I'm almost English. I couldn't exactly tweet my nationality. It's more of a kind of novella,' said Mendelson in an interview with Alex Peake-Tomkinson on Bookanista.com shortly after her place on the 2013 Man Booker Prize longlist was announced. As the novel's heroine finds herself similarly caught between middle-class Britain and the world of her Hungarian-speaking relatives, Mendelson's narrative voice plays the role of interpreter, explaining some of the more baffling aspects of her foreign characters, such as their accents, to the reader: 'Nothing you know, no rolled "r"s or recognizable sounds but either an entirely impenetrable language . . . or a distorted English, full of dactyls, which dust familiar words – "*Pee*-codilly", or "*vosh*-ingmochine" or indeed "*Vest*-minstaircourt" –

with snow and fir and darkness.' Interestingly, however, what Mendelson seems to have in mind is not the reaction of any common or garden reader but how the events of her book might appear, as she writes at one point, 'to the casual Englishman, were one present', a strangely quaint phrase suggestive of leather on willow and Edwardian picnics, and doubtless no more representative of the average reader of *Almost English* than the exotic characters being explained. Mendelson's British – or more specifically English – reader may not be everyone's cup of tea.

With increased travel and what Guibernau has called a 'proliferation of hyphenated identities', the concept of national identity seems to be getting ever more elastic – although a glance back down the centuries challenges the idea that this is an entirely new thing. As Thorlac Turville-Petre reveals in his book *England the Nation: Language, Literature and National Identity 1290–1340*, the massaging up of a common national sense of belonging has long been a fraught business:

> In 13th-century England it took considerable efforts of distortion to shape both the land and the people into a vision of a single community. While the sea marked the southern and eastern boundaries of England, the borders with Wales and Scotland in the 13th century were fuzzy, and the practical limitations of English lordship over people who had their own cultures and languages, their own legal practice and indeed their own origin myths were all too apparent.

Norfolk, according to Turville-Petre, had a dreadful reputation. Indeed, *Descriptio Norfolciensium*, a satirical poem written in Latin and thought to date from that time, paints the county as 'the vilest region in the world' and makes its inhabitants out to be villains and buffoons who eat dung beetles fresh from horse shit and get rid of unwanted visitors by shouting, 'We are not at home now.' Even today, with England's borders pretty much unchanged for centuries, debates about devolution and independence continue in the wider UK, with Scotland

narrowly voting to stay in the union in September 2014. Mor
socio-economic divide that sees unemployment rates at alm
times the London level in many regional cities leads numerous
tators to reject the idea of England as a single nation. 'The rea
London is a separate country. Perhaps we should make i
argued economics editor Larry Elliott in the *Guardian* in S
2013. Seen in this light, it's a wonder that the concept of En
let alone Britishness, has ever managed to exist at all.

*

The freedom to construct and control your own cultural ide
matter how fractured – is a luxury by no means available to al
regional characteristics are often superimposed on places
from outside. This is particularly the case for countries that h
tionally found themselves on the margins of the world map
figuratively or literally, as Chimamanda Ngozi Adichie d
when she first left Nigeria to go to university in the US at
nineteen. Instead of spending her first few months atter
decipher and fit in with life in a new country, the novelist-to
herself confronted with a view of who she was that she did
nise. Her American roommate met her with a range of preco
that made an even-handed friendship between them very dif
asked how Adichie had learned to speak English so well,
pointed to discover that her 'tribal music' consisted of
Mariah Carey songs, and assumed that the teenager – the d
an administrator and a university professor – would not kn
use a cooker.

What struck me was this: she had felt sorry for me even
she saw me. Her default position toward me as an Africa
kind of patronising, well-meaning pity. My roommate
single story of Africa – a single story of catastrophe. In thi
story there was no possibility of Africans being similar to

any way, no possibility of feelings more complex than pity, no possibility of a connection as human equals.[1]

It took several years for Adichie to make sense of her roommate's misguided sense of what was authentically Nigerian and the alien cultural identity that had been constructed for her. 'If I had not grown up in Nigeria and if all I knew about Africa was from popular images, I too would think that Africa was a place of beautiful landscapes, beautiful animals and incomprehensible people fighting senseless wars, dying of poverty and AIDS, unable to speak for themselves and waiting to be saved by a kind, white foreigner.'[2] Significantly, Adichie only began to describe herself as 'African' after arriving in America, as though this aspect of her identity had been crystallised in response to the rest of the world rather than arising purely from her experience of home.

Fellow Nigerian Chinua Achebe would no doubt have recognised her position. As a literature professor in the US, he had to challenge his students' preconceptions constantly, as he explained in a 1987 interview published in Jane Wilkinson's *Talking with African Writers*:

Here you are dealing with students who are coming out of a tradition where Africa is not really like anywhere else they know: Africa in literature, Africa in the newspapers, Africa in the sermons preached in the churches is really the Other Place. It is the Africa of *Heart of Darkness*; there are no real people in the Dark Continent, only forces operating; and people don't speak any language you can understand, they just grunt, too busy jumping up and down in frenzy . . . So I find that the first thing is to familiarize them with Africa, make them think that this is a place of people, it's not the Other Place, the opposite of Europe or America.

---

1 Chimamanda Ngozi Adichie speaking at TEDGlobal2009
2 Ibid.

Such narrow misconceptions about people from other cultures can be extraordinarily resilient. Like dominant genes, they get passed on from one generation of accounts to the next, reproducing tales in their own image. Indeed, once a story has gained ground, we human beings seem to prefer to work from it rather than go back to first principles, a phenomenon that slave-trade historian Philip Curtin documented in his 1964 book, *The Image of Africa*. In it, he describes how European explorers' perspectives were heavily influenced by the reports of their predecessors so that, rather than coming to Africa with fresh eyes, they looked for evidence that would corroborate the conclusions they had read, and were relatively blind to anything that contradicted what they thought they knew. 'They did not ask, "What is Africa like, and what manner of men live there",' wrote Curtin, 'but "How does Africa, and how do the Africans, fit into what we already know about the world". . . . The image of Africa, in short, was largely created in Europe to suit European needs.'

The problem with such superimposed cultural identities is that we human beings have a strong tendency to play the roles we're assigned. You only have to look at the dramatic contrast between the seasons of reality TV show *Big Brother* to see that. The rather staid first series, back in 2000 when the concept of filming strangers in a house constantly was unfamiliar, featured a bit of kissing and the dastardly 'Nasty Nick' – who was guilty of the momentous crime of writing down names on scraps of paper. Subsequent series, in which housemates, no doubt egged on by the production team, entered the show aware of the media circus that would await them when they left and conscious of how the stories might play out on screen, were full of nudity, sex acts and scandalous revelations as the contestants strove to be what was expected of them.

A century earlier, Leonard Woolf had picked up on a similar process. During his time as a government official in Ceylon, he began to wonder about the influence of stories on the society in which he worked, as he described in *Growing: An Autobiography of the Years 1904–1911*:

The white people were also in many ways astonishingly like characters in a Kipling story. I could never make up my mind whether Kipling had moulded his characters accurately in the image of Anglo-Indian society or whether we were moulding our characters accurately in the image of a Kipling story.

If this strangely symbiotic relationship between storytelling and identity was problematic for the white immigrants, it was potentially disastrous for the locals. Depicted as 'as incapable as a child of understanding what authority means' in Kipling's short story 'His Chance in Life', Indians were judged and dismissed in boarding-school dorms and libraries long before each generation of future colonialists got its postings to the remote corners of the British Empire. 'The tension existing in India has been bad for our race, and a conception of Indian life based upon the writings of Ethel M. Dell or Maud Diver, or even Kipling, has not helped,' wrote translator and historian Edward Thompson in 1925. Indeed, such stories imposed by outsiders may well have had a pernicious influence on events. As Allen J. Greenberger put it in his 1969 book on *The British Image of India*, 'In an age when "sparing the rod" was the equivalent of "spoiling the child", it is obvious that relations with a people considered to be children would involve a large degree of force' – and, as atrocities such as the Amritsar Massacre demonstrate, the rod was duly not spared.

While we may have come some way from the mindset of the Raj, we're dishonest if we tell ourselves that such blinkered attitudes are entirely a thing of the past. In spite of efforts to broaden cross-cultural understanding in recent years, we still live in a world where politicians can claim that the phrase 'Bongo Bongo Land' represents the views of 'ordinary people in a rugby club', as UKIP MP Godfrey Bloom did in 2013, and where 'Do They Know It's Christmas?' blares out in the shops in December – regardless of the fact that Christians make up more than a third of Africa's population.

The problem for us as readers is that these inadequate

representations of life in other places mean we rarely come to literature from faraway places with fresh eyes. Almost without our realising it, a range of partial, naïve and even downright false images of many regions of the world have accumulated in our imaginations throughout our lives, like limescale round the spout of a dripping tap, and these influence the flow of our thoughts. They sensitise us to certain aspects of life in different places and close our eyes to others. And they may lead us to think we know what a Nigerian or Namibian or Malawian story will be like before we've read a single word. Taken to extremes, they can make us hanker after simplistic, skewed or spurious representations of parts of the world in the misplaced belief that these are authentic – so much so that we become nostalgic for places that have never existed.

During and since my year of reading my way around the planet, I've come into contact with huge numbers of people engaged in world-reading quests of one kind or another. The projects are as varied as their creators, but a thread that runs through many of them is the desire to discover stories that are in some way representative of the different nations or regions encountered – to find books that, as several people have put it to me, capture the 'spirit' of a place. For many, authenticity is the key consideration. If we're reading books from far away, we want to be sure that we are getting a genuine sense of the culture that produced them; that we are, in some fashion, doing justice to their origins. When you delve into this well-meaning objective, however, a problem emerges: if you have no first-hand knowledge of a nation, how can you judge whether or not a particular story is likely to be representative of its 'spirit' (assuming of course that such a thing exists in the first place)?

Some readers think that the best way to guarantee the cultural authenticity of a story is to make sure that it is set in the country in question. In fact, a number make this the primary consideration, occasionally at the expense of all other factors, lumping books by British and American nationals in with works by writers more closely linked to the country, especially in the case of nations where few home-grown narratives are available in English. I've even seen Dan Brown's *Angels and Demons* billed as Vatican City literature.

You can understand the thinking behind it – in most cases at least. For many people, the impulse to read more widely arises when practical considerations do battle with a desire to see more of the world. Unable to afford the time or money that a real-life journey to every region would require, they make the decision to bring the world to them through books, using literature as a massive telescope to view things that are too remote to see any other way. In these circumstances, it makes sense that you should want stories set in the countries in question. How else are you going to find out about the Tuvaluan rain dances, Lesothan marriage rituals or Fijian kava ceremonies that you would dearly love to witness first-hand?

Indeed, as I discovered when I tried to slot books into the national categories on the burgeoning list of recommendations on my blog, there are odd examples where the setting of a story seems to tip the scales in terms of its cultural affinity. Oonya Kempadoo's autobiographical novel *Buxton Spice* draws heavily on the author's childhood in Guyana, which seems to make the book belong to that nation, instead of Grenada, the nation Kempadoo has claimed as her own since making her home there. At the opposite end of the scale, Neil Gaiman's *American Gods*, with its evocation of a nation made up of people originally from elsewhere and seen through the windshield of a road-trip tale in the mould of many of the classics, is arguably an American novel by a British writer – albeit one who has lived in the States for more than twenty years, is married to an American and has American children.

For the most part, however, just as residency in a place is only part of the picture when it comes to human beings' sense of national and cultural identity, so setting makes for a rather one-sided approach when it comes to the quest for authenticity in literature from around the world. After all, if national identity is as much about thoughts, feelings and perspective as it is about physical presence in a region, then surely the cultural uniqueness or specialness of a work is likely to be located as much in its voice and the mindset and assumptions underpinning it as in its setting, if not far more so. When you think about it, there's no reason why a Zimbabwean work about a kingdom under the sea couldn't be every bit as enlightening, thought-provoking and culturally specific as the most faithful portrayal of life in Mugabe's Harare.

It's not as if we expect British writers to keep their tales within the borders of the United Kingdom. If that were the case we'd have to relinquish our claims on many of the works we hold most quintessentially English – much of Shakespeare, Forster, Christie and Greene, to name but a few. *Our Man in Havana* would become *Someone Else's Bloke Over There*. And as for giving David Mitchell a British Book Award for his global and temporal odyssey *Cloud Atlas*, well, you can think again. The fact is that many of the greatest literary works past and present – the gems most people would include in the world-literature canon without a second thought – do not stay put and dutifully report on life in their neck of the woods. From Homer to Hemingway and from Cervantes to Beckett, stories rove around all over the planet and in and out of other worlds, appropriating experience wherever they see fit.

The danger with demanding authenticity, or 'spirit' of a place, in a book is that we look for what we expect to see and miss what is there. Instead of allowing the stories of a region to open our minds and lead us in new directions, we can become narrow and petty, demanding that regional literature conform to our expectations. Far from broadening our horizons, we risk shutting ourselves in a hall of mirrors where we see our version of the world reflected back at us ad infinitum. It's a theme Penelope Lively deals with beautifully in *Abroad*, a short, witty account of a young couple's trip to the Continent in search of inspiration for their creative endeavours:

Anyone artistic needed Abroad in the 1950s. You needed the Mediterranean, and fishing boats pulled up on sandy shores. Olive groves under blue skies. Romanesque churches. Market squares with campanile and peasantry. Sunflowers, cactuses, prickly pears, cypresses, palms.

By the end of the novella, the pair are forced to admit that 'You can have enough of authentic, eventually,' but not before the walking clichés with which they fondly imagined themselves to be surrounded have in fact proven themselves to be robustly rounded and canny to boot, managing to take advantage of the English duo's naïvety and squeeze a week's unpaid labour out of them.

Other, less amusing, consequences stem from too rigid a search for the authentic. By imposing what critic Shu-mei Shih has called 'the burden of collective representation' on individual writers, by demanding that they speak not only for themselves but for their compatriots, we risk squashing all individuality and daring out of their work. Well-meaning but misguided readers might even stop paying attention to the quality of literature from certain regions in their anxiety to champion the stories that are perceived to be somehow closest to the raw experience of life there (or at least to outsiders' conceptions of what that is). When the focus is on authenticity at the expense of almost all else, we can become strangely dishonest in our search for works we perceive to be 'true'.

Wole Soyinka observed this in the way that some Western publishers treated African literature in the late twentieth century. In several interviews recorded in Jane Wilkinson's *Talking with African Writers*, he shared his reaction to the changing profile of literature from the continent, focusing on some of the promotional ventures, such as Heinemann's African Writers Series, that sought to capitalise on a groundswell of interest:

> The series, of course, was very uneven; quite a large portion of it was total dross, but a fair amount, quite a good amount, was excellent literature . . . It occurred to me that the series was adopting a policy of anything goes because it's African and

therefore it must be published. If that series had been run by African intellectuals I would suggest that at least one-third of what was published would never have been published.

Paradoxically, it seems, an untempered mania for cultural authenticity can lead us to read not only books that reinforce the assumptions about other places we had all along, but poorly written stories that are likely to put us off venturing any further. Far from broadening our horizons, too slavish a desire to read the world can imprison us even more squarely in our own heads.

*

Given the myriad contradictions, ambiguities and problems that surround the question of cultural authenticity, it's perhaps not surprising that many writers advocate rejecting national distinctions altogether. 'We should give up, as fast and as thoroughly as we can, thinking in national categories,' the Austrian writer Anna Kim says. 'The idea of the nation-state has proven to be very dangerous. It leads to inclusion and exclusion, majorities and minorities, and to the horrible perception that there is only one real solution when it comes to dealing with minorities – and that is to get rid of them as they are disturbing the system.'

She is not alone. In fact Virginia Woolf put a compelling case that women should reject the idea of national allegiance on principle in her essay *Three Guineas*. In it, she argued that the only logical response to the historical discrimination that denied women property-owning and voting rights and legal status is to say that 'as a woman, I have no country. As a woman I want no country. As a woman my country is the whole world.' Any vestige of patriotism after this exercise, she wrote, would be down to 'some obstinate emotion . . ., some love of England dropped into a child's ears by the cawing of rooks in an elm tree'.

For others, national categories disturb the reading process too. Nigerian writer and Booker Prize winner Ben Okri spoke vehemently against carving literature up according to country:

My earliest readings were of folktales and myths, Greek myths, German myths, Roman myths, African myths, African legends. And my mother always told me stories. All of them were inter-mingled. I didn't separate one thing from the other. Aladdin was as African to me as Ananse. Odysseus was just another version of the tortoise myth. Literature depends first and foremost on the fact that one person can write something that another wants to read. How is it possible, if it weren't for the fact that essentially there's something that's shared? All this ghetto criticism ignores that essential point.

Twenty-five years later, Haitian-Canadian writer Dany Laferrière took up the theme in his novel *I am a Japanese Writer*, the story of a Haitian-Canadian author who, 'tired of cultural nationalism' and wanting to 'show that borders have disappeared', attempts to immerse himself in whatever Japanese culture he can find in his home town of Montreal as research for his new book, *I am a Japanese Writer*:

> I don't understand all the attention paid to a writer's origins. [. . . Growing up,] very naturally, I repatriated the writers I read at the time. All of them: Flaubert, Goethe, Whitman, Shake-speare, Lope de Vega, Cervantes, Kipling, Senghor, Césaire, Roumain, Amado, Diderot – they all lived in my village. Other-wise, what were they doing in my room? Years later, when I became a writer and people asked me, 'Are you a Haitian writer, a Caribbean writer or a French-language writer?' I answered without hesitation: I take on my reader's nationality. Which means that when a Japanese person reads me, I immediately become a Japanese writer.

For all his protests, however, Laferrière's protagonist is unable to escape from the perceptions of those for whom national categories do still have significance. When news of the book he is supposed to be writing sparks a cultural movement in Japan and the Japanese embassy wants to involve him in all sorts of literary ventures, the fictional author finds his statements about the meaninglessness of national borders count for very little. Whether he thinks nationality matters or not is immaterial – a significant number of others do and that in itself is enough to make it a reality. Oddly enough, Laferrière's outlandish scenario now has a real-life counterpart in the experience of American novelist and long-time Japanese culture enthusiast David Gordon. His debut novel *The Serialist* was published to modest success in the States in 2010, but when a Japanese translation (retitled *The Second-Rate Novelist*) came out, he was rocketed to superstardom on the other side of the Pacific, winning three major literary awards and being invited over for the glamorous premiere of the film of the book. The experience of being a celebrity in another country was rather disorientating, as he described in the *New York Times* in January 2014. Reflecting rather wistfully on his rapturous reception, Gordon noted that the rooms stuffed with books in which he spent his solitary writing life in the US were smaller than the hotel suite he'd stayed in for those few heady days in Tokyo. His quotidian washing facilities were distinctly lacklustre in comparison to the luxurious self-filling bath he'd enjoyed the use of in Japan. And the friends he met up with and the people he saw out jogging rarely if ever applauded him. Happy enough though he was in his day-to-day life, Gordon wrote, it was hard not to daydream occasionally about the glamorous life of his alter-ego, David-san, who was a sensation on the other side of the world.

When enough people proclaim that someone possesses a quality – whether fame, certain personality traits or a particular nationality – it can have the effect of creating a local truth. What other people say about us has considerable power to make things so. And while many writers such as Kim and Okri may reject attempts to pigeonhole books by country, the story of national identity persists – embedded deep in many people's understanding of who and what they are.

And so it seems to be today. Nearly 200 years on from Goethe's assertion that 'national literature is now a rather unmeaning term; the epoch of world literature is at hand, and everyone must strive to hasten its approach', the majority of us still assume a link between story and place. We still award book prizes according to region. We still think in terms of our culture's literary heritage and we argue passionately about what defines it – as numerous comment threads on newspaper articles attempting to give rundowns of British, American, Indian or other nations' greats will attest. Writers fuel this too, making cultural identity a recurring theme in novels and stories from *A Town Like Alice* to Therese Anne Fowler's *Z*, as characters struggle to define their place in the world. If nationalism with all its ugly associations is, in Einstein's words, 'an infantile disease' and 'the measles of mankind', it seems to be a childhood affliction through which many have to pass in order to mature as artists. For many authors, negotiating a relationship with the place, people or things in which their identities are grounded appears essential to the business of spinning tales. Indeed, as I discovered during the most moving and memorable encounter of my year of reading the world, the ability to root yourself in a culture and tie your words to the literature of a place can be the start of writing.

The meeting came about after I read *Why the Child is Cooking in the Polenta*, an autobiographical novel by Aglaja Veteranyi, and wrote about it on my blog. Born into a family of Romanian circus performers, Veteranyi spent her childhood travelling Europe performing tricks until she and her relatives were granted asylum in Switzerland, the country she came to adopt as her home. Illiterate because of her nomadic life, the teenage Veteranyi taught herself to read and write German before embarking on a career as a freelance writer in 1982. However, the abuse and exploitation of her early years had taken a lasting toll and the author drowned herself in Lake Zurich in 2002.

At the root of her novel's unease – in which the child-narrator and her sister insulate themselves from reality by masking one horror with another, creating a gruesome story about a child being cooked alive in a vat of polenta, which they tell themselves for comfort when the world becomes too frightening – is the search for home and identity. To the central character, 'every country is in a foreign country', and the family's history and allegiances shift depending on whom they are speaking to:

OUR STORY SOUNDS DIFFERENT EVERY TIME MY MOTHER TELLS IT.

We're Orthodox, we're Jewish, we're international!

My grandfather owned a circus arena, he was a salesman, a captain, traveled from country to country, never left his own village and was a locomotive engineer. He was a Greek, a Romanian, a farmer, a Turk, a Jew, an aristocrat, a Gypsy, an Orthodox believer.

My mother was appearing in circuses even as a child so she could feed her whole family.

Another time she runs away to the circus with my father against her parents' wishes.

As I discovered when Jens Nielsen, Veteranyi's former partner, offered to meet me after reading my response to the novel in late 2012, this quest for home and rootedness was central to the story of the author's writing itself. We met in a bar in Covent Garden, where Nielsen, a playwright in his mid-forties, with a shaved head, glasses and kind eyes, told me the story of his turbulent seven-year relationship with Veteranyi, which began when she was his teacher at drama school in Zurich. The high point, he said, came when the original *Warum das Kind in der Polenta kocht* first appeared in 1999, the year after Nielsen graduated. Having collaborated on numerous projects throughout their relationship, the duo turned their attention to developing a performance piece to accompany Veteranyi's readings from the novel and spent nearly two years touring Europe with it.

The show went through ten or twenty incarnations in that time as the pair experimented with images that would complement the book without commenting on it. In one version, the action consisted of

Nielsen eating a grilled chicken suspended on an empty stage; in another, he would serve inedible food in the manner of a circus artist to places set at a table. There were variations involving Swiss folk songs and knife dances, and other forms using salad and vegetables. Many of the ideas received an airing only once or twice before the duo cast them aside and moved on to something else.

'It was really about finding elements that create images,' said Nielsen. '[It was] similar I guess to modern expressive art where you find an installation and some of them are crap and you see through it right away and others you're taken in with. That's what I was searching for.'

This dedication to finding the right image to interact with the text reflected in some small way Veranyi's tortuous route to publication. *Polenta* was the result of twenty years of abortive literary attempts carried out from the time that Veranyi taught herself to read and write aged seventeen. Yet for all the 'hard suffering' Nielsen knew it had cost her, the decision to be a writer and to adopt Switzerland and the German language had been a watershed moment in the young woman's life. Having grown up in an anarchic group that moved from the fringes of one place to the next, shunning rules, ties and stability – at least as far as her immediate family was concerned – she had at last found something in which she could ground her identity:

'What connected her so strongly to Switzerland was that she was [illiterate] before she came there. Her mind was all in this area and also in the language. Meanwhile all the belly things – the mother, the food, the home of the child – were back in Romania and were in a way the lost items that she would always search for. There was a constant threat in her life of being sucked back into this. This was always a danger because it was associated with her mother and the relationship between them. She said she always expected that her mother would go crazy one day. It happened the other way around, I guess.'

In August 2001, while the couple were sharing a studio in Berlin, Veteranyi, who battled with eating disorders for much of her life, began to show signs of slipping into severe mental illness. In the months that followed, they moved back to Zurich, where Veteranyi's anxiety and phantom ailments increased. The pair consulted a large number of doctors and therapists, and Veteranyi also engaged a variety of alternative healers and practitioners with dubious credentials, flitting from one to the next with dizzying haste.

In early February 2002, Nielsen finally convinced her that she should go into a clinic and see the course of treatment through. After a retrogression session with yet another mysterious shaman the Saturday before she was due to be admitted, Veteranyi and Nielsen went to bed for the last time.

'That night I remember her waking me up several times and then there was a point where I pretended not to wake,' he said.

When Nielsen woke again at around 5 a.m., he found the bed empty beside him and the door to the flat ajar. The door to the building had also been wedged open with a broom. Not knowing where to start, he went out to look for Veteranyi. Then he remembered a place on Lake Zurich with a little pier where they always used to go. He found her floating in the lake, already dead for several hours. She had left her shoes and some sleeping pills on the pier.

In the ten years since Veteranyi's death, her work had been Nielsen's constant companion. From preparing her unfinished second book, *Das Regal der letzten Atemzüge* (The Shelf of Last Breaths), for posthumous publication with the help of her mentor Hannes Becher, to having input into numerous stage and film adaptations of the *Polenta* novel and a documentary about the author's life, Nielsen's thoughts had rarely been far from Veteranyi's writing since her novel came out. When I met him he had recently returned from trips to Budapest to view an award-winning Hungarian film of the novel, and Amsterdam, where a new stage adaptation was in production.

Things were about to change, however: when he left London, Nielsen would be handing Veteranyi's literary estate over to the Swiss National Archive, where it was to be preserved and made available to the public for at least 300 years. After a decade of looking after it single-handedly, he would have a chance to let go. 'I will cry one more last time. It's OK to grieve but there comes a point where you either have to carry on or dissolve. I will be honoured and grateful to pass it on.'

Not that Nielsen expected Veteranyi's influence and fascination for readers to end any time soon.

'The way she would take people's stories and tell their stories on the belly level – this book does the same to people. Her legacy is the stuff that happens to people after she died [because of her work]. There's a great inner correspondence that makes great sense.' He smiled for a moment. 'And obviously many people also dislike the book and think it's rubbish.'

A few days after our meeting a package arrived through the post. For once, it wasn't book-shaped. It contained two CDs Nielsen had burned for me – one of them featuring an episode of *Musik für einen Gast* (Music for a Guest), the Swiss version of *Desert Island Discs* on which Veteranyi had appeared after her book came out. I sat and listened to the author talking in her high, almost childlike, voice about her life, and about how writing her novel enabled her to 'play with reality' and become father and mother to the characters. Speaking in the adopted German language that had enabled her to take control of her story, she had the air of a national treasure in the making. Some seventeen years after she had arrived on the planet, rooting herself in the Swiss nation had given her the means to grow and thrive, at least for a while. And although it couldn't save her in the end, it had provided a starting point – and a place for those who loved her to lay her estate to rest.

4

Following the trade routes
publishing around the world

Here's a challenge: go into your local bookshop and count up how many nations are represented on its shelves. If you don't have time to tot it up, ask someone behind the counter. Assuming they're able to tell you, I'll warrant you won't find literature by authors from more than around seventy, or roughly one-third, of the world's nations available to buy. When I asked blog visitors to do the same thing a while ago, that was the highest number that anyone came across, with many shops only offering works from twenty or thirty countries. From the glossiest emporium to the quirkiest wordmongers, the story was the same: the majority of the world was off limits.

The truth is that the odds are stacked against most books from elsewhere ever reaching us, particularly when they are written in languages other than English. With just over 4 per cent of fiction, poetry and drama published in the UK and Ireland (according to research by Literature Across Frontiers), in the region of 3 per cent of all texts released in the US originating from other languages, and a mere half a dozen or so translations published every year in Australia – as International PEN reported in 2007 – the proportion of translated titles on the average English-language bookshop's shelves will only ever be tiny.

When you consider the implications of these statistics for the number of books reaching us from specific language groups, the results are sobering. Literature Across Frontiers found that only twenty-two of the books published in the UK and Ireland in 2008 were translations of literary works originally written in Arabic, twenty-one were Chinese and a mere eleven were Polish – six fewer than the seventeen works carried over from Latin in the same period. Even with Stieg Larsson becoming the second-best-selling author in the world that year (after Khaled Hosseini), a mere forty-two of the books we saw in that twelve-month stretch were Swedish. Small beans when you think that 129,057 new and revised titles came out in the UK during that time.

The upshot is that there are many nations with work by only one or two writers available to buy in English and plenty that have no literature at all represented in the anglophone market. With books from elsewhere forced into a Darwinian struggle to make it through the bottleneck and attain the incomparable reach that release in the world's most published – and most translated – language makes possible, competition is fierce. By and large, only those titles with the shrewdest and most powerful backers stand a chance of landing an English-language deal. As a result, countries with weak publishing traditions or economies that make it impossible to put up the funding often required to persuade a British house to take a risk on an unknown foreign author lag woefully behind. Though French might be the language most frequently translated into English, coming top in all of the three sample years in Literature Across Frontiers' study (with well over 100 literary texts each time), the majority of these books will be from French-speaking countries with strong networks. Francophone Africa will largely not get a look in.

In fact, much of Africa rarely gets a look in when it comes to translation. Leaving aside works written in the continent's numerous indigenous tongues – which, despite making up around one-third of the planet's languages, are hardly ever translated – you'd be hard pushed to get hold of English versions of anything written in the European languages that are official in many states there. To date, you won't find a single commercially available translation of a Malagasy novel – even though, judging by the array of extracts, short stories and poetry published in the 2002 anthology *Voices from Madagascar*, there are numerous interesting French-language writers in this nation of more than 22 million people. Look for work from Burkina Faso, Cameroon, Gabon and Guinea and, beyond a handful of classics and trailblazers – Mongo Beti and Norbert Zongo among them – you'll draw a blank. It's a similar story with Equatorial Guinea, Africa's only hispanophone nation – November 2014 saw the publication of Jethro Soutar's translation of Juan Tomás Ávila Laurel's *By Night The Mountain Burns*, only the second novel ever to make it into English from there.

When it comes to African writers working in Portuguese, the situation is laughable. Records show that seventeen Portuguese-language literary works were published in the UK and Ireland in 2008. That's seventeen books picked from the literary output of Portugal, Mozambique, Angola, Guinea-Bissau, East Timor, Cape Verde, São Tomé and Principe and Equatorial Guinea (Portuguese is spoken there too), not to mention the behemoth Brazil. Seventeen books to cover the literary productions of a combined 260 million or so people. And 2008 was a bumper year: in 2005 and 2000 the number was just ten. Things are no better across the pond in the US: figures from the Center for Books Culture show that just six works of fiction from Portugal and seven from Brazil were published between 2000 and 2006. The table I saw doesn't even include the African lusophone nations.

In cases such as these, the only works an anglophone reader can hope to come by are those off the beaten track of the commercial thoroughfare – unpublished translations and self-published works in English, which may be shared at the discretion of their creators. From the decade-old translation of a novel by the Comoro Islands' first published novelist, Mohamed Toihiri, buried in the hard drive of an academic in Vermont, to the self-funded rendering of Panamanian novelist Juan David Morgan's *The Golden Horse*, sent by the author himself, when reading the world I repeatedly found myself reliant on the kindness of strangers for access to areas of the globe the English-language publishing industry doesn't reach. These unofficial versions sometimes included startlingly significant works. Along with the first ever novel to be translated directly from Turkmen into English, Ak Welsapar's *The Tale of Aypi*, I was lucky enough to read a manuscript of a novel that was voted one of Africa's best books of the twentieth century by an African jury in 2002 – but is otherwise off-limits to those of us who read only English-language texts.

I would never have discovered it existed were it not for a timely comment on my blog from a Portuguese literature fan. Having read Mia Couto's novel *Under the Frangipani* as my Mozambican choice, I was limbering up to write a blog post about it when a comment flashed up from someone called Miguel. He had a recommendation for Mozambique: '*Niketche* (Paulina Chiziane); because it's a cliché to only read Mia Couto and she needs more attention ☺'.

The smiley did little to lessen the sinking feeling that the words inspired: I was going to have to go back to the drawing board and thereby miss my weekly target of reading and blogging about four books. Still, the alternative was even less palatable. I might be many things, but a cliché I was determined not to become – at least, not if I could possibly avoid it. I took a deep breath and googled Paulina Chiziane.

The early signs were promising. Information in English about Chiziane – the first Mozambican woman to publish a novel and the winner of the 2003 José Craveirinha Prize – topped the search results. What's more, an English translation of *Niketche*, billed as a farce in which six women get their revenge on a lying polygamist, was listed on Amazon with a publication date of 10 February 2010.

The only fly in the ointment was the fact that the book was apparently 'currently unavailable' and did not appear to be for sale through any other retail outlet. Still, this seemed like a minor obstacle. The book had a publication date, it had ISBN numbers and it had a cover – I had seen it on the web. It could only be a matter of time until it was in my hands. Nothing daunted, I looked up the publisher – a small independent house called Aflame Books – and sent them an email asking how I could obtain a copy.

A few days later, a reply came back from Richard Bartlett, co-founder of the company and also the translator listed in the information about *Niketche*. He was sorry to say that Aflame had gone bust before it had managed to publish the novel and only a third of it had ever been translated. He was a big fan of Mozambican literature, but as far as he knew, the only writer from the country with commercially available work in English was . . . Mia Couto. Under the banner of Aflame Books, Bartlett had published various titles in translation from other parts of Africa, Iraq and parts of Central and South America. He was hesitant to recommend them as they were going out of print, but he would be happy to give me copies of what he had if I was interested.

A few days later, I was standing on a doorstep, glancing slightly nervously around the south-east London estate Bartlett had given as his home address, hoping that I wasn't making a foolish mistake. The door opened and a slight, bespectacled man with a beard looked out.

'Richard?' I said hopefully.

He gave me a warm smile and shook my hand. 'You found it all right?' he said.

Over tea in the living room, surrounded by books, artefacts and bright wall hangings, Bartlett told me the story of Aflame Books. He and a colleague had founded the company in 2006 while they were working as subeditors for the *Financial Times*. They ran the business in their spare time for the next four years – meeting its shortfalls from their own pockets without any external funding – and somehow managed to produce a catalogue of beautiful books by writers in countries including Iraq, Brazil, Guatemala and South Africa. There was a pile of them on the table between us and, flicking through, I couldn't help being impressed by the hours of work that had gone into them. Bartlett smiled with a mixture of pride and sadness as I marvelled at the volumes – he was in the middle of studying for a master's with a view to starting a new career as a geologist in southern Africa and, while Mozambican literature would always be a love, soon all this would seem a world away. In the course of our conversation, Bartlett mentioned that he had an unpublished translation of a novel called *Ualalapi* by Mozambican writer Ungulani Ba Ka Khosa. This he promised to email to me, and I left bearing my pile of books and the hope that my quest to find an alternative to Mia Couto had finally borne fruit.

When I got home, my hope blossomed into excitement. A cursory internet search told me that this Khosa fellow was really rather a big cheese in Mozambican literary circles. Not only was *Ualalapi* included on the list of Africa's 100 Best Books of the Twentieth Century, it had also won the 1990 Grand Prize of Mozambican Fiction. I plunged into Bartlett's manuscript and was quickly engrossed in the mesmerising rise and fall of the legendary historical leader Ngungunhane, who presided over the region now known as Mozambique until the Portuguese conquered it in the nineteenth century, and who was driven by the impossible longing to be 'the first protagonist and the only one that History will record while men will be on the earth'.

Being one of the few English-language readers ever to encounter this momentous tragic hero, who exits the narrative to take up his place among figures of the stature of King Lear and Okonkwo, was both a huge privilege and a shock. It felt like getting a glimpse through the keyhole into a locked garden full of astonishing plants flourishing out of reach. There was all this world out there that the majority of English-speakers knew nothing about – worse, that most of us couldn't begin to imagine. There were references and figures that were the touch-stones and rocks of consciousness for many millions of people, yet meant less than nothing to us. There were images and ways of thinking and feeling that those of us trapped on the anglophone side of the fence would probably never know. It seemed a monumental shame.

Yet, instead of expressing concern that literature like this should be beyond our reach, most of us seem unmoved by such omissions. With so many books churning out of anglophone presses every year – not to mention the vast array of self-published titles appearing each day – many of us seem to feel we simply don't need any more words, no matter how good. Moot the possibility of encouraging more texts from, say, China and you'll often find people protesting that there is already too much anglophone literature available as it is, apparently unmoved by the fact that fewer than 1 per cent of works published in the world's most populous country are translated into any other language. Far from being alarmed at the fact that, for example, according to English PEN, in British schools and universities there is no chance of gaining sufficient grasp of a foreign language to become a translator, we talk in terms of the 'self-sufficiency' of the English-language publishing scene, as though our parochial reading habits are somehow virtuous, on a par with sustainable fishing and buying local produce.

The implications are worrying. A glance at the careers of some of the world's leading writers shows the damage that such literary isolationism can cause. Throughout history, many of the planet's leading wordsmiths have made no secret of the debt their writing owes to stories from elsewhere. Gabriel García Márquez – himself a huge influence on magical realist writers in many languages – wrote extensively about the effect that reading foreign authors had on him when he was learning his craft, in his autobiography of his early life, *Living to Tell the Tale*. The works of William Faulkner, Luis Borges, Franz Kafka, D.H. Lawrence, Aldous Huxley, Graham Greene, G.K. Chesterton, William Irish and Katherine Mansfield all nourished him like 'bread warm from the oven'. And when it came to James Joyce's *Ulysses*, the novel gave him not only 'the discovery of a genuine world that I never suspected inside me, but it also provided invaluable technical help to me in freeing language and in handling time and structures in my books'. Without being able to access books in translation, it seems likely that Márquez would not have had the reputation that he has today. He was by no means the only one to feel this way. For many the belief that, in the words of Josep Bargalló, director of Barcelona's Institut Roman Llull, which campaigns to promote the Catalan language, 'translation is the lifeblood which sustains and nurtures literatures' is one of the cornerstones of the creative process – a vital exchange that enables not only talent but language itself to grow. German theologian and philosopher Friedrich Schleiermacher, for one, observed that 'just as it is perhaps only through the cultivation of foreign plant life that our soil has become richer and more fertile and our climate more pleasing and milder, so too do we feel that our language, since our Nordic lassitude prevents us from exercising it sufficiently, can most vigorously flourish and develop its own strength only through extensive contact with the foreign'. It was a sentiment that his contemporary, *Weltliteratur* champion Goethe expressed in yet more emphatic terms. 'Left to itself, every literature will exhaust its vitality if it is not refreshed by the interest and contributions of a foreign one.' From this perspective, the 'self-sufficiency' of the English-language publishing industry looks less like good housekeeping and more like a recipe for intellectual impoverishment, malnutrition and eventual starvation.

When you set the tiny numbers of translations entering the anglophone world against the proportion of foreign-language literature published in other countries, the prognosis looks more worrying still. Although you might expect nations with less widely spoken languages like the Czech Republic, Estonia, Lithuania and Finland to import and translate around half their literature – which they do – it's perhaps more surprising to think that translated fiction makes up around 45 per cent of books published in the Netherlands, 40 per cent in Turkey and one-third of the literary output in France. Germany, on the other hand, takes things further still. A nation of book lovers, printing around 500 million volumes a year (or just over six per person), it has a track record of publishing more translations than any other country and has frequently seen non-German fiction making up more than 50 per cent of its bestsellers. What's more, in most countries English-language works make up by far the biggest chunk of texts converted into the national language.

The resultant imbalance is bad for everyone. With a trickle of titles flowing into English and a deluge gushing out, writers everywhere are being exposed to increasing numbers of books written by people with access to a similar range of linguistic tools, perspectives, styles and ideas. Should the status quo continue indefinitely, it seems likely that wordsmiths around the planet will suffer: the give and take of international literary exchange so vital to the development of literary greats looks set to atrophy and become stunted under the weight of anglophone texts. As US-based translator Esther Allen puts it, 'the tendency of an integrated world market to privilege the translation of English fiction and poetry into other languages for reading or listening enjoyment may damage the production of world literature and *in this respect* makes us all worse off'. When translation works too much in one direction, we all lose.

*

When Katherine Rucker, a postgraduate student at the University of Rochester in New York State, decided to broaden her horizons by seeking out literature from under-represented Spanish-speaking Latin American countries to translate in early 2014, she encountered a problem. No matter how hard she looked, she could not find comprehensive information on the titles released in many South American nations. Even where some records existed online, the data was patchy at best. Writing on her university's Three Percent blog (named after the much-quoted US translation statistic), she described some of the frustrations she'd encountered. These included a Uruguayan publisher who wanted her to collect the book she'd ordered from their offices, and a national list of publications from one country so short that she assumed it was a rundown of the 'Best of 2013' until she read the small print. 'I guess what I might be experiencing here is something that other translators have confronted before,' she wrote. 'Even if I'm actively seeking out books from particular countries, I'm going to have a hard time finding them. And if I'm not actively looking for them, I'm never, ever going to find them – and books that are invisible to translators stay invisible to everyone else, too.' The experience prompted her to consider setting up a database of publications in the absence of any other comprehensive source.

Such scant records are not the sole preserve of South America. When it comes to the details of published translations, many anglophone nations are every bit as lax. Unlike several of our European neighbours, such as Belgium and Slovenia, which maintain extensive databases of what's come into print from other languages, we have traditionally had a rather laissez-faire approach to literary bookkeeping. Although there are registers such as the British Library's British National Bibliography and UNESCO's Index Translationum – a compendium of information on books translated in about 100 member states since 1979 – they are incomplete, difficult to search and sometimes inaccurate: hardback and paperback editions can appear as two separate entries, translator names are missing, and some books are included that never made it into print in the first place. Lists kept by commercial bibliographic metadata service providers such as Nielsen BookData face similar problems and are often dependent on publishers taking the time to input data – time that the majority of small presses can ill afford to spare. In fact Bowker, Nielsen's counterpart in the US, stopped publishing information on translation in 2000 when it switched to a new database. As Chad Post of US-based translations publisher Open Letter Press puts it, when you compare the amount of data held about translations in his nation to records kept in many other places 'we come off as an ass-backward, second-rate country' – a statement that could no doubt be applied to the UK too.

It's not just the registers of publications and translations that are incomplete. Books themselves often keep mum about their origins, with many translators credited only among the copyright information, and some not mentioned at all. It's almost as if publishers worry that acknowledging the language shift might put us off, as though we might hurl the copy down in disgust and demand our money back, repulsed by the thought that the story we are reading has been filtered through someone else's consciousness. In fact, out of the 144 hard copies of texts I read during my year of reading the world that are still sitting on the bookshelf across the room, I can only see one translator's name featured on a spine: Michael Emmerich, translator of Hiromi Kawakami's *Manazuru*.

The lack of readily available information about translations can make the hunt for titles from further afield extremely difficult. In many cases, those looking for work from neglected countries will be forced to rely on long-out-of-print editions, such as Bernard M. Dulsey's 1964 translation of Jorge Icaza's 1934 Ecuadorian classic *Huasipungo*, Helen R. Lane's 1986 rendering of Paraguayan great *I the Supreme*, or John Buchanan-Brown's 1970 version of Bambote's *Daba's Travels from Ouadda to Bangui* – a children's story from the Central African Republic written shortly after independence, which, but for leopard sightings, crocodile hunts and lion-tracking, might have sat very comfortably alongside Enid Blyton's novels in a British child's bedroom forty years ago. Often available only as second-hand copies from closing or stock-clearing libraries (I read twelve such books during my quest, most of them in mint condition as if barely or never opened), these volumes lurk among the unknown bindings on retailers' sites, with scant information to their names. On occasion it isn't until they arrive that you can be quite sure of whether you're buying a translation or an oeuvre originally written in English, and whether the work in question is fiction, a memoir, a history, a children's book or something else. Perpetually shifting ground as new tides of books wash in to submerge what was there before, these patchily available second-hand works allow us glimpses of perspectives that are otherwise cut off. Sometimes the only stories that we can read from a particular time or place, these narratives reach us like light from long-dead stars: a message from a land that no longer exists to a world that hadn't been conceived of when it was written.

*

In July 2011, outgoing executive editor of the *New York Times* Bill Keller published a provocative column. Titled 'Let's Ban Books, or At Least Stop Writing Them', it set out his lament that almost everyone he knew seemed to aspire to be a published author. Despite his best efforts to dissuade them, his friends and colleagues persisted in their ambitions:

> Every month, it seems, some reporter drops by my office to request a leave of absence to write a book. I patiently explain that

book-writing is agony – slow, lonely, frustrating work that, unless you are a very rare exception, gets a lukewarm review (if any), reaches a few thousand people and lands on a remaindered shelf at Barnes & Noble. I recount my own experience as a book failure – two incompletes, and I'm still paying back a sizable advance with a yearly check to Simon & Schuster that I think of not as a burden but as bail.

But still the reporters – and editors, too – keep coming to sit in my office among the teetering stacks of *Times*-written books that I mean to read someday and to listen politely to my description of book-writing Gethsemane, and then they join the cliff-bound lemmings anyway.

If getting your stories into print is tough in downtown Manhattan, it's exponentially more difficult in places where the infrastructure simply doesn't exist to gather, edit and sell words. Indeed, Napoleon Bonaparte's claim that 'a country's foreign policy is dictated by its geography' might very well apply to publishing too: in many parts of the planet, the business of producing books and transporting them to readers is complicated by a nation's size, shape and location. In such places, the issue is not whether books get noticed or make it out to the wider world, but whether stories get published at all.

In some areas, it's nigh on impossible. Canadian-born writer Susan Kloulechad discovered this when she tried to form a writers' group in Palau, where she has lived with her Palauan husband and children for more than twenty years. Eager to find like-minded people with whom she could develop her craft as she got her teeth into her first, as yet unpublished novel, she set up a Yahoo Group and waited for aspiring writers to get in touch. She's still waiting.

In many ways, it's not surprising. With a population of just under 21,000, spread over some 250 islands, Palau is hardly a promising setting for anyone looking to develop a publishing industry. The books that are produced are largely pamphlets for tourists, who are the nation's primary source of income. In all her time living there, Kloulechad can only recall one work of fiction created by local writers: a collection of short stories written during the Festival of Pacific Arts, which takes place annually in a different island nation in the region and in 2004 came to Palau. As she sees it, the only route to traditional publishing lies thousands of miles away in New York.

It's a sentiment that many writers on small islands (certainly those more of the microstate, rather than Bill Bryson, variety) would recognise. In the Caribbean, where close on 40 million people are spread across nearly thirty states and territories and more than a million square miles, those keen to see their words in print have traditionally resorted to publishers elsewhere, following in the footsteps of such notaries as V.S. Naipaul, Sam Selvon, George Lamming and Edgar Mittelholzer. Although there are a few Caribbean-based presses, such as Ian Randle in Jamaica, these tend to focus on textbooks and other non-fiction works, obliging creative writers to seek outlets across the sea. Arguably the most successful Caribbean publishing house, Jeremy Poynting's Peepal Tree Press, is based several time zones away – in Leeds, West Yorkshire.

Even with an upsurge of interest in writing and a growing clutch of Caribbean-based writers making it into print in recent years, the geographical challenges of marketing and moving books from island to island continue to limit opportunities closer to home. According to Nicholas Laughlin, editor of the *Caribbean Review of Books* and programme director of the Trinidad-based NGC Bocas Lit Fest, there is, in all senses, a long way to go. Short of a technological development that would make print-on-demand technology affordable for the general stores and stationers that double as bookshops in many of the smaller nations – or that would enable the wider use of ebooks – he doesn't see the logistical barriers to local publishing being broken down any time soon.

'It's a problem of critical mass,' he says. 'These are small islands scattered over a large expanse of sea. That's not going to change.'

As with translation, when it comes to publishing in such remote communities, getting accurate data can be a challenge in itself. And where hard information fails, speculation rushes in to fill the vacuum, often peddling some dubious fictions of its own.

'Some people will tell you that people in the Caribbean or people in Jamaica don't read,' said Kellie Magnus, Jamaica-based coordinator for the Caribbean Literature Action Group, CaribLit. She goes on:

> 'I think that's complete hogwash. People read and buy books. They may not be buying the books that our local publishers create because that's not what they're interested in. One of the things we have to do is develop a detailed reader interest survey to find out what people are doing so we can put hard numbers around this stuff instead of speculating about it. We need to find out what people are buying, what people are reading and what they have an interest in buying that they aren't currently finding and then share that information with the publishing community so we can start making smarter choices.'

For Magnus' money, smarter choices would include developing other channels of the local fiction publishing industry, which, as far as it goes, has traditionally focused on literary works. Alongside the growing line in Caribbean sci-fi pioneered in the novels of writers such as Tobias Buckell and Karen Lord, she wants to see more emphasis put on mass-market commercial fiction, which might help make local ventures more sustainable and allow them to play the Anglo-American publishing industry at its own game.

Yet it's not just remote or relatively recently independent nations that sometimes struggle to establish effective networks in publishing and the arts. When I tried to track down a book from the microstate of San Marino, said to be the world's oldest sovereign state, I spent months contacting anyone who might have an opinion on the subject – Steve even joked that I must have been in touch with every one of the 30,000 or so residents. At one desperate moment, I even found myself caught up in a baffling phone conversation with the Sammarinese Ministry of

Culture, during which the pleasant but slightly bewildered woman on the other end informed me that Mr Morri, who a contact at the EU in Brussels had told me was the minister of culture for San Marino, was not around any more and no one was quite sure who held the position now. 'You should ask Mr Morri,' my interlocutor told me with a laugh, before dictating a phone number for the former secretary of state amid giggles and a whispered argument about how to say numbers in English. Needless to say, when I tried to call Mr Morri's number, it didn't work. It hardly seemed a great loss – I couldn't help feeling that the Sammarinese publishing industry and the translation of its literature into English, or any other language for that matter, might be some way down his priority list. (In the end, I had to resort to a yellowing pamphlet about the story of San Marino – translated and published some decades before and dug up for me by someone at the University of San Marino – which, among several other things, went into some detail about the reasons the microstate decided not to become a nuclear power.)

The San Marino case is by no means the rule. In fact, several European microstates boast thriving literary scenes and writers who have gained considerable recognition beyond their national borders. The only problem is that they haven't made it into English yet. The diminutive state of Liechtenstein, for example, which has only some 4,000 more citizens than San Marino, has hatched an impressive brood of German-language writers, including Iren Nigg and Stefan Sprenger. Nigg was one of the European Union Prize for Literature winners in 2011, but this distinction sadly did not bring an opportunity to see her work published in English beyond a brief extract in the ceremony brochure. In fact, the only Liechtensteiner to have had a whole book translated into English in recent years was Prince Hans-Adam II von und zu Liechtenstein. And his political treatise, *The State in the Third Millennium*, cannot really be considered a narrative unless, as Sprenger has joked, you think of it as a horror story.

In some cases, wordsmiths in microstates have achieved international celebrity status. *The Teacher of Cheops* by Andorran writer Albert Salvadó has sold well over 100,000 copies in Spanish and Catalan – no mean feat for an author living in a nation of fewer than 80,000 people. When I wrote about it on my blog, I was amazed at the reaction: within a day or so of my broadly appreciative review going live, a tide of Andorrans flooded on to the site, extolling the virtues of Salvadó's novels and expressing great jubilation and excitement that his work had finally got some attention from an English-language audience. Salvadó was clearly a leading figure. His work was something that people cherished, and the fact that it was possible for it to be conveyed into another language and brought to readers around the world was important – important enough for people to go through the headache of registering on a website they would probably never visit again and drafting comments in a foreign language to show their support.

*

In some parts of the world, the technological advances that Nicholas Laughlin anticipated revolutionising Caribbean publishing have already played a significant part in bringing books to audiences that would otherwise never get them. Few people can feel this more keenly than Justin Cox. When he joined the African Books Collective, a global marketing and distribution company for books from the continent, back in 2001, Cox found himself facing an unusual challenge. Translation wasn't an issue – the titles he was in charge of selling were largely in English or other widely spoken European languages – but there was a problem nonetheless. 'We didn't know what was going to be published. Books would just arrive at Heathrow and there was no clear line of supply. We could try and push a book but we could never be sure that we would ever get any more of that book once we'd sold it, so we were really limited. We could only go so far.'

With communication difficult and big time lags between exchanges with publishers, it was tricky for the distributor to build up any kind of momentum – let alone buzz – around a book. Had it not been for the advent of ebooks and print-on-demand technology, which now means the African Books Collective delivers all bar a handful of the hard copies it sells by way of wholesaler-printers in countries such as Germany, the UK, the US, Australia and South Africa, the enterprise would probably have folded when it lost its funding in 2007. Yet that year's developments gave the African Books Collective the ability to be a much leaner, self-sufficient operation, ditching the Oxford warehouse and office for home-working and reducing overheads. (Among other things, it saw the world's first so-called 'Espresso Book Machine', which can deliver bound paperbacks from a computer file in a single operation, installed in the New York Public Library.) The move to digital technology brought in a whole new raft of prospective clients, including libraries in places as far afield as Taiwan.

Nowadays, the major challenge for the African Books Collective is not distribution but whether the 147 publishers in twenty-five nations whose books the company currently markets will continue to send titles. This depends on many things. With prohibitive paper taxes and spending cuts that have seen many libraries and universities reduce their book-buying dramatically in recent years, income has dropped significantly for many of Africa's presses. Anecdotal evidence suggests that literature lecturers at universities in some parts of the continent have switched from teaching full texts to extracts in order to get round the fact that neither faculties nor students can afford the books. Additional pressure comes from the stiff competition local presses face from international firms, which are sometimes not averse to engaging in underhand tactics to secure the bread-and-butter academic contracts that still keep many small publishers afloat. In the past five years, for example, both Macmillan and Oxford University Press have been fined for bribes offered by their local representatives or subsidiary companies in the hope of securing deals in Sudan and in Tanzania and Kenya respectively. In addition, there's the political instability that threatens freedom of the press in many parts of the continent. The 1999 *African Writers' Handbook*, for example, features a section on 'Getting on with the State', alongside the advice on cover letters, contracts and agents you'd expect to see in comparable British publications. All in all – when you take into account that, given literacy rates and regional linguistic diversity, the average African press publishes for only about 20 per cent of the population – the sub-Saharan books game looks less than promising. Small wonder that, in the mid-nineties at least, only twenty books were making it into print per million Africans, as opposed to around 800 titles for every million Europeans.

Yet, as I discovered when I embarked on my quest for a book from Burundi, infrastructure, networks and financial issues are only part of the story. I always knew getting a Burundian book would be challenging. One of the five poorest countries in the world and the scene of unrest and ethnic persecution since its independence in 1962, the nation has been the site of two genocides: in 1972 when the Tutsi-dominated army massacred Hutus and in 1993 when the Hutu community turned on Tutsis. Even now, nearly ten years after the UN shut down its peacekeeping mission, tensions simmer beneath the surface and the problem of how to address the widespread war crimes and crimes against humanity committed over the last five decades remains unsolved.

As with several war-affected nations, the book I read was by someone who had left the country – and it came to me by way of a number of others who had done so, in the shape of the United Burundian-American Community Association. Amid a deluge of emails from its members in response to my request for help – offering suggestions of academic titles, works by non-Burundians and novels in French, as well as, in one memorable case, the opportunity to help someone write a book – there came a message from a man who had gone to school in Burundi. He remembered that an old classmate of his had published two novels in English. Her name was Marie-Thérèse Toyi.

Although her novels are not commercially available, Toyi, who is now a lecturer at Benson Idahosa University in Nigeria, offered to courier one to me. A few days later I was holding a battered copy of her novel *Weep Not, Refugee*, complete with a greeting from the author written inside the cover. Following the fortunes of refugee-camp inhabitant Wache Wacheke Watachoka (a Kiswahili name that means 'Let them keep laughing, one day they will get tired and eventually cease'), it explored 'the overpowering burden of forcing oneself to live in a foreign land where you are most undesirable':

> Just for you to have an idea what it was like, take a cup of ground red pepper, pour it on your bleeding wound and you will have a little idea what it was like. If you have no wound, well, we cannot discuss again, because there are things which you will never be able to understand.

But it was only some months later, when I spoke to Toyi over the phone after a year or so of intermittent email correspondence, that the source of the book's power and the scale of Toyi's achievement in writing it became clear.

Born in 1965, Toyi grew up as one of thirteen children in a home with no books except for the Bible. The first non-religious writing she came across was a non-fiction title by a Burundian author, which she found in a bin. It wasn't until she was at secondary school that she encountered novels, in the shape of nineteenth-century French classics such as Hector Malot's *Sans famille* and Jules Verne's *Le Tour du monde en quatre-vingts jours*.

At the time of the 1993 genocide, Toyi, who had lost several relatives in the first genocide two decades before, was a student at the University of Burundi. Having been encouraged to give up on her ambition of becoming a doctor because of the stiff competition for jobs, she had chosen to study English literature. She was living at a house on a main road near the campus when the trouble started, and what she saw when the killing spilled on to the streets changed the course of her life. 'Living in fear is not an easy thing. I saw someone being cut into pieces. It took me more than three years before I could concentrate. It took me more than three years before I could forget the people screaming and the person dying.'

Once she was able to focus on her studies again, Toyi found that the scholarship opportunities she had hoped to apply for no longer existed because of the war. The only option open to her was in Nigeria and so she reluctantly moved there in 2001, grateful at least that she had been spared the no man's land of the refugee camps to which many of her friends and family had fled. She was in for a surprise.

'When I went to Nigeria, I saw that everyone in Nigeria was motivated to do something,' she said. 'They said to me: "You are going to publish books." I said: "Is that what this means?" They said: "Yes, you are going to publish books." So it gave me confidence and I tried it.'

Had it not been for that assumption on the part of her Nigerian peers, Toyi suspects she would probably never have attempted to write for publication. Although she had drafted a novel in French in Burundi, she wouldn't have dreamed of taking it further, a mental barrier she put down to the lack of precedent for publishing fiction in her homeland and an almost non-existent reading and writing culture in Kirundi, the language spoken in daily life as opposed to formal, school-based French.

According to Toyi, this has had significant psychological effects on those who might otherwise put their words on the page. 'I have discovered that we don't trust ourselves. Some writers, like Joseph Conrad, were not born English speakers but they produce something good. I know in my brain how to translate something, but we don't trust ourselves. We believe that those who write are particularly gifted people, European people, not a typical Burundi.'

Yet, although her novel had largely positive responses from its non-Burundian readers, Toyi's compatriots were not enthusiastic about it. 'Among Nigerians and among foreigners everyone encourages me,' she said. 'They are surprised that the novel could be produced by a Burundian, and the topic about refugees' experiences is quite unique. They encourage me a lot. But Burundians are not encouraging. They say why should I write in English, not in Kirundi or French and they say no one's going to read it.'

To Toyi's mind, there is another reason for her compatriots' negative response to her novel too. 'We are reserved. Even the truth, we don't want to talk about it. It is very difficult for some people to say what happened among Burundians. So many women were raped but no one talks. It is taboo. You are disgracing yourself by narrating your story.'

Toyi is not the only African author to receive a less than lukewarm reception at home while garnering more enthusiastic responses elsewhere. As Professor Charles Larson of the American University in Washington, DC points out in his 2001 book *The Ordeal of the African Writer*, in which he analyses responses to questionnaires sent to writers across the continent, even leading lights like Chinua Achebe and Amos Tutuola, author of *The Palm-Wine Drinkard*, owe their careers largely to international recognition rather than support from their compatriots. Indeed Amos Tutuola – praised by Dylan Thomas, and hailed by many as the grandfather of magical realism and of Nigerian literature in English – never received much local celebration or remuneration for his work throughout his life and a collection had to be taken to pay for his funeral when he died in 1997. When the American critic Eric Larrabee went in search of Tutuola, who worked as a messenger in the Nigerian Department of Labour, to get his copy of the novel signed in the early 1950s, the writer seemed amazed at the thought that anyone would want his autograph. The experience prompted Larrabee to pose readers a challenge in his review of *The Palm-Wine Drinkard*, which was published in *The Reporter* on 12 May 1953:

> As an exercise in imagination, try to conceive of an author who (1) probably has never met another author, (2) owns no books, (3) is not known to his daily acquaintances as an author, (4) has no personal contact with his publisher, (5) is not certain where his book is on sale, and (6) does not think of himself as an author.

He might have added '(7) has to suffer the suspicion and even hostility of his compatriots' to the list, for news of *The Palm-Wine Drinkard*'s success abroad prompted a wave of indignant responses from

Nigerians. Even those who had never read Tutuola's work felt entitled to weigh in. On 5 June 1954, the journal *West Africa* published a letter from one I. Adeagbo Akinjobin, who, despite admitting not having seen a copy of the novel, expressed numerous grave reservations. Tutuola's book would shore up European misconceptions about Africa through its fantastic and improbable tales, he wrote. It was no wonder that the creation was so popular in England and France because it was no doubt precisely the sort of writing calculated to appeal to the ignorant imaginings of people in those places. It might be all very well for the author, who no doubt would enjoy wealth and worldwide fame as a result, but the book would be very damaging for his peers: Africans obliged to travel to Europe would suffer as a result. 'I am not being unduly anxious,' he signed off ominously.

As Marie-Thérèse Toyi was to discover some sixty years later, writing, in some people's eyes, is akin to letting the side down. To tell stories, at least to tell the wrong kind of stories, is to threaten the pride and dignity of those around you; those who, rightly or wrongly, believe their reputation or character might somehow be compromised by association.

Given such challenges, it's perhaps astonishing that Amos Tutuola found the will to continue with writing at all. Yet his efforts and those of the generations of outstanding Nigerian novelists who came after him created a vibrant literary culture that has put Nigeria at the forefront of the African literary scene. Even with Charles Larson noting a decline in the nation's publishing industry during the nineties, the country's literary tradition was still strong enough in the early twenty-first century to make a woman from Burundi with an impulse to write stories believe that getting her words into print was possible. And it's been enough to inspire her to continue writing.

5

Venturing off the beaten track

writers commercial publishing doesn't reach

If accessing texts from countries with weak literary traditions and networks is difficult, it's nigh on impossible when it comes to countries that have published no books at all. Such was the case when it came to South Sudan, the world's newest country, which sprang into being on 9 July 2011, a mere six months before I was due to start reading the world.

Establishing a publishing tradition was the least of the nation's challenges. Still reeling from the after-effects of the Second Sudanese Civil War, which saw an estimated two million people killed between 1983 and 2005, the newly independent state lacked hospitals, schools and even the basic infrastructure most of us take for granted. On top of this, although it had chosen English as its official language as part of a move to distance itself from Arabic-speaking Sudan, the country is home to some 300 other languages and dialects. With so much else to think about, I very much doubted that anyone there would have had time to get a publishing industry up and running in the months since independence. Although there was a fleeting mention of a Writers' Association of South Sudan on the web, the only evidence I could find of it was a draft constitution, dated 8 July 2011, and there were no contact details.

Luckily, however, I had a man on the ground.

I first met Deng Gach Pal in early 2011 on a visit to the University of Exeter. He was studying for a master's in public administration in preparation for returning home to take up a role as a senior civil servant in the new administration of South Sudan. I interviewed him later that year, around the time of independence. As we sat in a fried-chicken shop in Wood Green, he impressed two things upon me: the magnitude of the task facing those trying to build his country from the ground up and his excitement at being part of it.

'We don't even have roads,' he said, grinning and shaking his head. 'The only tarmacked road you'll find is in Juba, going from the airport to President Salva Kiir Mayardit's office. And without roads, how do you get goods in?'

Pal's own story was pretty amazing. Having fled to a refugee camp in Ethiopia as a child in 1986 with his mother and father, a separatist fighter in the First Sudanese Civil War, Pal had eventually been recruited into a spartan military camp for child soldiers under the pretence of being sent to school. The fall of the Mengistu regime in 1991 saved him from being sent to fight, but also left him stranded many miles from home, with no idea where his parents were. Over the next few weeks he made his way back to southern Sudan, walking at night to avoid capture and navigating by asking people if they knew how to get to the lands of his tribe, the Nuer. Astonishingly, he managed to find his family, but the brutal civil war in his homeland meant that it was not safe to stay put. He spent his teenage years travelling between Sudan, Kenya and Ethiopia, trying to get an education as best he could. In spite of it all, though, there he was, studying in the UK on a scholarship and about to take up a pivotal role in his new country.

If anyone could help me find something to read, I was sure Deng Gach Pal would. So, during the last weeks of 2011 – as I gathered recommendations, stockpiled stories for the first months of the project and laid the groundwork for finding books from what I thought would be the toughest countries – I sent Pal, now back in South Sudan, an email asking him if he could recommend any writers who might fit the bill. It didn't take him long to reply. Book publishing was non-existent as far as he knew, but there was someone he'd like to put me in touch with: Dr Julia Aker Duany, a former refugee who had been a research associate at the University of Indiana. She had returned to South Sudan in 2005 to help prepare for independence, spending five years as undersecretary in the Ministry for Parliamentary Affairs. Duany had published her memoirs, *Making Peace and Nurturing Life: Memoir of an African Woman about a Journey of Struggle and Hope*, in 2003. The book wouldn't count for my purposes because it was published before South Sudan existed, but Pal thought Duany might be prepared to write something specially for my project.

I spoke to Duany a few days later, having had to dial using the old Sudan country code because the new nation's number wasn't working yet. She agreed to write me a short story drawing on her experience of South Sudan's declaration of independence. A few weeks later, I recorded her reading it and used it to launch my year of reading the world on 1 January 2012, South Sudan's first New Year's Day. The story – a simple, autobiographical account – spoke of Duany's reasons for returning to Sudan, which she described as a 'pantomime of hell', and the horror of discovering that everyone she asked after had been killed, including two of her brothers. But it also brimmed with optimism for the future of the new country and Duany's desire to use her mixed tribal heritage (her mother being a Dinka and her father a Nuer, two of the ethnic groups on opposite sides of the fighting during and since the civil wars) to overcome the impulse for revenge. She found a striking local simile:

'Kudu [a species of antelope native to east-central Africa] goes all day looking for its special plant. When it gets one of these bushes, it will not leave it alone. Kudu will strip the bush almost to death. But this plant has a special natural mechanism that protects it from being stripped to death. When there are few leaves left on the plant it feels the sun's rays and the leaves turn bitter. When kudu continues eating the leaves, they will taste bitter and the kudu will spit them out and leave the bush and go on to look for more bushes while the plant will have a chance to grow more leaves.

'As humans we are just like that plant. When someone touches us in a vulnerable place, we turn bitter just like those bushes, ready to jump out of our skin and get hold of that person's neck.'

In various ways, the story broke my rules. It was not a book – it was a mere handful of pages long. It was not published. In fact, I wasn't even sure it was a story; it felt more like an essay or an op-ed piece for a newspaper. Bits of it, read in Duany's soft, lilting voice, sounded like *Thought for the Day* on Radio 4 (indeed, when South Sudan plunged into violence two years later, forcing Deng Gach Pal and many of his colleagues to flee for their lives when the government ordered their arrest, Duany recorded several moving and harrowing interviews with Radio 4 from Juba after a producer asked me to put them in touch). The story Duany wrote for me was some way from my conception of what I thought I'd be including in my project, but, as I was discovering, my rules and categorisations for the world I thought I lived in were proving to be increasingly flawed and sometimes even downright foolish. Instead of me reading the world, it seemed the world was reading me – and forcing me to rewrite the bits with which it didn't agree.

*

In places where commercial publishing does not exist or does not provide a reliable route to get their stories out, writers have little option but to explore other channels – and readers who want to find them often have to go to great lengths to track them down. For many authors, this means going it alone and publishing their work themselves. Yet, while self-publishing makes it possible for many authors in places usually overlooked by commercial publishers to realise the dream of seeing their efforts in print, it rarely makes it easier for such authors to get their voices heard by the wider world – or for interested readers in other places to seek out their work.

This is not helped by the fact that in regions that have a strong publishing industry, such as Western Europe and North America, self-publishing has long been a dirty word. In September 2013, US author

Jonathan Franzen published an extract from his latest book, *The Kraus Project*, in the *Guardian*, under the title 'What's Wrong With the Modern World'. Rather than a novel, the book is a series of annotated translations the writer made of the essays of relatively obscure *fin-de-siècle* Austrian satirist Karl Kraus – a figure whose work, though written a century earlier, Franzen feels speaks to 'our own media-saturated, technology-crazed, apocalypse-haunted historical moment'. Known in his day as 'the Great Hater', the Viennese writer's words provide the notoriously world-weary Franzen with the perfect platform for airing some of his pet peeves, using extensive footnotes and some creative glossing to steer the arguments as he wishes. Chief among the issues in the firing line is self-publishing – a vacuous, error-riddled practice carried out by 'yakkers and tweeters and braggers' who spend more time promoting themselves than reading or writing meaningful work, according to Franzen. 'What happens to the people who want to communicate in depth, individual to individual, in the quiet and permanence of the printed word?' he asks.

Franzen is by no means alone in his views. In the last fifteen years or so, as advances in technology have made sending your work out into the world for all and sundry to read ever easier, numerous people have expressed alarm and disdain at the mass of unfiltered words self-publishing has the potential to produce. Armed with the knowledge that works such as E.L. James's notorious *Fifty Shades* trilogy started life as self-published fan fiction on the web, these detractors rail against the dumbing-down effect that unvetted works could have on the literary market. They recall the words of another nineteenth-century writer: Oscar Wilde's declaration that, 'In old days books were written by men of letters and read by the public. Nowadays books are written by the public and read by no one.' Even with a softening of attitudes towards alternative modes of producing books, as evidenced by initiatives such as the very same *Guardian* newspaper's Guardian Legend Self-Published Book of the Month award – 'as DIY publishing gains respectability and established authors join the throng, the *Guardian* is joining forces with Legend Times to find the best self-published novels, in any genre, every month' proclaimed the newspaper on the launch of the scheme in April 2014 – the idea that books launched by any means other than the commercial route are simply not good enough to land a deal persists in many quarters.

Self-publishing can seem to be the poor relation of the literary world, but it was by no means ever thus. In fact, the concept predates the commercial ventures that have long since become the holy grail for most aspiring authors. Although commonly used in connection with journalism, the phrase 'freedom of the press' was in circulation long before the modern newspaper industry cranked into life towards the end of the nineteenth century. Coined in the 1660s, not long after pamphleteering had reached fever pitch around the time of the English Civil War, it originally had little to do with professional writers and everything to do with any Toms, Dicks or Harriets who might take it into their heads to put their thoughts into print. The 'press' it referred to was not the media but printing equipment, and the 'freedom' was the general right of every person to have access to this equipment and use it to spread his or her ideas without intervention from licensors or censors.

It was an idea that Milton had argued for passionately two decades before in his polemical tract *Areopagitica: A Speech . . . for the Liberty of Unlicenc'd Printing, to the Parliament of England* (1644). Good, bad and indifferent books should be allowed to circulate freely, he claimed, because truth and integrity would win out over lies, 'And though all the winds of doctrine were let loose to play upon the earth, so Truth be in the field, we do injuriously, by licensing and prohibiting to misdoubt her strength. Let her and Falsehood grapple; who ever knew Truth put to the worse, in a free and open encounter? Her confuting is the best and surest suppressing.'

In the centuries that followed, many English-language writers embraced the original sense of press freedom. From the court of Charles II, where the Earl of Rochester and his libertine cronies circulated obscene rhymes for their friends' amusement, to the Hogarth Press founded by Leonard and Virginia Woolf in 1917, many of literature's most famous –

and infamous – figures have not been averse to a spot of DIY when circumstances dictate or allow. Though the phrase 'vanity publishing' may long have had a touch of the cringes about it, it's largely in recent times that, in the anglophone world at least, the practice has evoked the sort of outrage that sporadically brings literary heavyweights like Jonathan Franzen lurching out of their corners to swing a few punches at the 'yakkers and tweeters and braggers' they seem to see assembling beneath the banner of self-publishing. As technology makes freedom of the press possible for more people than ever before, some of those within the citadel of the literary establishment are adopting a siege mentality, readying the vats of boiling scorn and vitriol to pour on the heads of the advancing, zombie-like masses intent on admittance.

But the stigma that is attached to self-publishing is by no means the rule in all parts of the planet; as I discovered when I met Vincentian writer Cecil Browne, in many places it is often the only way for an author to get his or her words into print.

Born and brought up in a village of about 500 people on the Caribbean island of St Vincent, Browne's course was set early in life when he won a scholarship to a local grammar school. In 1970, at the age of thirteen, he left St Vincent for the UK, eventually taking up a place to study maths at the University of London and going on to be a maths teacher at a further education college in Hillingdon. Yet the feeling of being rooted in the Caribbean never left him:

'I feel that sense of being a scholarship boy coming from a village where adults and children mingled easily as a strong identity. I've always seen myself as a villager and even if I go back now, people don't see me as different. As soon as they see me, my friends say, "let's go to the shop and have a drink. Let's go and play dominoes. Let's go and have a race round the village," or whatever it is.'

This sense of the importance of identity was one of the things that set Browne on the road to self-publication. Having looked for Vincentian literature during his trips back home, he was disappointed to find only books from overseas on the island. In the absence of a home-grown literary scene, he set about trying to create one, encouraging friends and acquaintances to put pen to paper and drafting a novel himself by a process of trial and error. In the end, he found that digging back into his childhood memories of Caribbean music and folklore provided a good starting point.

'I've always liked telling stories. I like to make people laugh. When I was a child the Mighty Sparrow [a Grenadian calypso singer] was a major influence. Those are my first memories of storytelling: stories in song. I used to memorise them. Some are quite improper and I couldn't possibly repeat them. Gradually I got braver to put it on paper.'

Writing was one thing, but when it came to publication there was very little option. With no Vincentian publishing industry and having received feedback that his themes and settings weren't commercial enough for UK publishers, Browne had no choice but to go it alone, particularly as the first books he felt ready to publish were short-story collections – still notoriously rarely published in the UK, even though Alice Munro won the 2013 Nobel Prize for Literature.

Putting his first book, *The Moon Is Following Me*, out through academic publisher Troubadour's self-publishing imprint Matador in 2010, Browne realised he would have to market his work himself. He focused his efforts on St Vincent, arranging book launches at the University of the West Indies and fixing up interviews on local radio and television – using these opportunities to encourage others to take up writing too.

'We're getting people interested,' he said. 'But I suspect we really need to be revolutionary, go out to the villages, read to people and say, "here are some stories – do they sound familiar?"'

Already, Browne is encouraged to see a lot more of his compatriots engaging with the idea of local literature. 'When I went back last year, I was really quite amazed at the number [of self-published authors] who have sprung up everywhere. There is now a big drive to read local and to get our stories down for our own entertainment.' This transformation has no doubt been helped by initiatives such as NGC Bocas Lit Fest and CaribLit elsewhere in the Caribbean.

As a Caribbean writer, Cecil Browne is in good company when it comes to self-publishing. Given the relative scarcity of local presses in the region, several internationally famous writers first made their names there under their own steam. Indeed, one of Browne's heroes, Derek Walcott, famously launched his career by self-publishing his first two collections of poetry and selling them to friends in the late 1940s, with the help of a $200 loan from his seamstress and schoolteacher mother.

Elsewhere too, especially for writers in minority and little-published languages, self-publishing is still pretty much the norm. It has traditionally been the case in Laos. There, one of the legacies of French colonial rule – the institutionalisation of secular education in South East Asia during the twentieth century, which separated the Buddhist temple from the arts of which it was traditionally the major patron – has combined with the state's more recent turbulent politics and rugged geography to engender a very sluggish publishing tradition. Although the first printed works appeared in Laos in the 1920s, a Lao-language newspaper did not come out on a regular basis until the early 1940s, much later than in most of the neighbouring nations. State-subsidised publishing since the Communist victory of 1975 has traditionally comprised works by writers whose literature is seen to serve the regime, with most established authors working as civil servants or reporters for government newspapers and magazines. Even now, those wishing to describe politically sensitive issues are best advised to send their works to be published in Thailand, if they dare to write at all. As it is, with the recent collapse of state funding, only a handful of Lao texts make it into print every year.

Back in the mid-1960s, when writer Outhine Bounyavong penned his first collection of short stories, *Sivith Ni Ku Lakone Kom* (Life is Like a Short Play), there were only two bookshops in the capital, Vientiane: one that sold Thai-language works and one selling books in French. Publications in Lao were extremely scarce and almost exclusively funded and distributed by the authors. Seeing no other way forward, Outhine paid to have 2,000 copies printed, and walked the streets, leaving books in hotel lobbies, coffee shops and other places where he thought readers might find them as a way of getting the word out about his book. He ended up selling roughly half his print run, although the success that eventually saw some of his work translated into English no doubt has more to do with the various government posts he held throughout the late twentieth century than with his intrepid self-promotion as a young man.

It's not just writers in countries with poor publishing track records who often have to take things into their own hands. India is a case in point. Although the nation boasts more than 17,000 publishing houses – producing the world's third-largest number of English-language books (after the US and UK), and acting as a hub for literature from smaller South Asian nations such as Bhutan, Nepal and Sri Lanka – these books can often only be bought through Indian distributors and the country offers relatively few opportunities to speakers of its minority languages. More than half of its presses churn out exclusively anglophone texts and unless authors are of the standing of, say, Malayalam writer and film director M. T. Vasudevan Nair – recipient of India's highest literary honour, the Jnanpith Award, and generally acknowledged national treasure – those working in most of the twenty-one official languages and as many as 300 other tongues that are used in addition to Hindi and English can expect to have to distribute their work themselves.

In recent years, a number of companies have sprung up to facilitate publication for these authors. Goa-based Cinnamon Teal is one of the longest standing in the region. Although the majority of the titles it publishes are in English, the press carries work in five or six other Indian languages, with a Hindi self-help book among its most successful releases. According to Leonard Fernandes, who founded the company with his wife Queenie in 2007, the service came about in response to demand from visitors to his online bookstore, who repeatedly requested help with launching and marketing their own work. Keen to capitalise on this evident gap in the market, the Fernandeses modelled their business on the international self-publishing company Lulu. In the first six years of trading they have seen queries escalate from an average of one a week to one a day and now publish up to twenty books a month. Although most of the readers who buy their books are located in India, some 30 per cent of their authors are based in twenty-three other countries around the world.

Success stories such as former banker Amish Tripathi's self-published *Shiva* trilogy, which has become India's fastest-selling series ever, shifting more than two million copies to date, only look set to accelerate the trend. Indeed, the potential for profit is such that some traditional publishers have been tempted to rethink their historically stand-offish stance on the practice, as demonstrated by the launch of Penguin Books India's self-publishing imprint, Partridge, in 2013.

And for all the grumbling from the literary establishment, self-publishing is gathering momentum in the anglophone world too. Some 391,000 self-published titles came out in the US alone in 2012 – more than double the UK commercial industry's output. This represents a 422 per cent increase in American self-publishing since 2007 – although that percentage is probably on the conservative side of the truth. Visit the websites of some of the major players and you'll more than likely do a double take when you realise that the counter on the homepage refers not to visitor numbers but total books published. When I was drafting this chapter, for example, Lulu's figure stood at 1,589,637, although it is probably well past the two million mark by now – if you refresh the page, the number climbs by one every two minutes or so (when I checked back some two months later the figure had already risen to 1,614,212).

Many self-published titles undoubtedly sink into the ocean of words without a trace, but a number do make a splash. These days self-published ebooks account for around 20 per cent of sales in the genre market, with romance leading the field. Indeed, in 2014, Mark Coker, founder of independent publishing platform Smashwords, went so far as to predict that 'indie books will account for 50 per cent of ebook sales by 2020'. The arena has even seen a number of stars surface – success stories like that of Welsh teenager Beth Reeks, who secured a three-book deal with Random House after her self-published romance novel *The Kissing Booth* scored more than 19 million hits online, or Violet Duke, whose *Falling for the Good Guy* and *Choosing the Right Man* took two spots in the Apple iBookstore's top ten bestsellers list in August 2013, rubbing shoulders with J.K. Rowling. The water looks so inviting that some published authors and celebrities are even abandoning ship and jumping right in, with names like crime writer John Pye, playwright and director Steven Berkoff and hit TV writer G.F. Newman striking out on their own. In recent years, self-publishing converts have become regular fixtures at industry events such as the London Book Fair, where booths resound with once-contracted authors sharing their Damascus moments and exhorting crowds of hesitant wannabes to see the light.

From a world reader's perspective, the difference between many traditionally and author-published works is often far from clear-cut. This is particularly true when you venture off the beaten track of Anglo-American publishing and into areas where your cultural compass is out of whack. Company names alone won't help you. Is Pothi a self-publishing house? What about Zorba Publishers, Glas, Kachifo Limited, Sub-Saharan Publishers and PressGang? Have books with Weaver Press on the spine been funded by an author or a commercial venture? And do we care?

The sceptics suggest that we should, because, having been through less of a vetting process, self-published works are likely to be of less reliable quality. Like food produced by an unlicensed vendor instead of a Food Standards Agency-approved firm, critics imply, self-published works may be unwholesome and unsavoury. They may be poorly executed and lack vital ingredients, and we may have to sift out stray commas and typos in order to be left with something we can digest.

Increasingly, however, the reading experience doesn't bear this out. In many parts of the world, battered copies riddled with typos might just as easily originate from a small, cash-strapped press as from someone's back bedroom (indeed the premises might also be indistinguishable), while the ongoing improvements in print-on-demand technology mean that glossy, good-looking books need not necessarily have much in the way of money behind them. Ebooks muddy the waters further, with formatting betraying little about their provenance. In addition, many publishers, including several multinational houses like Penguin, are embracing the financial opportunities aspiring authors represent by launching their own self-publishing imprints, making a virtue of a previously scorned source of competition and thereby producing self-published works with a production quality comparable to that of commercially published titles.

The similarities don't end on the superficial level. Although huge numbers of unvetted – and sometimes terrible – manuscripts flood on to the market every day through self-publishing firms intent purely on maximising the number of authors paying to use their services, many companies offer editorial guidance designed to knock books into better shape. Some even insist on it. At Cinnamon Teal, for example, Leonard and Queenie Fernandes refuse to distribute books that have not been edited. Depending on their assessment of a manuscript, this may range from simple proofreading and copy-editing to substantive reworking. This can either be undertaken in-house for a fee or by a third party of the author's choosing, but it is a non-negotiable part of the deal. This stance has cost Cinnamon Teal a considerable number of potential customers over the years, but the Fernandeses feel the short-term financial sacrifice is worth it to maintain the long-term integrity of their brand, which they are keen to shield from negative connotations. 'We believe a lot in what self-publishing can do, but we know where it might fail. It might fail if it's bracketed with the slush pile. It might lose its credibility altogether if it is understood that only bad books come out of self-publishing. Therefore we are a bit selective. More than that, we are absolutely sure that we want books that we publish to go through a certain process.'

The upshot of processes like these is that, instead of there being a sharp divide between conventionally published and self-published books, most of the distinctions are to do with availability and distribution, and stand far outside the pages themselves. While it's fair to say that the need for publishers to make a return on the work they put out usually acts as a filter to block the most unreadable efforts from the commercial route, it by no means guarantees the calibre of the stories churned out by traditional presses and certainly doesn't preclude excellence in books released through other means. Indeed, the necessity of limiting risk-taking in traditional publishing can restrict the opportunities for experimentation – something the self-publishing arena enables, by contrast, because the marketability of books is not a determining factor in whether or not they are made available. Self-published writers are free to produce niche work that might appeal to a very tiny readership without worrying about where it will sit on the bookshop shelves.

It can have some surprising results. Samoan housewife Lani Wendt Young's Young Adult Telesa series, for example, has taken the Pacific region by storm. Ask for recommendations from that part of the world and everyone – from the Auckland Libraries service to the Director for Economic Governance of the Pacific Islands Forum Secretariat – will mention it, usually saying it has created a sensation. In some ways, it's not hard to see why. Following misfit American-Samoan eighteen-year-old Leila, who returns to her mother's homeland in search of her roots only to discover that the very things that made her an outsider at her Washington high school are the source of supernatural skills that may enable her to save the world, the novel is more than a little reminiscent of teen hits such as *Buffy the Vampire Slayer*. What sets it apart is Wendt Young's use of Polynesian myths and culture as the framework within which Leila's powers exist. Discovering that she is *Telesa* (a kind of spirit woman with powers connected to Mother Earth), Leila has to learn to inhabit the mythology of her island heritage to gain control of her gifts and head off disaster. Samoan culture plays a fascinating role in other aspects of the novel too, with *siva* songs and dances and *malu* tattoos all featuring in the plot. Perhaps Wendt Young's boldest choice, however, is to make one of Leila's best friends, Simone, a *fa'afafine* (one of Samoa's 'third gender', as Leila's uncle explains). For all its boundary pushing, I don't recall a transgender teenage boy appearing in *Buffy*.

The novel's fusion of two very different cultures and genres clearly struck a chord with young readers as the trilogy has sold thousands of copies worldwide, attracting nearly 1,400 ratings on Goodreads alone. Yet it would probably never have made it off Wendt Young's desk if she hadn't taken matters into her own hands. The manuscript of the first novel in the series, *Telesa: The Covenant Keeper*, was rejected by more than thirty agents and publishers before she decided to have it edited herself and printed in Tauranga, New Zealand. Its subsequent success confirmed to her the role self-publishing can play in disseminating some of the world's more unusual tales, as she explains on her website, laniwendtyoung.me:

> I am passionate about seeing more of our Pacific stories taken to a global audience and believe that digital publishing is an exciting avenue to make it happen – it's the fastest, cheapest and simplest way to get our stories to the world. Self-publishing makes it possible for the artist to be in control of every step of the creative process – from packaging, pricing, distributing, marketing to promoting their book. It makes it possible for the artist to be in control of the financial returns of that book. I do not see it as a replacement for traditional publishing – but rather, as another option – particularly for those of us writing for a 'niche market' . . . Love it or hate it, the TELESA publishing story demonstrates what most of us already suspected, there is a hunger for stories from the Pacific. Contemporary, 'fanciful, fun' stories written by us, about us and for us. It's a hunger fuelled by our Pacific people worldwide but it's also a hunger in Western readers who are intrigued by the richness of our unique cultures and mythology.

When we see self-publishing through the prism of – albeit unusual – successes like the *Telesa* and *Shiva* trilogies, it's tempting to wonder whether it might just be the corrective the global publishing industry needs. Perhaps it has the potential to counteract the 'disquieting homogenization of world literature' that Steven Roger Fischer, former director of the Institute of Polynesian Languages and Literatures in Auckland, New Zealand, identified in the early 2000s. This is a trend characterised by the fact that, in his view, 'only a small coterie of established English-language authors, it seems, swells the shelves of the world's bookstores and libraries with primarily children's books, romances and thrillers according to a standard set of conventional plots within politically correct frameworks (as determined by corporate accountants)' and a trend which, he claims, 'promises to increase until [. . .] English-language originals alone are left'.

At their best, the advances of the last ten years or so afford writers who might otherwise have been denied publication because of their cultural milieu or subject matter the kind of reach of which previous generations could only have dreamed. And while they may not allow a full-scale assault on the global literary establishment's citadel – were such a thing desirable – they certainly give a lucky few the tools to slip in through the side door, scramble up the stairs and crow loudly from the parapet.

*

Steven Roger Fischer's comments may sound extreme, but he is right about one thing: English is a force to be reckoned with on the international stage. Not only is it the source language for more than half of the texts translated into most other widely spoken tongues, but it is also the lingua franca for around 85 per cent of international organisations. Mandarin and Spanish might beat it in the native-speaker stakes, but when you look at the numbers and geographical spread of people with some degree of competence in English (around one-seventh of the world's population, by many estimates) no other mode of verbal communication comes close in terms of reach and influence. Such is the language's clout that speaking it is regarded as a significant ingredient for success in many non-anglophone regions. In 2003, for example, the Chilean government announced its intention that the nation should be bilingual within a generation, and launched its 'English Opens Doors' programme, making English lessons mandatory for all secondary-school-age pupils. Meanwhile, in Spain, Italy and South Korea, the first decade of the twenty-first century has seen the creation of a series of 'English villages' offering students the opportunity to immerse themselves in an English-only environment for days or weeks at a time. The team behind the Spanish venture – Valdelavilla – even created a *pueblo inglés* in the cyberspace game 'Second Life', where avatars were obliged to communicate only in the Queen's mother tongue.

It's a situation that might have pleased Winston Churchill were he alive to see it (even if he might have been a bit nonplussed by the 'Second Life' dimension). Speaking as he accepted an honorary degree from Harvard University on 6 September 1943, he set out his stall for the promotion of a distilled version of English – termed 'Basic English' – as a global means of communication. Reacting warmly to the news that the Harvard Commission on English Language Studies was working with schools to promote the use of Basic English in teaching, he described the advantages he thought it would bring:

'Gentlemen, I make you my compliments. I do not wish to exaggerate, but you are the head-stream of what might well be a mighty fertilising and health-giving river. It would certainly be a grand convenience for us all to be able to move freely about the world – as we shall be able to do more freely than ever before as the science of the world develops – and be able to find everywhere a medium, albeit primitive, of intercourse and understanding. Might it not also be an advantage to many races, and an aid to the building-up of our new structure for preserving peace?

'All these are great possibilities, and I say: "Let us go into this together. Let us have another Boston Tea Party about it."

'Let us go forward as with other matters and other measures similar in aim and effect – let us go forward in malice to none and good will to all. Such plans offer far better prizes than taking away other people's provinces or lands or grinding them down in exploitation. The empires of the future are the empires of the mind.'

Though the evidence of the intervening decades roundly contradicts the rather jingoistic idea of English as the lynchpin of world peace, the spread of the language has been every bit as formidable as Churchill could have wished. These days it's nigh on impossible to avoid being spoken to in English in many parts of the world, whether you want people to do so or not. On a recent holiday to Crete, Steve and I exulted when we finally found a café where our unopened Greek phrasebook had to be pressed into service – it was pretty much the only place where we got a chance to use the language during the whole fortnight.

When it comes to self-publishing, the ubiquity of English has surprising consequences. With the internet offering distribution potential on a scale that would have been unthinkable for many wordsmiths of previous generations, those with some degree of competence in the language have a choice: write in their mother tongues and limit themselves to a local readership, or try their hand at a story in English on the off chance it might catch the imagination of the hundreds of millions of people able to read it.

For Kuwaiti blogger Nada Sheshtar, or 'Danderma' as she is known online, the decision was a no-brainer. Having developed her irreverent heroine Dathra – an obese thirty-two-year-old junk-food addict who is more than a little out of place in image-conscious and marriage-obsessed Kuwaiti high society – through her English-language blog (danderma. co), Sheshtar felt it made sense to stick with the same medium when it came to writing her *Chronicles of Dathra* trilogy. Even when she discovered that, as most of her local presses work exclusively in Arabic, writing in English would mean she had to self-publish, Sheshtar felt it had an advantage with which her mother tongue simply couldn't compete, as she explained to me: 'Had I written *Dathra* in Arabic – or blogged in Arabic – I would always be confined in the Arabic-speaking world. But there is an entire world out there, from east to west, who are all potential readers and English would be a much better medium to tell the story since its [*sic*] a more universal language, almost the universal language everyone speaks. Had I written my *Dathra* in Arabic, I wouldn't be writing this email to you.'

Having learned English when she attended school in London during the 1990 Iraqi invasion of Kuwait – when troops ransacked her family home – Sheshtar folds Persian Gulf culture into the language she believes will make it go further, to make a rich concoction. Most striking of all is her use of Arabish – a method developed for chatting in Arabic online using Roman characters. This she achieved with the help of her Twitter followers, to whom she turned for advice on translating the Arabish phrases into English footnotes. The following extract is a good example:

'Yumma![1] Would you want me to take trifles from some married guy and become his mistress? You should be angry about THAT! I wanted to throw them at the door. But the gazebo looked so pretty. And you know. Futhool.'[2]

'Futhool?'

Dathra kept silent.

'Why do you have a mother?'

Dathra stayed silent.

'You have a mother who is still alive but you will apparently kill soon, so that when things like this happen, you come t oher [*sic*] and tell her. Walla ya Yumma Jumbo made a pass at me. Your mother, who to you is nothing more than a decoration in the house, 6ar6oor y3ni,[3] would lift up the phone receiver, call him [*sic*] mother and deal with her. You do NOT go to the guy yourself! You do NOT ring their house bell. You DO NOT hide

---

1 Yumma: Mom in Kuwaiti dialect
2 Futhool: Curiosity
3 6ar6oor y3ni: Like a clown you mean

in their gazebo. Where is your brain? When you act, you are not alone in your actions! You are attached to a family, and every action you do is an action that refect [*sic*] on your entire family. Fahma?'[4]

Dathra nodded whispering 'I am so sorry Yumma. It will not happen again. Wallah el 3atheem o rab il Ka3ba!'[5]

However, for all the enthusiasm that the first *Dathra* novel was met with – including a buzzing book launch in June 2011 at chic concept store 52 Degrees, where a long line of blog fans queued to get their copies signed – Sheshtar found the experience of self-publishing a book in her second language tougher than expected. Although the logistics of registering it, getting the necessary approvals from the Kuwaiti Ministry of Information and finding a local printer were relatively straightforward, she hadn't bargained for the level of editing the text might need – or the negative comments made by many readers in response to the book's errors.

'Many of them had very strong opinions,' she told me. 'To be frank I never thought it was that offensive to publish an unedited book. Everyone would go "It's so funny, I couldn't stop laughing but the mistakes . . .!". . . a friend of ours actually threw the book away after reading the first few pages saying the mistakes were too much to bear. Even though my book made it to a famous bookstore in Dubai and to Amazon, I began to feel ashamed of myself.'

As a result, Sheshtar engaged a professional editor and designer to oversee the production of her second book. Indeed, the necessity of taking charge of the process seemed to have become something of a virtue in her eyes.

'If I could find anyone willing to publish an English book in the first place I'd have to wait for a long time for there would be a long queue

---

4   Fahma: Do you understand?
5   Wallah el 3atheem o rab il Ka3ba: Swearing by God the almighty and the master of Kaaba

with changing priorities,' she wrote. 'Besides, the *Dathra* book is a child of the internet era and many publishers cannot understand that. Had I searched and looked and tried to convince, I'd be still waiting for it to see the light and the next big internet thing after blogs and Instagram would be here. It just wouldn't do for a person used to post[ing] her thoughts online with the speed of clicking the "publish" button. I cut the chase short and published it on my own.'

Yet, while it can produce joyful fusions in the hands of some non-native authors, for others the sense that English is the only medium that can broadcast ideas effectively proves deeply restrictive and even damaging. Speaking at the Literary Seminar at the 2004 International PEN Congress on 'Writers in Exile – Writers in Minority Languages' in Tromsø, Norway, the Lebanese-born French author Amin Maalouf expressed his concerns about the impact that feeling obliged to trade stories in the world's most common verbal currency could have on the work of people with no long-standing affinity with the languages. The experience of using English as a non-native writer could often feel superficial, he said, as though the significance of what was said never went deeper than the surface level. For many of those preparing written documents, this presented a problem because the choice of words was so personal and individual to each wordsmith. And yet, for a huge array of reasons, more and more people working in diverse fields around the planet were opting to express their thoughts and discoveries in languages other than their own. The upshot was that increasingly writers, scientists and academics who hailed from minority – and even some majority – language groups felt obliged to present their work and conduct the most vital transactions of their professional lives in a medium that did not belong to them for fear that if they did not do so they would otherwise be ignored by the international community and fail to be heard.

International Federation of Translators vice-president and chair of the Norwegian Association of Literary Translators Bente Christensen is only too aware of the problem. In his work as a lecturer at the University of Tromsø, he frequently sees evidence of the toll that working in

113

a second language can take on students. In a letter to one of the leaders of the American Council of Learned Societies' Social Science Translation Project, in response to its 'Plea for Social Scientists to Write in Their Own Languages', he described the impact that the bias towards English was having on academic study in his country. It was a constant struggle, he said, to try to get university text books and study materials that were written in Norwegian, rather than working purely from English-language sources. The upshot was that in numerous cases students did not fully understand what they were reading. Many times he had observed people parroting concepts in English which sounded convincing enough until he asked them to explain what they had said in their native language. The students would then be at a loss.

In the long-term, commentators worry, this trend for academics to express themselves in English regardless of their linguistic background may mean that other languages are denuded of the specialist terms needed to express complex ideas and discoveries – or never given the chance to develop them in the first place. In some languages, the tools to formulate new concepts could be quietly stripped away.

When it comes to fiction, some fear that the damage could go even deeper. Not only could writers be stunted linguistically by forcing themselves to express their ideas in English, but they might well also try to ape the structures of the widely translated Western literature to which most will have been exposed from an early age. It's an issue that concerns British-Chinese writer Xiaolu Guo. Speaking at the 2014 Jaipur Literature Festival, she argued that the rush to read and write in Western terms could lead to other regional modes of storytelling being pushed to the margins. In many parts of Asia, she said in a panel discussion on the global novel with other writers including Jonathan Franzen and Jhumpa Lahiri, people's reading habits had been twisted out of all recognition. Gone was the tendency to favour the less narrative-led works more typical of the region, and in its place was a drive towards Anglo-Saxon and American-style stories. Realism and plot were crowding out poetry and the alternative approaches that gave many works their local distinctiveness, forcing everything towards the mainstream.

As windows on a wider cross-section of writing than makes it on to traditional publishers' lists, the world's self-published novels provide unexpected insights into these issues. Often acting as spies from the slush pile – for all the efforts of firms like Cinnamon Teal to distance their products from these connotations – they sometimes reveal the struggles of those who would otherwise remain unheard. And, at least among writers opting for English over their mother tongues, they can reveal dark secrets. Indeed, as the only two truly bad books I read during my quest whispered to me under torture (mine, not theirs), the desire to reach a global audience can sometimes encourage aspiring authors in more overlooked parts of the world to make appalling compromises. Both framed as Western-style commercial fiction, these novels by writers from Bahrain and Brunei made no secret of their authors' desire to ape English-language blockbusters, even as their plots, settings and sentences creaked and cracked under the strain of being crammed into an alien form. In one, the murder mystery *Four Kings* by Christopher Sun (aka Sun Tze Yun), a clue even drops out of a copy of Dan Brown's *The Da Vinci Code* left lying around in a house in a French city – peopled with characters called things like Bruno Culruthers, Hugh Jetter and the unfortunately spelled Rouseeau – that is about as culturally specific as an airport terminal.

And yet, in both novels it is the weird anonymity of the setting that provides the key to what is really going on. It forces the reader to wonder why the writers decided to pen stories in a language not their own and set in parts of the world with which they clearly have no great affinity. Peering through the cracks in the flimsy settings and the poor motivations and the clumsy aping of popular genre fiction are the faces of authors who feel they have no option but to try and write Western-style novels in English if they are to reach a larger audience around the world.

While there is no doubt a generous helping of opportunism in the choice of style and subject matter, there is more to this than two cynical hacks leaping on a bandwagon in the hope of making a quick buck. According to an interview with him in the *Brunei Times*, Sun has written and published books, *cerpen* (short stories) and *sajak* (poems) in his first language, Bahasa Melayu. Similarly, Ali Al Saeed – who despite my misgivings won the Bahraini Outstanding Book of the Year Award for his effort, *QuixotiQ,* and has gone on to publish other books in English – makes fretful comments about authenticity and truth towards the end of his novel that point to an authorial sense suggesting that, if he'd written in his mother tongue with more revisions and better editorial support than the self-publishing company he used could offer him, he might have made richer capital out of his material.

Both authors, you can't help feeling, have more to offer than the alien medium they feel driven to work in allows. But for the moment, in English at least and with the international publishing playing field tilted against them by the disproportionate quantity of anglophone works hitting the world's shelves each year, writers like this are reduced to telling a single story: that of English-language privilege. It is a tale of a world where, instead of the conversation Goethe envisaged when he first got to grips with the idea of *Weltliteratur*, a small number of voices are shouting through powerful amplification systems at the expense of many others – and where a significant number of those not favoured with a fair shot at an audience feel they must distort their performances and mimic those dominating the arena in order to be in with a chance. It means that you and I are limited in what we can access, hemmed in by walls of works written by writers raised on and sustained by the same relatively small pool of ideas, stories and assumptions. And it suggests that right now, out there, there is probably an author at work on a masterpiece of which the vast majority of the planet's readers will never hear. Unless the balance shifts, for many, the tale seems unlikely to have a happy ending.

6

Taking alternative modes of transport

oral narratives

One evening during the rush hour, the woman sitting next to me on the East London line tapped me on the arm. 'What are you reading?' she asked, peering at me under the rucksack of the person standing over us. 'It looks so unusual. I've never seen a book like that before.'

I looked down at the copy of *Marshall Islands Legends and Stories* balanced on the bags heaped on my lap. Now I came to think of it, the book was rather strange. It featured photographs of the people who had told stories to the collection's editor and line drawings by a local artist. There were margin notes translating certain bolded words, and stage directions in italics peppering the text. And the whole thing was organised using headings in a strange, chunky font, more suggestive of letters etched in wood or stone than those usually printed on a page.

The contents of the fifty stories contained in the book were every bit as unusual too. Featuring whales sleeping on the roofs of houses, flying women, children born twelve at a time and kingdoms at the bottom of the sea, they presented an intriguing and broad picture of Marshallese folklore. Some of them contained fable-like explanations of aspects of island life – such as how turtles first came to the nation or how women learned how to survive childbirth – and together they wove a complex web of duties and preoccupations, in which the importance of hospitality and respecting customs and authority jostled with a love of ingenuity, wit and cunning. Among some of the most striking tales in the collection were those of the *iroij* (chief) who strikes a deal with demons and gets washed out to sea when he fails to keep his side of the bargain, and the fishermen who lose the art of magic fishing because they do not pay attention to their elders.

Fittingly, the story of the creation of the book was just as extraordinary as its form and contents. The project began back in the early nineties when, in his capacity as Honolulu Theatre for Youth's director of drama education, Daniel A. Kelin II was asked to go to do some work with a youth health programme in the Marshall Islands, the tiny nation of some 60,000 people distributed among more than 1,000 islets in the North Pacific. Keen to engage the young people with their community and culture in fresh ways, Kelin hit on the idea of dramatising some of the local myths and legends. But there was a problem.

'I kept feeling like it was being poorly done because I was finding this stuff in books,' he told me. 'I thought "why am I finding this stuff in books that were created by outsiders when I'm here in this place itself?" So I asked their help in trying to find stories.'

What followed was a ten-year, self-funded 'labour of love', during which Kelin travelled to the Marshall Islands every summer and spent time going from island to island in the company of local contacts, trying to record, transcribe and translate stories. It wasn't easy. Leaving aside the logistical and financial challenges of moving between tiny communities spread over 750,000 square miles of ocean, Kelin had no guarantee that the specially designated storytellers charged with remembering and narrating Marshallese folklore would speak to him. Technically this decision was in the hands of the local *iroijes*, who have the power to instruct the narrators to grant or withhold a performance.

In practice, however, Kelin found things were rather less clear-cut. Having followed protocol on the island of Ujae and received the *iroij*'s permission to hear stories from local storyteller Nitwa Jeik – a storyteller so rigid in his adherence to the rulings of the *iroij* that even many of his peers had not heard his tales and loitered curiously in the background while Kelin was with him – he was dismayed to discover that Jeik was planning to leave the island two days later. As Kelin had arranged to spend a week there, he might have been looking at a lot of wasted time had he not bumped into another storyteller, the rather mischievous Jorju Arre.

'I asked if I would have to get permission to hear stories from him,' recalled Kelin. 'And he said, "These are my stories. I don't care what anyone else says. I'll share them with you if I want to." I just found it really engaging. Here I am on this island that has 800 or 1,000 people living on it and here's this guy with this wry sense of humour who's challenging the status quo. No one in the world's going to know this guy except for the people here and yet to me he's as entertaining as anything I've ever seen anywhere.'

As it turned out, no *iroijes* refused permission for Kelin to hear stories, although he did encounter resistance from storytellers on a few of the islands. On Jaluit, for example, two or three of those he approached were upset that he was asking for tales and refused to speak to him; despite spending a week there, he came away with just two stories. The reasons for the storytellers' refusals were not clear, although Kelin put it down to his visit to that island being less carefully arranged than usual: whereas he would normally have made approaches through a local intermediary, this was less easy to set up on Jaluit.

Where his trips were successful, exchange was a key part of establishing a rapport with the storytellers. Instead of simply expecting legends to be told to him, Kelin shared anecdotes about his home and, where he could, offered lifts to those wanting to travel between islands. He also pledged to send copies of the book to each of the eighteen storytellers featured, a promise he honoured by returning to the Marshall Islands when the collection was published and waiting at the airport to get people flying to each of the destinations to hand-deliver the volumes (at this point in our conversation, I made a note to ensure I sent him a copy of this book when it came out). In turn, Kelin was often welcomed with great excitement and showered with hospitality and gifts of food. And when he arrived at Kiat Benjamin's house on Maloelap with a bunch of balloons to hand out to the local children, he caused quite a stir. 'Kiat was beside himself. He was just so happy that we weren't just there to get him to tell stories but we were there to interact. Those are the kind of things that made a difference to me. It was getting to know other people and spending time with them and feeling valued.'

This reciprocity chimed well with the ethos of Marshallese storytelling: the local term for legend or story, *bwebwenato*, is the same as the word for conversation, implying that the relation of a narrative is a two-way process. In fact Kelin found these incidental episodes and the atmosphere surrounding the telling of the stories to be every bit as important as the words themselves. So when the invitation came from Hawaiian publisher Bess Press to compile the material he'd collected into a book, it seemed natural to draw on his theatre background to introduce into the text stage directions and extraneous comments made by the storytellers (as well as their photographs and biographies) in an attempt to capture as much of the experience as possible. These additional details included how one storyteller, Tonke Aisea, invited Kelin to visit another island to see the pit where a boy wrestled a demon to death, and some personal interpretations of the morals of a few of the tales, which many of the narrators spoke about as historic fact, no matter how fantastic the events.

Kelin thinks that every story is influenced by factors such as mood or place, and says: 'I wanted to get a sense of that so that it's not just me taking a story and saying "here's a great story," but here's the person who told it, here's where it was told, here's how it was told, here's some of the funny little things that went on to give a real sense of place – culture in a sense, although I can't say I'm translating culture directly – to have more of a sense of what this experience is like here in this place that makes it different than other places in the world.'

This view that the atmosphere and interaction of each individual performance are important is something that many oral storytellers and literary performers around the planet would agree with. The late South African writer Mazisi Kunene, who described himself as working in the tradition of the Zulu poets from praise singers onwards, told critic Jane

Wilkinson he rarely enjoyed performing to Western audiences because of their staid and formal reaction to staged events. 'I hate to read, for instance, especially in Europe, because there you are reading to audiences that are sober and sitting down,' he told Jane Wilkinson. 'I would prefer to perform to people who are not so sane, who are *engaged*, even drunk! Yes . . . because then there is an involvement.' For Kunene, the exchange he experienced with those who listened to his work and the way each piece landed in the context of the specific event was a vital part of the whole.

Capturing such subtle distinctions presents challenges for those trying to represent spoken narratives in written words. And, in Kelin's experience, it can be possible to take the attempt to capture everything too far. 'There are some people who try to get every nuance of an oral story – all the intonation. To me that's extreme. That could change if you have a cold, for God's sake.'

He took a similar approach when it came to the question of recording the definitive version of each tale. 'When has a tale ever been one way? It depends on how somebody hears it, where they are at the time, etcetera, etcetera. For me it's the experience of it in the now. It's like, here we are and this is this moment. And if I came a week later or a year later the moment would be different and the story would be different.'

Kelin's openness and creativity, combined with his honesty about the limitations of the written form's capacity to contain the storytellers' renditions, may go some way to explain why *Marshall Islands Legends and Stories* is one of the most widely available books to come out of the smaller Pacific island nations in the decades since independence. Consulted for research by several filmmakers and writers, it is known among the Marshallese diaspora and was used by US parents as a tool to educate children adopted from the islands about their heritage. Even ten years after its publication, Kelin hears from people who have just discovered it and want to share their enthusiasm for it (although he confesses he'll be lucky if he ever breaks even after all the money he spent collecting the tales).

The fact that the book was striking enough to persuade a stranger on the Tube to break the unwritten rule of pretending everyone else doesn't exist speaks volumes in itself.

*

For all Kelin's efforts, reading the book was a bittersweet experience. At lively moments in the narratives, I found my ears straining in vain to catch the voice speaking or singing far away across the sea. When the italics informed me of a storyteller's laugh or exclamation, I wished that I could be there to witness it for myself. Creative and imaginative though the layout was, the fixedness and formality of the written format couldn't help but get in the way of the spontaneity and immediacy so central to the tradition, like a po-faced interpreter relaying a stand-up comedian's routine.

This awkward fit between presentation and content raises the issue of what impact such transcriptions have on the traditions they seek to record. Indeed, several of the storytellers visited by Kelin expressed their sadness at the decline of the oral storytelling culture with the encroachment of Westernisation, just as their words were being recorded for use in a Western form. Even if these comments contained a healthy dose of what Kelin described to me as 'old people bemoaning that young people aren't like them', their inclusion in the text presents an uncomfortable irony, which begs the question whether the book itself may in fact represent the hammering of yet another nail into the coffin of the proud traditions it seeks to celebrate.

After all, one of the major elements that historically contributed to the prestige of the storytellers was the fact that they were among the select few entrusted with remembering and imparting locally and nationally significant stories. They were essentially curators of the nation's heritage and the final arbiters when it came to managing and presenting their compatriots' literary culture. Without any other source to refer to, they were precious repositories of shared memory, and their status and the lavish feasts and parties that commonly accompanied their performances bore witness to this fact. No bluffer's guide for them; no revision notes to mug up on or internet databases to refresh a hazy memory. Their nations' histories and legends lived through them.

Writing these stories down inevitably changes that. In the last two centuries or so (at least since anthropologists began recording these oral folk legends, often developing written alphabet systems for the purpose), transcribers have created independent records against which the narrators' performances can be checked. The written copies also mean that, in theory at least, people no longer need the narrators if they want to access the tales. This may have the consequence that the legends are told less and less, providing fewer opportunities for the practice that keeps the sagas alive in the tellers' minds. Given this trend, it's conceivable that storytellers face changing from central figures in their communities into benevolent uncle types, wheeled out on occasion to perform their party pieces. And that their tales, rather than being organic, living things that change with each telling, will shrink and crystallise. Even with outside influences rapidly changing life on the islands and a high chance that whatever isn't recorded may well soon be lost, it's hard not to wonder whether ink and paper sometimes have the unintended effect of fossilising the practices they seek to preserve.

This impression becomes stronger when you compare the lively collection of Marshallese tales with the nation-building stories published by several Pacific states around the time of independence. When islands such as Tuvalu and Vanuatu gained their sovereignty in the seventies and eighties, the writing of some form of national story as told by the islanders themselves seemed to be regarded as a central part of the assertion of identity, at least by officials in the new governments and representatives of the former colonial powers and other big English-speaking countries nearby, which often fielded academics to help with the recording process. In *Tuvalu: A History*, which draws together workshop-generated accounts by seventeen Tuvaluans, for example, a sense of the gravity of the task the writers are undertaking runs throughout the narrative. This is established from the very first page in the Foreword by Prime Minister Tomasi Puapua, who describes the book as being of 'considerable significance in the history of the young nation of Tuvalu' because the accounts are, for the first time, 'written by Tuvaluans interpreting events as they themselves see them'.

This interpretation of events turns out to be a blending of personal stories and historical research and gives rise to some wonderful moments. We learn, for example, how to hitch a ride on a turtle's back – apparently the trick is to hang on without getting your fingers jammed between the neck and the shell or too near the mouth – as well as the islanders' rather alarming traditional methods for dealing with trouble-makers, which involve a leaky canoe without a paddle. As in the Marshallese stories, the narrators often appear to make little distinction between factual and symbolic truth. The accounts rove back and forth between myth and history, mingling tales about cannibals and magical eels with maps, diagrams, and explanations of the islands' names, geography and politics. Indeed, the fantastic and the factual sometimes blend together, with anecdotal accounts about chiefs who could charm fish and the story of the old woman who had power over the weather:

Taia Teuai, an old woman who died in 1982, was generally recognised as having inherited from her grandparents the power to make it rain. Shortly before her death she explained how she did it:

'If there is a long drought then I will make the rain fall. First I go to the bush to gather coconut leaves and flowers with which to weave myself a garland. Later, towards sunset, I put oil over my body and wearing a clean dress and with a garland on my head go down to the beach to meet a team of "rain-makers". These are little clouds sailing towards the setting sun. I look at them and dance, and sing a song such as this one:

'Little clouds, little clouds!/Bring rain to me,/To moisten my body.

'In about three days [*sic*] time there would be heavy rain. This sort of rain can easily be recognised because the drops are much thicker than those of ordinary rain.'

Yet for all the rhetoric about these written accounts being a way of islanders taking ownership of their national story, it's hard not to feel the hands of the non-Tuvaluan workshop leaders on the shoulders of the writers. The islanders may have felt this too because, at least as far as I have been able to discover, no other prose book by a Tuvaluan writer has been published in the thirty years since this one came out. The same seems to be true on Nauru. Since the 1990 University of the South Pacific workshop 'organised so that a conscious effort would be made to encourage Nauruans to write and to record their folklore in the attempt to build up a Nauruan literature' – according to the Foreword in the resulting collection, *Stories from Nauru* – nothing further seems to have appeared, despite some promising pieces in the first anthology.

There are of course exceptions to these orchestrated publications from the region. In particular, anyone looking for a truly joyful and personal account of independence will find it in Sethy John Regenvanu's memoir *Laef Blong Mi: From village to nation*. Its narrative bubbles with pride as it weaves together political events and the former Vanuatuan government minister's own story to reveal what it means to build a nation from the ground up.

As a rule, however, the published historical accounts have a hollow, formal feel. Tonke Aisea grinning and offering to show Kelin the ditch where the heroes of his story hid from a demon seems a world away, and it is as though we are looking at a school photograph showing everyone dressed in their best and smiling politely, desperate for the moment when the shutter clicks and they can all scatter back to their normal lives. The written word feels cramped and inflexible, like a badly fitting pair of new shoes, pinching and distorting the thoughts of people who for generations experienced storytelling as an immediate, shared event and stories as living, mutating, performative things. Reading these books, it feels like you're missing a much livelier party going on elsewhere.

*

Across the world, wherever there is a tradition of communicating tales by methods other than writing, you'll normally find an attendant cluster of – often Western – anthropologists, literary critics and other interested parties agonising about the best way to get what's being said or sung down on the page. From the dastans of Central Asia to the 2,000-year-old Pandavani tradition of Madhya Pradesh, stories that are performed rather than published present a particular challenge to those of us used to taking our narratives in printed form.

This issue is compounded by the speed with which many of the languages that frame these tales are being eroded. Although the world is home to more than 6,000 tongues, some 90 per cent of these are thought to be in danger of extinction, with a good 3,000 or so predicted to die out in the next 100 years. According to Professor Nicholas Evans, head of the Australian National University's department of linguistics and author of *Dying Words: Endangered languages and what they have to tell us*, 'on best current estimates, every two weeks, somewhere in the world, the last speaker of a fading language dies'. Evans, who has spent large chunks of his career researching and recording Aborigine languages such as Kayardild – which, at the time his book came out in 2009, had only eight known surviving speakers, all of them aged over sixty – writes powerfully about what the loss of a spoken form means:

No one's mind will again travel the thought paths that its ancestral speakers once blazed. No one will hear its sounds again except from a recording, and no one can go back to ask a new question about how the language works.

Even with speakers of allegedly extinct languages turning up now and again – as happened with Kusunda in Nepal in 2000 – and many governments now enshrining the rights of once-maligned minority-language speakers in law and funding programmes to promote and protect them, the trend seems inexorable.

With vast numbers of these languages not yet transcribed, the loss of a mode of speaking often means the destruction of the stories that were couched in it. Though some languages move into written circulation fairly organically, as English did after the publication in 1258 of the 'Provisions of Oxford' (the first documents ever issued in the King's name in English, as opposed to in French or Latin), many languages in small communities remain without a written form. In these cases it is often down to individual anthropologists armed with notebooks, recording equipment and a great deal of patience to try to crack the grammatical code and find a method of notation that will enable another person to reproduce the sounds of the words from the symbols on the page. Failure to do so in time can have devastating results; as Malian writer Amadou Hampâté Bâ memorably put it in an address to UNESCO in 1960, 'an old person dying is a library burning' – and in the case of speakers of the world's rarest languages, the library in question may contain the last copies of works about which we can only guess.

With the pressure on, scholars have scrambled to find satisfactory ways of recording stories that might otherwise be lost. In doing so, they have had to contend with challenges ranging from inadequate standardisation methods, which sometimes mean that a written form may privilege a particular dialect and be almost intelligible to speakers of another strain of the same language, through to the issue of how to capture the multifaceted nature of an oral performance. Sticking to the Western habit of assuming that words take precedence over all else can have serious consequences, as Ruth Finnegan noted in her seminal 1970 work on *Oral Literature in Africa*: 'Thus the public is still given the impression of African oral literature as a kind of written literature manqué – apparently lacking the elaboration of wording and recognisability of association known from familiar forms, and without the particular stylistic devices peculiar to oral forms being made clear.' Treating oral works in this way risks leading us into the trap of 'substituting for an awareness of the shallowness of our own understanding an imaginary picture of the shallowness in literary appreciation and development of the people we are attempting to study'.

As Daniel Kelin discovered in the Marshall Islands, there is also the puzzle of how you go about creating a permanent version of something that shifts from one day to the next. This is particularly difficult where improvisation plays a key role in the realisation of a story. In the early twentieth century, the American classicist Milman Parry studied the work of the Yugoslavian bards. Rather than memorising their poems word for word, these performers would ad-lib from a set base of material, adapting scenes to different settings and using certain stock phrases and formulas to fill out the lines as required. There was no definitive version, only a series of renderings stretching across time, influenced by the whims of each performer and their audience. As Parry's successor Albert Lord noted in his 1960 work on the subject, *The Singer of Tales*, 'the truth of the matter is that our concept of "the original," of "the song," simply makes no sense in oral tradition'. Trying to record a single sample of one of these performances would be like taking a photograph of a pattern seen in a kaleidoscope: you would capture what you saw at that moment, but miss the essence of the thing.

Then there's the issue of the many subtle tonal and vocal variations for which most languages simply don't have a standard means of notation. Anthropologists such as Dennis Tedlock, who spent much of the sixties and seventies recording the stories of the Zuni Indians in New Mexico and Quiché speakers in Guatemala, have gone to great lengths to find ways of capturing these extra-verbal markers. In Tedlock's view, as he explains in his 1983 book *The Spoken Word and the Work of Interpretation*, 'a translation of an oral narrative should be presented as a performable script'. To this end, he developed a complicated system – using line breaks, spacing, italics, dashes, brackets, exclamation marks and capital letters, among other symbols and signs – in an attempt to reflect the different sorts of tone, pitch, emphasis, gesture, tempo and audience participation in the stories he heard. The texts in his book bear witness to his diligence, at times seeming to blare from the page, as in this example transcribed from his 1971 recording of a worker in the American Midwest:

'That was the HARDEST job because
up there in Kansas
the weather is too HOT
even around nine o'clock, ten, twelve o'clock
bo——y that's hot.
(*staccato*) The héat cómes úp to yóur FACE
and the héat cómes ón yóur BACK—
(*throaty*) gosh!
And you're pressing on
on the hot ground with your BARE HAND
your KNEES—
(*fading*) we almost gave up on it.'

For all his efforts, though, even Tedlock concedes that 'no score can ever be so detailed and precise as to provide for the re-creation of the full sound of the tape'.

In light of this, attempts to record non-verbal forms of expression in writing can seem like an awful lot of trouble to go to for an exercise that is doomed to fail. Yet, before we dismiss these as simply more trouble than they're worth, perhaps we should reflect that one of Britain's greatest men of letters, had he decided to turn his hand to anthropological pursuits, might well have set a lot of store by the intonation of the world's oral narrators. Although chiefly remembered for his magnificent written *oeuvre*, Charles Dickens was by all accounts a nifty performer of his own work. According to biographer Peter Ackroyd, he included notes in the margins of the texts he read out loud, reminding himself of the tone and gestures to use: 'Cheerful . . . Stern

. . . Pathos . . . Mystery . . . Quick on', along with 'Beckon down . . . Point . . . Shudder . . . Look Round in Terror'. In advance of his extensive reading tours, the first of which began in August 1858 in Clifton and ended in Brighton, taking in some forty towns along the way, the writer spent months preparing. And by the end of a reading he was usually drenched in sweat, having put so much effort into his performance. He certainly seemed to gain satisfaction from the added influence over readers that performing his work afforded him, as a letter to his wife Catherine in which he described reading his short novel *The Chimes* demonstrates: 'If you had seen Macready last night – undisguisedly sobbing, and crying on the sofa, as I read – you would have felt (as I did) what a thing it is to have Power.'

Former prime minister Margaret Thatcher certainly seemed conscious of the power that tone and inflection can carry when on 19 October 1988 she imposed a ban on the media broadcast of Irish Republican leader Gerry Adams' voice, along with those of representatives of eleven other Republican and Loyalist organisations. The purpose of the ban was ostensibly to 'starve the terrorist and the hijacker of the oxygen of publicity on which they depend', but in practice it only increased the Sinn Fein president's notoriety and his fascination for a generation of British children brought up watching his mouth move to the accompaniment of a voice that was not his, wondering what illicit verbal flourishes and emphases lay beneath the deadpan tone of the actor hired to dub him.

Yet, although gestures and vocal modulations can add extra layers of significance to words, some anthropologists worry that too scrupulous a desire to capture every inflection could compromise the authenticity of the telling itself. In *Dying Words*, Nicholas Evans cites the warning of Bob Dixon, who used his acceptance speech for the 2006 Bloomfield Award – for his written grammar of the Amazonian language Jarawara (which required lengthy recording and study to compile) – to caution young anthropologists against embracing innovations willy-nilly. Junior researchers embarking on their own projects should be wary of rushing after the latest gadgets and gizmos, he said, because these impressive-looking bits of kit could well let them down at crucial moments or compromise their position in the communities they were trying to work with. His best advice was to eschew digital machinery in all its guises and limit equipment to pens, pencils, spiral-bound notebooks and a decent quality tape recorder or two, as he had done when preparing his grammars not only of Jarawara, but also Dyirbal, Yidin and Boumaa Fijian. Even laptops, he felt, were unnecessary and potentially detrimental to meaningful anthropological work and the recording of linguistic patterns.

Fogeyish and somewhat arbitrary as this sounds – after all, why should a tape recorder be any less likely to fail, seize up in humidity or clog with dust than digital equipment or a computer? – there is a serious point to be made about the limitations of recording equipment when it comes to preserving stories. With technology moving as fast as it does, many digital recordings become obsolete within ten years of their creation, meaning that unless their owners take care to transfer them to the latest formats, they may quickly become inaccessible. Even trusty old ink and paper will fade, curl, rip or burn, in time. As Evans puts it: 'In this regard, Sumerian clay tablets still remain unsurpassed for archival stability and long-term "interpretability".'

All this assumes, of course, that you've got the permission of the owners of the stories to preserve and disseminate them as you see fit. But when it comes to oral stories, the question of who has the final say in what happens to the intellectual property can be extremely complicated, as linguists Nora Marks Dauenhauer and Richard Dauenhauer discovered when they embarked on a project to reverse language shift among the Tlingit, Haida and Tsimshian peoples in south-east Alaska. Conscious that of twenty native languages historically spoken in the state only two were still being passed down from parents to children, the pair set out to attempt to tackle the reticence that years of discrimination against minority-language groups had fostered – until 1995, Tlingit children in the Alaskan capital Juneau were routinely put in special education and speech therapy to correct their accents when speaking English. The Dauenhauers began work on a series of projects, which included trying to record local legends, only to encounter a level of distrust that sometimes had disastrous consequences:

> There is a real and legitimate fear of traditional ethnic materials being appropriated, exploited, trivialized, or desecrated by outsiders, and this fear has led many elders and communities in the direction of secrecy.
>
> . . .
>
> There have been cases where one relative sabotaged another elder's attempts to have an event video-taped. There have even been situations where children interfered with recording sessions, with the result that after the death of the parent, there was no record of what he knew and wanted to preserve for them. Only with the death of the elder did the younger people realize the enormity of their loss. They assumed that 'somebody' knew 'the stories', but this was not the case.

In the face of such extreme cases of 'linguistic and cultural suicide', the Dauenhauers found themselves pretty powerless to achieve their goal of re-engaging the community with its heritage. 'We can document the stories, but we cannot create them out of nothing; we can produce grammars and instructional material, but they are nothing unless people actually speak the language to each other in the home and community,' they wrote sadly, estimating that, based on current trends and with so much that is specific to the language group's culture leaching away, Tlingit would be extinct by 2050.

Such negative experiences, coupled with the shrinkage of language diversity around the planet, tend to throw a pall over the question of oral literature. Even in the face of occasional success stories – such as the resurgence of Maori-language education in New Zealand in the late twentieth century, or the groundswell of support for protecting the twenty-nine Mayan languages spoken by some six million indigenous Maya spread across Guatemala, Mexico, Belize and Honduras – the thought of telling stories rather than writing them down seems to have a nostalgic, wistful air. Echoing with the footsteps of Vaughan Williams trudging the country lanes to harvest the last remnants of Britain's folk songs more than a century ago, the idea of oral narratives seems quaint and distant – a hangover from a previous era that must inevitably fade into obscurity with time. 'The two traditions – the foreign literate and the indigenous oral – are usually worlds apart and, as the transcriber of *Beowulf* discovered around 1,300 years ago, fundamentally irreconcilable. Only the one prevails in the end: the written word, its manifold advantages irresistible,' writes Steven Roger Fischer in *A History of Reading*, concluding that all roads lead ultimately to 'the reading monoculture of the twentieth century'. Seen in this light, it is as though narrated stories are local ephemera, doomed to be drowned out by the grinding of the printing presses and the tapping of computer keys. We can appreciate them and admire them as we might admire a quill pen or an Elizabethan mask in a museum, but we should never be so silly as to forget their fragility and otherness. We should understand them in their context and celebrate them as precious links to ways of thinking and speaking that might one day be lost to us. Because surely such delicate and endangered practices could never have any real relevance to our modern-day lives in the West?

*

When Penn State University lecturer Thomas Hale tried to get music lessons in Niger in 1981, he was in for a surprise. As he recounts in his 2007 book *Griots and Griottes*, the academic took the three-stringed *molo* (a sort of lute) he had purchased from the shop of the Musée National in the capital Niamey to a young performer or *jeseré* called Zakary Hamani, only to find his prospective teacher wasn't satisfied with it. The instrument needed to be modified. Hamani took it away, promising to return it within a week.

When the *molo* came back, it looked almost identical. The only modification was that the original wood of the neck had been replaced with slightly abrasive hardwood, which would help to maintain the tuning of the strings. Minimal though it was, as Hale recalls, the difference revealed an important reality about the lives of the performers and storytellers he was spending a year recording:

> The change to the instrument was hardly noticeable, but it represented an evolution, a modernization – what we might call an equipment upgrade. Though I thanked Zakary for his work, I was not delighted by the change because I viewed it as technologically incorrect. I didn't realize that in Zakary's eyes the instrument was not a museum piece, but a working *molo*. He had, in fact, high hopes that I would pay him for lessons and learn how to play it – hence the need for the latest version.

Hale has been in a great position to observe how the West African storytelling tradition has adapted in recent decades. It is more than fifty years since his first trip to Niger, as a Peace Corps volunteer in 1964, and nearly thirty-five years since his twelve-month stint there recording legends such as *The Epic of Askia Mohammed*. That work, which had been narrated over two evenings by famed storyteller Nouhou Malio, recalls the life and times of the sixteenth-century ruler of the Songhay Empire, Mamar Kassaye, and took Hale and a team of Nigerien scholars ten years to transcribe and translate from Songhay into French and then into English. Since then, he has maintained contact with various people in Niger, Mali, Senegal and The Gambia – nations whose storytelling traditions have been one of the major focal points of his research.

His long association with the region has given Hale ample opportunity to study the enigmatic figure of the griot – also known as *guewel*, *jali*, *jeli*, *jeseré*, *gawlo* and *iggiw*, among other terms, depending on which part of West Africa you go to. Traditionally born into the profession – which has no direct Western equivalent – griots are, in Hale's

words, 'time-binders', repositories of cultural history, personal genealogies and myths and legends. They have central roles to play in all the
ceremonies marking rites of passage and the power to make or destroy
a reputation with a word, responsibilities that give them a rather ambig-
uous status, as Hale explains in his book:

> On one hand, griots appear to be the respected keepers of the
> heritages of families, clans, and societies. On the other hand, if
> one were to stop a hundred people on the street in Bamako and
> ask if they would be happy to have a daughter marry a griot, the
> response would likely be a mixture of laughter and disdain.

Yet despite being part of a tradition that is documented as existing more
than seven centuries ago and probably stretches a lot further back than
that, griots are by no means stuck in the past. As soon as radio became
widespread in West Africa, they took to the airwaves. More than sixty
years later, you can find them on YouTube and although the handful
of English transcriptions and translations available focus almost exclusively on stories of heroes who lived between the eighth and eighteenth
centuries, contemporary performances incorporate recent events and
modern technologies. One griot, Al Haji Papa Bunka Susso, was even
asked to serve as minister of youth, sports and culture in the Gambian
government in 1994, an invitation he declined; nevertheless, it demonstrates the ongoing relevance of the art to the nation's life. Pragmatic
and innovative, these wordsmiths, it seems, are past masters in anticipating what is expected and adapting their practices accordingly. As
Hale puts it, griots are 'preservers of tradition who are often eager to
change their ways'.

When you look at the kind of storytelling that griots practise, this
malleability makes perfect sense. Although sometimes vaunted as
keepers of immutable historical records, they more usually present what
Hale calls 'a reading of history' – a culturally relative account of events
past, crafted to glorify a certain figure or clan or make a particular point.

Indeed, as Hale discovered when he went to record the Zarma people's *Epic of Mali Bero* in the palace of the Zarmakoy in 1981, these renditions can change emphasis according to the whim of the person holding the purse strings or wielding the most influence. During the performance, the chief told Hale to stop recording and then instructed the *jeseré* to shift his narration in a slightly different direction. 'He wanted to be sure that I had the "right" version from his perspective – a version that included or excluded some episodes about his family or was deemed particularly appropriate for the foreign researcher.'

This pragmatism and ability to adapt may be one of the key qualities that has enabled the griot tradition to weather the rapid changes of the twentieth century and a host of attendant challenges. These include the rise of large numbers of 'fake' and substandard griots who flock to naming ceremonies and weddings, eager to profit from the rewards given to those commissioned to sing the praises or tell the genealogies of those involved. The problem became so severe at times that in 1980 a report commissioned by the Niger government even recommended abandoning the term 'griot', as part of an effort to sanitise the profession, which President Seyni Kountché felt was becoming too parasitic on the resources of others.

Even so, the griot tradition shows little sign of dying. Indeed, with the increase in travel and migration, griots have travelled with their communities, spreading out to serve the ceremonial and cultural needs of the diaspora, as well as profiting from the interest of other communities and scholars around the world. Nations such as the US and France are home to many of them, along with instrument manufacturers who may never have visited West Africa, yet construct molos, koras and balafons to the highest standards using traditional and modern techniques.

In fact Thomas Hale and a griot based in New York – the very same Al-Haji Papa Bunka Susso once offered an opening in the Gambian government – have a long history of collaborating. They have done several tours together, performing at cultural venues around the US, with Hale talking about the griot tradition in between recitations and songs from Papa Susso (as he is popularly known).

But it's not just those with a direct connection to West Africa who find meaning in embracing the griots' legacy. As Californian-born African-American Eric Cyrs found when he began to look into ways of tackling crime and violence among the young black population in and around Long Beach during the late eighties and early nineties, the story-telling tradition can hold the key to a new way of life. Having been trained as a classical percussionist at Chapman University, Cyrs took on the role of teaching history and self-awareness through drumming, music and storytelling as part of a local Rites of Passage programme designed to mentor young people. But when members of the Guinean dance group Les Ballets Africains attended one of his sessions, Cyrs was in for a surprise. 'When they saw what I was doing, they said: "Hey! You're a griot! You're a griot!" So I started researching the griot tradition.'

A key influence on Cyrs' research was Alex Haley's 1976 book *Roots*, a work partly inspired by an encounter the African-American writer had with a griot in The Gambia when he went to research the history of his ancestors, who were abducted by slave traders. Although criticised in some quarters for its blending of fact and fiction, or what Haley himself called 'faction', the account did much to kindle interest in West African storytelling. As Thomas Hale puts it in *Griots and Griottes*, 'Haley probably did more than any other individual to create an interest in griots throughout the world.' Much like the culturally relative readings of history moulded by griots to fit each audience and occasion, *Roots* is effectively a symbolic account of the bitter family history of many African-Americans. Whether or not it is factually accurate is almost beside the point.

For Cyrs, it opened up powerful possibilities. 'I started seeing that there was value in utilising something cultural because the children connected with it. The deeper I dug, the more I adapted my storytelling. Because the majority of African-Americans come from West Africa, I adopted West Africa and started doing research for the children to introduce them to their cultural lineage.'

Teaching himself the kora, a bridge-harp commonly played by griots, and the West African language Bambara, Cyrs created the persona of Baba the Storyteller, the name under which he works today. But it wasn't until he put up a young Senegalese man that Baba got the opportunity to take his craft to the next level. Grateful for the American's hospitality, the house guest insisted that his host accept an invitation to stay with his family back home. In 2000, Baba packed his bags and set off for Senegal, eager to learn from the masters. But things didn't go entirely according to plan: 'It was my very first time to that part of the world and it was a trying experience. I was a very foolish young man.'

Looking back, he recognises that the main issues arose from approaching the learning experience with a Western mindset. Armed with tape recorders and notebooks, he was keen to study in the way he was used to doing in the US. But the teaching process he encountered was rather different.

'It wasn't instruction the way I understood it. I butted heads quite a bit saying "I want to learn! I want to learn!" when it [the learning process] was just part of living everyday life. I had to learn to relax and accept the way learning happened. That was a challenge for me because I was raised in the West where there's a respect for time and there's the order that you're used to. None of that served me well when I first started learning.'

For all the teething problems, though, Baba found he was welcomed during the months he spent in Senegal – sometimes as a curiosity, but more often than not as a serious student of the griot tradition. And when he went to fulfil his personal ambition of walking back through the Door of No Return on Gorée Island, the final exit point of many slaves from Africa, all those he met respected what it meant to him. 'Everyone was so accommodating. Everyone understood what I was trying to do. It was a homecoming most of the time. They would say, "our ancestors were taken away hundreds of years ago but you've come back. You show the strength of spirit to return." I would have celebrations in my honour. I was accepted.'

Further trips to Mali, Guinea and The Gambia followed, during which Baba stayed with the son of Papa Susso, who had become his mentor back in the US, and taught English and bought rice in exchange for the hospitality he received. During this time, he continued to learn from those around him by a process of osmosis, attending as many weddings and naming ceremonies as he could to hear the storytelling (or *jaliyaa*). Opportunities to broaden his repertoire also cropped up organically: going to the market to get a new kora made one day, he found himself engaged in a long session of song-swapping with the craftsman.

These experiences gave Baba a great stock of material to draw upon back in the US, where he now supports himself entirely by storytelling and gives up to twelve performances a week – many of them in schools. Working in English, French and Spanish, with chunks of Bambara thrown in for good measure, Baba translates and adapts the stories for his audience, much as West African griots have done for generations – although he occasionally finds that cultural differences require more than a little poetic licence.

One such story concerns an overweening servant girl, who impersonates her princess mistress and gets her put to work in the fields. In the African version, when her trick is discovered, the servant is tied to a pole in a hut and burned to death. 'It's a beautiful story, but in the West I can't sit with a bunch of children and tell that. So I change the story so it becomes more of a fable where there's a lesson to learn at the end. For example, we tell children lying isn't good. The servant girl has lied and what I usually end up doing is that she is punished but not so violently.'

Alongside his work in schools, Baba gets invited to tour further afield, and has performed in several South American countries, Poland and the Dominican Republic (where he was a guest of the First Lady). He teaches kora and storytelling to a number of students in the US and abroad, using Skype where distance is prohibitive, and was named artist of the year by the City of Long Beach in 2001.

Although he tends to leave ceremonies in West African communities to home-grown griots like Papa Susso, Baba often finds himself called upon to bring a cultural flavour to the funerals, weddings and baby-naming ceremonies of compatriots keen to include some historical material in the proceedings. Those who ask him to perform are usually 'African-Americans who are very culturally aware', he says. 'They're looking for something based in ancestral roots and because I've studied and done so much they bring me for that connection.'

For Baba, stories and storytelling have a central role in building a sense of identity and strengthening ties among communities; being 'time-binders', as Thomas Hale puts it. Their dynamism is the very thing that keeps them going, necessitating telling after telling as each new generation moves through the stages of life. Whether creating self-awareness among disaffected youth, educating a Western audience or celebrating a marriage, they are useful and welcome statements about who those narrating and those listening are. It's for this reason that Baba believes the tradition he adopted will continue:

'There's always going to be some form of storytelling. Our minds build story as a response to existing – they scaffold our understanding according to stories – so human beings are always going to have some form of story.

'As far as the griot tradition is concerned, it's constantly in flux so I don't know what it's going to look like tomorrow, but I do know that in some way it will exist. It may no longer be called *jaliyaa*, it may take on some other form, but I know that what we know as story is part of our existence.'

He may well be right. Walking along the South Bank one evening not that long ago, I heard an oddly familiar sound: a voice singing over a harp-like accompaniment. As I rounded a corner and walked through the next archway, I saw the singer, standing with his back to a historic picture of Blackfriars Bridge originally published in the *Illustrated London News*, his fingers busy on the strings of a wooden instrument that he held in front of him, jutting up from his stomach. Then it hit me: the man was playing what appeared to be a kora. I stood and listened for a few minutes, as the evening commuters pushed past. Perhaps when the song finished, I thought, I would ask the performer how he came to be there and whether or not he was a griot. But the song continued and I was beginning to shiver, so at last I turned and carried on my way. I would leave the questions for another day, I decided. Besides, I had a hunch it might be a long story.

7

Encountering roadblocks

censorship, propaganda and exiled writers

One January evening in the late 1980s, sitting in the glow of the gas fire in our living room, I saw something I'd never seen before. The news was on and for once Sinn Fein leader Gerry Adams wasn't on the screen. Instead, a group of men with beards was gathering around a book suspended from a pole on a bit of wire. They seemed angry. They were shouting. And around them stood people holding handwritten signs, including one boy with a placard on which 'Ban Satanic Veses' was scrawled – an offence against spelling that, even at the age of seven, made me purse my lips. Then, amid a roar from the crowd, one of the men put a burning piece of wood to the book and the pages caught fire. The people cheered, waving their fists in the air, and jerked the book on its pole, making sure the TV cameras could get a good look. I watched as the lovely, shiny blue cover turned black and began to flake. To me, burning that book seemed about the naughtiest thing you could do.

Over the weeks that followed, more pictures of burning volumes and people cheering appeared. Sometimes they involved protesters in the UK – you could tell by the bus stops and pillar boxes in the back-ground – at other times they were in various other parts of the world, but the book they were burning was always the same: *The Satanic Verses* by Salman Rushdie. It wasn't just single copies, either. In many places, the people had heaped up piles and piles of the novel – copies that, put together, were worth more pocket money than I could imagine – and made them into great big bonfires.

But if burning the books was supposed to achieve something, it didn't seem to be working. The people just got angrier and angrier and the men with the microphones standing in front of the cameras sounded more and more solemn. I began to wonder whether it would keep going until the angry people had burned their way through all the copies in the world.

Then on 14 February 1989, a man called Ayatollah Khomeini, who seemed calmer than the others but it turned out was the angriest of all, issued something called a fatwa, ordering the death of Salman Rushdie. He meant it too, promising to pay whoever carried out the killing $2.8 million and saying that there could be no second chances.

Salman Rushdie had no choice but to disappear, assuming an alias and receiving round-the-clock protection from the police. He didn't vanish from my thoughts, however, and, a few years later, when I heard a rumour that his son was attending my brothers' school, my interest was piqued. Every time I accompanied my mum on the trip to collect my siblings, I would sit in the car and keep a lookout for Salman Rushdie. I didn't know what I'd do if I saw him. Perhaps I'd smile and wave in a quiet way that wouldn't attract the attention of any assassins lurking nearby. Maybe I'd give him a thumbs-up from behind one of my exercise books. However I did it, I hoped I'd be able to find some secret way of telling him that I was sorry about his books being burned and that I hoped he'd manage to keep alive.

It seemed likely to me that Salman Rushdie would probably come to pick up his son in disguise – perhaps wearing some of those joke spectacles that made you look short-sighted. Maybe a false beard over his own beard as a clever double bluff. At the very least, I was sure, he would be wearing dark glasses and be moving surreptitiously, using things like postboxes and parked cars for cover. I kept a close eye on anyone who vaguely fitted that description (more than you might expect, it turns out). I also watched any hatted and bearded Orthodox Jewish men I saw closely – it struck me that this might be a particularly cunning disguise.

I never did spot Salman Rushdie, but a year or so later when I happened upon a copy of *The Satanic Verses* in W.H. Smith, I nearly burst with excitement. Here was one they hadn't got! I bought it quickly and hurried home, thrilled that at last I would find out what all the fuss was about.

I was in for a disappointment. Precocious reader though I was, the dense weave of Rushdie's sentences was too much for my eleven-year-old brain to unpick. The text glittered with references I didn't know how to weigh or value, and the giddy flitting of the action from one thing to another made my head spin. I wished that Rushdie would make his narrator sit down in one place for a moment with no fidgeting and tell me calmly what was going on. All the same, I pushed myself on to the final page with the same sense of duty I applied to Brussels sprouts on Christmas Day: the thing just had to be got through. On some level, I knew it was good for me, if only because every paragraph I read was like a cup of water thrown on the bonfires I'd seen on the news. 'Take that,' I thought as I turned each page, my brain throbbing, 'and that, and that.' When at last I finished it, I set the volume on my bookshelf alongside Jane Austen and the Brontës. I was pleased that at least here it was safe from the flames.

*

It seems likely that for as long as people have been telling stories other people have been trying to shut them up. It's certainly been the case as far as printed books are concerned. Pretty much as soon as Gutenberg's movable type got, well, moving, the Catholic Church and governments of the various nations to which the printing press rapidly spread set about trying to work out how to stem the dangerous tide of words. As the Argentine-born Canadian writer, translator and editor Alberto Manguel so memorably puts it, 'like no other human creation, books have been the bane of dictatorships' and, as a result, 'the history of reading is lit by a seemingly endless line of censors' bonfires'.

He can write that again. With attacks on printed material and people's access to it including everything from General Pinochet's banning of *Don Quixote* in Chile in 1981 to the attempt to wipe out Bosnian culture by bombarding the National Library in Sarajevo in 1992, there can be no question that books are often on the front line in the war of ideas. People have had their ears cut off and letters branded on their cheeks because of what they wrote, as happened to the luckless English lawyer and pamphleteer William Prynne in the 1630s, when his book against stage plays, *Histriomastix*, was judged to contain criticism of Queen Henrietta Maria, a keen actress. Other writers have been imprisoned for long stretches, deprived of basic human rights and tortured. And, as happened to the Burkinabe journalist and author Norbert Zongo when a bomb detonated under his car in 1998 (one of the Compaoré regime's favoured methods of silencing its critics), they have been murdered for daring to express their ideas. In the Preface to later editions of his biting, yet deeply human, novel *The Parachute Drop*, the book that first led to him being labelled 'a serious threat to the State', Zongo describes his interrogation by Burkina Faso's special police. The ordeal marked the start of three months of solitary confinement in 1981 and a career marked by persecution and assassination attempts. As if foreseeing the violent death to which it would all lead, Zongo wrote that it was 'like the beginning of time for me, the day my life began to melt like butter on a hot skillet'.

In many places, some of the titles to draw down the wrath of the censors have seemed oddly arbitrary in the context of what else has been allowed through. In the 1960s, the Soviet minister of culture Ekaterina Furtseva put a limitation on productions of Shakespeare for fear of their portrayal of power struggles, and yet Aleksandr Solzhenitsyn's overtly political *One Day in the Life of Ivan Denisovich* was, albeit briefly, published in the USSR. Other states have had an all too systematic approach. The burning heaps of paper that appeared in German streets throughout much of the 1930s as Hitler sought to rid the nation of the work of Jewish authors and all foreign influences bore witness to the terrifying efficiency of his regime, even in the face of resistance efforts such as the Library of Burned Books, set up by a group of anti-Fascists in Paris and containing copies of all the titles destroyed by the Nazis.

Elsewhere, morals and public decency have been the watchword for those who seek to curb people expressing themselves in print. The greatest writers have not been above suspicion – Vladimir Nabokov's *Lolita*, Henry Miller's *The Tropic of Cancer* and D.H. Lawrence's *Lady Chatterley's Lover* were all delayed for publication in the US or the UK by several years because of claims that the works were obscene. And had it not been for the gumption of American ex-pat Sylvia Beach, who opened the original Shakespeare & Company bookshop in Paris in 1919, James Joyce's *Ulysses* might never have made it into readers' hands. Unavailable in Ireland and banned in the UK and the US, the novel had no chance of finding a publisher until Beach undertook to put the book out through her business in 1922, using the services of Dijon-based printer Maurice Darantière. The first print run comprised only 100 copies, forty of which were mailed to Canada and then smuggled into the US by a friend of Ernest Hemingway's, who took them on the ferry from Windsor, Ontario to Detroit over a number of weeks, carrying a few copies each day.

Indeed, in the era of prohibition – and for a good few decades either side – many titles fell foul of those who had set themselves up to protect the moral sensibilities of the American reading public. Chief among these guardians was United States postal inspector Anthony Comstock who, with funding from the YMCA to the tune of $8,500 (no small change in 1872), founded the Society for the Suppression of Vice, effectively the US' first censorship board. Not a great fan of books in general – he once observed that 'Our father Adam could not read in Paradise' – Comstock was also not a believer in doing things by halves. Towards the end of his life, he boasted to a journalist that he had destroyed some 160 tons of obscene literature and convicted enough people 'to fill a passenger train of 61 coaches, 60 coaches containing 60 passengers each and the 61st almost full'. Fast work – although perhaps less surprising when you consider that the titles on Comstock's hit list included pretty much the entire literature of Italy and France, which he regarded as 'little better than histories of brothels and prostitutes in these lust-crazed nations'.

The zeal of people like Comstock has traditionally been matched by the effort and energy that many state-funded organisations put into developing writing that flatters and furthers their work. While the most obvious examples come from extreme right-wing or left-wing regimes – such as the literature penned in the wake of Mao Zedong's talks at the 1942 Yan'an Forum on Literature and Art, in which he specified that creative work should serve politics and advance the cause of socialism – these are by no means the only places that have embraced such practices at times. Britain itself has dipped its pen in the propagandist's inkpot on more than one occasion. In the interwar years, arranging material selectively to broadcast a positive image of Blighty both at home and abroad was talked about openly and seen as not merely a positive virtue but a necessity. One-time Foreign Office head Sir Arthur Willert, for example, wrote about 'the growing demand for an adequate system of national advertisement' as Britain's influence waned with the decline of its empire. Foreign secretary Sir Samuel Hoare was blunter still, stressing that it was 'particularly desirable for British cultural propaganda to secure as firm a hold as possible in the minds of the population'.

On the face of it, things look rather different these days. Since freedom of expression was first proclaimed as part of the 1948 Universal Declaration of Human Rights, a raft of legislation has been brought in to safeguard people's ability to communicate their ideas in many countries around the world. As of 5 July 2012, when the United Nations' Human Rights Council unanimously adopted a resolution to protect individuals' free speech on the internet, this has in theory extended to the virtual world too.

In practice, however, things are not so simple. Though China was one of the forty-seven members that approved the UN Human Rights Council's resolution on internet free speech (despite, along with Cuba, expressing some reservations), its approach to censorship is rather different on its home turf. With its dedicated 'Fifty Cent Party' – so named because this is thought to be the rate the state pays for each positive comment an employee posts to defuse a negative story about the regime – the Chinese government is notorious for the lengths to which it has gone to control its citizens' ability to express themselves and access information online. Its 'Golden Shield' internet censorship programme is thought to involve more than 100,000 Chinese, who comb websites to delete and limit suspect posts almost as soon as they appear. And at the sharp end of it all are social media. A study published in March 2013 by Dan Wallach and a team of researchers at Rice University in Houston, Texas found that some 4,200 censors monitor the 70,000 messages posted every minute on Weibo, the Chinese version of Twitter, which launched in 2010. Working in eight-hour shifts, they study the site continuously, deleting and blocking sensitive posts. Already, their activities seem to be making China's netizens more reluctant to share their views online: some 28 million users abandoned Weibo in 2013 in the wake of new legislation that led to the arrest of numerous microbloggers.

Furthermore, as online censorship methods grow more sophisticated, even the controls themselves become harder and harder to detect. In years gone by, if you googled the Tiananmen Square uprising of 1989 inside China, you'd be presented with an error message and a blank page. (Indeed the blackout was so comprehensive that a lecturer on a UK-based international journalism course once told me that he had to allow for a Tiananmen session each year to accommodate the discussion that always blew up when, about three weeks into the course, one or more of the Chinese students stumbled upon news of the events about which they had never heard.) These days if you plug in any terms related to the protest in China you're more likely to be presented with pages of innocuous photographs and trivia about the square. Even the fact that there is something to hide is now hidden. The censors have succeeded in cutting themselves out of the story so that few people would ever guess there was anything more to read on the subject –

much as, if this book is ever published in China, these paragraphs will most likely be cut and the words below moved up so that no one will guess they were here.

Extreme cases aside, however, the truth is that nowhere is completely censorship free. For one thing, though freedom of expression may be a universal right, it is not an absolute one. It can go a long way, but as soon as it begins to trespass on someone else's rights things start to get tricky. This is not necessarily always a bad thing – in wartime, for example, an overly informative news broadcast might lead to loss of life, as happened in the Saudi Arabian town of Al Khafji in 1991, when a CNN news report showed the area to be undefended, prompting Saddam Hussein to order his troops to invade. Indeed, as William Shawcross wrote in his Preface to campaign group Article 19's 1988 *World Report*: 'fundamentally, almost everyone is in favour of some sort of censorship. Almost everyone believes that there are some things, personal or otherwise, which he or she would rather were left unsaid.' Though we might find inspiration in philosopher J.S. Mill's passionate assertion in *On Liberty* that 'if all mankind minus one were of one opinion, and only one person were of the contrary opinion, mankind would be no more justified in silencing that one person than he, if he had the power, would be justified in silencing mankind', most of us would be unlikely to go along with it if push came to shove. As the Edward Snowden affair demonstrated, we disagree on where the line should be drawn. Say something that insults a member of the armed forces in Germany and you could find yourself on the wrong side of the law; criticise the Thai royal family and you may find yourself barred from Thailand, as happened to Rayne Kruger when his 1964 book, *The Devil's Discus*, asked questions about the mysterious death of twenty-year-old King Ananda Mahidol, the present monarch's older brother; appear to be inciting people to commit suicide, or express doubts about the Holocaust in France and you may well be bang to rights.

The anglophone world is no exception. Though we might associate censorship with coercion, manipulation and dictatorship, we are as riddled with freedom-of-expression wrangles as the next language group. For example, in 2012 South Africa's proposed Protection of State Information Bill, which technically would have allowed any government official to declare any piece of information a state secret, was described by Wendy Woods, widow of anti-apartheid journalist and editor Donald Woods, as more damaging to press freedom than apartheid-era censorship. Meanwhile, the Canadian government's growing list of research topics that its scientists are forbidden to talk about – including salmon, the ozone layer and, of all things, snowflakes – prompted calls for protests in sixteen cities in September 2013. And if such deliberate attempts to curb freedom of expression weren't bad enough, there's always the chance that ham-fisted, if often well-meaning, legislation could inadvertently make certain things unprintable. In 2005 the attempt of the Labour government in the UK to make it an offence to incite hatred on the grounds of someone's religious or racial background, for example, drew widespread criticism from comedians and writers, who saw it as a threat to free expression. Indeed, it seems self-censorship is a growing problem in Britain, with the Index on Censorship's 2013 conference report, *Taking the Offensive: Defending artistic freedom of expression in the UK*, arguing that there is an increasing tendency for individuals and arts institutions to limit what they say, write about or publish for fear of media outrage, loss of funding or police intervention if they cause offence. More worrying still, Prime Minister David Cameron's knee-jerk suggestion that the government should look into the possibility of a social media shutdown at times of crisis in the wake of the 2011 London riots neatly demonstrated how quickly censorship and restriction can suggest themselves as acceptable, even preferable, options when our minds are on other things.

In reality, when it comes to the issue of censorship, most of us demonstrate a strange brand of doublethink. Because, as Nigel Smith writes in his Preface to *Literature and Censorship*, the belief that our written tradition has triumphed over different forms of repressive authority is 'crucial to our sense of history', and 'usually assumed to be one guarantee of a tolerant society, and a major factor in the richness of English literature', we can often take these freedoms for granted – and censor for ourselves the times when our societies fail to live up to the ideals on which we pride them. We treat advertising as a form of art, often sharing witty videos and campaigns on social media, but view propaganda as a dirty word. We rail against censorship and yet protest when the British National Party gets invited on *Newsnight*. We attack unduly positive coverage of political events as 'whitewash' while the British Council runs a 'GREAT Britain (and Northern Ireland)' campaign to promote our country to the rest of the world. And we blithely ignore these contradictions because they do not fit into the stories we tell ourselves and others about who we are.

*

In nations where people have less freedom to shape their stories as they see fit, writers face three choices. They can conform, leave or go underground – and each of these options usually takes a hefty toll. In the case of writers who opt to go underground, integrity comes at a high price. It can also require every bit as much ingenuity as the creation of literature itself. The *samizdat* works that banned writers like Bohumil Hrabal produced in Communist Czechoslovakia during the sixties, seventies and eighties are a prime example. Although *samizdat* is commonly translated as 'self-published', these books bore very little relation to most of the self-funded stories you'll find on Amazon today. Usually made and circulated by hand, they not only had to appeal to potential readers but also to escape detection by the secret police by a number of artful means. The manuscript pages of Egon Bondy's *Notes on the History of Philosophy*, for example, were photographed and put inside a folder of photographic paper; there were 'tamizdat' books that were published in Germany and smuggled back in (in Czech, *tam* means 'there'); there were palm-sized books that came complete with magnifying glasses tucked into the spines; and there were books made from wallpaper, office binders, calendars, insulation, and lots more besides.

To understand why writers went to these lengths, however, doesn't take such great efforts of imagination: the plaque commemorating the victims of torture under Communism on the building that housed the secret police's interrogation centre in Prague tells its own tale.

Second languages sometimes provide the cover needed to get a writer's work out to the wider world. Though much maligned for the limiting effect it has had on speakers of regional languages in many parts of Africa, English provided a relatively free space for Zimbabwean writers during the turbulent period after the Unilateral Declaration of Independence in 1965. According to one of the nation's leading writers, Musaemura Zimunya, most of Zimbabwe's serious works were written in English because they 'could be published abroad and there was no way the Censorship Board could stop publication of things abroad'.

For those eager for books that challenge the state to be read openly on their home turf, the preferable option is to write anonymously. When it works, this provides authors with the best of both worlds in that they can continue with their lives while enjoying the freedom of expressing themselves. However, as septuagenarian clergyman Luigi Marinelli found out when he set himself up against the administration of the world's smallest but in some ways most powerful country, the results of discovery can make this a course for only the most determined – or foolhardy – of authors.

Marinelli is the only person to have acknowledged contributing to *Gone with the Wind in the Vatican,* or *Shroud of Secrecy,* as my edition has it – a sort of collective memoir-cum-exposé published in 1999 in Italy by an anonymous group of Vatican prelates calling themselves The Millenari (although Marinelli's anagrammatic last name makes you wonder quite how many other people were in the group). Having worked at the Vatican for forty-five years, he spent the last months of his life facing the wrath of the Catholic Church.

It's not hard to see why. Right from the start (in the subtitle, in fact), the book sets out to tell 'the story of corruption within the Vatican' and propose measures to help the secretive and hierarchical institution 'cleanse what has become a festering wound'. It then proceeds to allege that almost every kind of malpractice and intrigue – blackmail, fraud, sexual favours, links with Freemasonry, spying, drug abuse and even satanic rituals – was rife among the elite clergy at the top of the Holy See in the late twentieth century, leaving those who wanted to advance their careers no option but to play the same games. The most compelling passages of the book centre on the descriptions of the mechanisms within the 'dictatorship' of the Holy See and the way 'the diplomacy of the Vatican immediately influences any states with which it has diplomatic ties'. At times cynical, sardonic and even peevish, the 'many voices' behind the narrative cite numerous instances of favouritism and petty rivalries advancing the careers of unsuitable (and often unqualified) candidates and blighting the prospects of deserving clergy. Perhaps most chilling of all are the allegations that those high up in the hierarchy controlled and manipulated the Pope for their own ends:

> To create a power vacuum at the top, they encourage the Pope to immerse himself in apostolic visits . . . Once back in Rome, bewildered and dazed by the rush of the crowd, ears still ringing with delirious hosannas, it is virtually impossible for the Pope to discover the intrigues of the court . . . When the Pope returns, steeped in glory, he is too tired and distracted to notice the insidious conspiracies hidden in the documents he signs. Everyone drafting the documents knows that the aging Pope won't absorb the notes on the report.

Among the 900 or so citizens living in the 0.2 square miles of the Vatican City – home to the world's only ATM with instructions in Latin – the book ruffled more than a few feathers and cast a dark shadow over its one known author's final year. Investigated by the Roman Rota, the Holy See's court, Marinelli claimed he was persecuted by the Vatican for the rest of his life. When he died of liver and bone cancer in 2000, his funeral was conducted in a church in his home town of

Cerignola, his family having been told not to try to hold the service at the local cathedral.

Living with persecution is difficult enough, but when writing freely is a matter of life or death itself, many authors have no option but to flee. Such was the choice facing Uzbek writer Hamid Ismailov when he discovered there was a bounty on his head in 1992, shortly after the collapse of the USSR. Having grown up under the strictures of Soviet censorship, Ismailov was well versed in the power of words. As a teenager in Tokmok in what is now Kyrgyzstan, he felt his first inklings that something was missing in the literature he was allowed to read after his mother died and he and his siblings were left in the care of his grandmother. With no income, the children were forced to do what they could to support the family alongside their schoolwork. It was a struggle to survive, but when Ismailov turned to literature for comfort, he found nothing of his experience reflected in Soviet books.

'For me, this was an impossible life because all the books around me were telling me that we were living a wonderful life,' says the writer, who has lived in the UK for some twenty years. 'I was thinking that something was wrong with my life. It shouldn't be like that. I couldn't come to terms with this abnormality.'

It was only when, as a student in Tashkent in the 1970s, Ismailov began to read underground translations of American writers such as Steinbeck and Faulkner that things began to make sense for him. He sourced the texts through an unofficial book market that took place every Saturday in the city. The copies he found could sometimes cost as much as two months' salary, but it seemed worth it for the insights they contained.

'When I started to read this foreign literature, all of a sudden I realised that not everything was according to the propaganda of the Soviet Union, that people were living the same life as me. I started to understand the abnormality of this propaganda life.'

At the time, Ismailov was leading a rather schizophrenic existence. Having signed up for a career in the military as the best and quickest way of making money to support his youngest sister, who had come to live with him when he was seventeen, the writer-to-be found himself working for the USSR one day in four and spending the rest of his time with artist friends. It was, as he puts it, a rather 'hippy' life, which consisted of reading Western books, listening to rock music, drinking and talking about revolutionary ideas. 'My wife jokes that when she found me I was truly anti-Soviet,' he laughs.

The contrast between his two incarnations proved to be stimulating. 'It was the most creative part of my life because of this controversy, because of these scissors between one life and another.'

At this time, Ismailov began work on a novel. It was to be a wide-ranging and ambitious book, restoring the prominence of Central Asian heroes such as the Sufi saint Khoja Akhmet Yassawi and Tambur-laine the Great – figures Ismailov spent hours cloistered in libraries researching even though studying them at the time was banned. Yet when he showed an early draft to a writer who had been arrested during the Stalin purges, the response was pessimistic: he advised Ismailov that no one would publish the work in Uzbek and his only hope would be to write it in Russian.

A move to Moscow followed in 1980, where he took up a post in the Union of Soviet Writers, an organisation formed to increase the state's control of literature. Work on the novel continued, along with numerous poems, but, even writing in Russian, Ismailov found it nigh on impossible to get his words into print. In the event, his language skills provided him with an outlet, and he worked as a translator of Uzbek classics into Russian, and Western classics into Uzbek.

Eventually, however, a collection of Ismailov's poems was published in 1984 when the writer was thirty. Too decadent for the tastes of the regime, the works might well have gone the way of his other creations had it not been for the intervention of the famous Uzbek writer and journalist Timur Pulatov. He wrote a Foreword to the book, the publi-cation of which coincided with a degree of relaxation of censorship rules, and the work made its appearance.

Ismailov continued to work as a representative for Uzbek literature in Moscow and Uzbekistan until 1992. When the BBC decided to make a programme about Central Asia, he became the man-on-the-ground for them, fixing up interviews and forging connections with various *personae non gratae*, including radical Islamists, opposition leaders and former political prisoners. He also devoted a lot of his time and effort to publishing articles on democracy and the future of Uzbekistan.

But it wasn't long before Ismailov's activities drew the attention of the Uzbek authorities. An attack on his house followed and the state began to prepare several cases against him. Summonses arrived for him to present himself at the Ministry of Justice, the prosecutor's office and the Ministry of the Interior. When an insider told Ismailov that a price had been put on his head, he knew it was time to get out.

The family fled to Moscow, where they spent several months hiding in different places. It was what Ismailov calls 'a sort of Salman Rushdie life'. Then a French poet friend arranged a three-month scholarship for Ismailov in France. There was only one drawback: to be able to get out of the country, he and his wife would have to leave their twelve-year-old daughter behind in Tashkent.

Feeling that there was no option, as Ismailov's arrest was imminent, the couple fled. The three months extended to six months, then a year. Then Ismailov's wife got a scholarship in Germany and they moved there, all the while keeping in close contact with their daughter, who warned them not to return to Tashkent because the prosecutor was at their house every day, looking for Ismailov. It was a time of great fear and uncertainty about the future; all the family could do was wait for things to calm down.

Eventually, they concocted a plan that would enable them to be reunited. Their daughter would travel to Moscow and leave for the West from there, posing as someone else's child. It required enormous courage from all concerned. The parents followed the trip to Moscow obsessively, calling every few minutes to check that everything was all right.

Once the family was reunited, plans for the future began to open up. The BBC had approached Ismailov, asking if he would be interested in working for its new Central Asia service. He accepted and relocated to the UK with his wife and daughter. His writing progressed too, with the completion of his novel *The Railway*. Instalments of this were originally due to be published in a journal in Uzbekistan, but the nation's censors took exception to the narrative's irreverence towards authority and banned the publication of the second extract, closing down the magazine at the same time. Eventually the book was published in Moscow in 1997 with a print run of 500 copies – tiny in the grand scheme of things but a huge number to a writer used to working with experimental poetry collections that were published in batches of fewer than twenty.

More than two decades on from his escape, Ismailov still hasn't rationalised its effect on him, although he is conscious of a different attitude to the concept of home. 'Something has changed in me. I have started to appreciate where my family is. Living in Moscow, I was always counting the steps to Tashkent. I would wonder, if no planes flew or trains ran, how many steps would I have to make in order to get to Tashkent. Not any more.'

Ismailov's life in the West has changed his attitude to writing too. Whereas in his earlier work, including *The Railway*, he favoured great complexity and what he describes as a Russian style of 'texts with floors of references that go up to three or four floors – reference to reference to reference', he now takes a different approach:

'I am becoming more digestible. In a way my work is becoming more Western. I started to realise people must relate to it. There was criticism of my books [from Russian and Western readers] that people couldn't relate to them, although sometimes they couldn't relate to them because of the issue of otherness. Sometimes we are not well suited to put ourselves into the shoes of others. It is not about highbrow references; it's about otherness.'

Nevertheless, taking a leaf out of the novels of globally successful writers such as Stieg Larsson and David Grossman, Ismailov has decided that the key to international success is mingling familiarity with 'something exotic, something unknown as well . . . That's the secret of these books. You start to keep your references to yourself, but to work for the reader as well. My golden formula is to satisfy myself first and then the reader, whereas with *The Railway* I didn't give a damn about the reader. It was pure self-indulgence.'

The formula seems to be working. For several years now, Ismailov has been Writer in Residence for the BBC World Service – a role that requires him to produce material in English, and transmits his words further than they would have been likely to go had he stayed in Uzbekistan.

Such international recognition, however, is by no means assured for writers obliged to leave their homeland. For fellow ex-Soviet Union poet, novelist and journalist Ak Welsapar, a career spent playing cat and mouse with the censors came unstuck when the USSR collapsed in the early nineties and he was forced to flee after being declared an 'enemy of the people' in Turkmenistan.

Writing under the watchful eyes of the somewhat erratic Soviet censors was never easy. Nevertheless, 'one decent paragraph' in the Soviet censorship guidelines – a stipulation that, in cases of ambiguity, the benefit of the doubt should be given to the writer – afforded some room for manoeuvre in creative works. It was for this reason that Welsapar found himself drawn to poetry and fiction.

'It was possible to by-pass censorship, using Aesopian language – the language of metaphor and allegory,' he told me during our email correspondence after I'd read a manuscript translation of his novel *The Tale of Aypi* for my project. 'So I was much more interested in writing fiction than journalistic articles. In literature, one can always broaden the horizons and get out of tight-binding boxes. I was always able to pass seditious thoughts under the watchful eye of censorship in the Soviet era. Once I even managed to get through an idea of the need to create an independent Turkmen state in my book *A Long Journey to a Place Nearby*. For such an idea, under unfortunate circumstances, at least in Turkmenistan, the writer could get imprisoned. Or one could simply encounter an accident, according to the principle of Stalin: no man, no problem.'

After the fall of the USSR, however, the benefit of the doubt disappeared and, according to Welsapar, freedom of speech returned to the level it had been at during the darkest days of the Stalinist era. Already on the watch list for a series of investigative articles he had written about damaging agricultural practices and malnutrition among the rural population, Welsapar was expelled from the national writers' union and his books were withdrawn from libraries and bookstores and burned. Ostracised and shunned by colleagues and friends, Welsapar and his family escaped to Sweden, where the writer was forced to rebuild his career from scratch.

More than two decades later, even though he has achieved some recognition – with books published in Sweden, Russia and Ukraine, among other countries – Welsapar remains unknown to many readers in the West, and his work continues to be blacklisted in his homeland. Despite being the first novel ever to be translated directly from Turkmen into English, *The Tale of Aypi* remains unpublished in our language at the time of writing. As he explained in an interview when he was chosen as the Turkmen representative for Poetry Parnassus, a cultural event organised to complement the London Olympic Games, the position of the exiled writer is often a precarious one:

> Being separated from the native land is a tragedy for a human being. It is even a greater tragedy if one who is involved in the art of speech has to leave his country. For poets and writers deal with daily words. The pain of separation affects even practical affairs. A writer who leaves his country, [*sic*] loses both his reader and publisher. Some time is needed to find them in a new country; it may take many years. But life is limited: would you want to write a new work or learn a new language? Would you

want to read a new book or look for a new publisher for yourself?! As a result the writer remains face to face with problems of
the simplest life – problems of survival looms over him [*sic*].
Then with the bits [*sic*] between his teeth he has to seek his daily
bread. These are your own problems, you have to solve all of
them yourself. If you can solve them, you will exist as a writer, if
not, you will not.'

The question of doing what it takes to safeguard your survival as a writer
would no doubt be familiar to those authors who opt to obey the wishes
of the powers that be in the world's most oppressive regimes. Indeed, for
some, the image of the valiant wordsmith locked in a battle for truth
against the government might seem to be more romantic Western fiction
than achievable reality. Where there is not room – or at least mental
space – to carve out the underground networks beloved of spy-thriller
authors elsewhere, writers face the stark choice of either conforming and
producing work in keeping with the prevailing ideology or doing something else altogether with their lives. It's a theme that Hungarian writer
Miklós Haraszti takes up in his dark classic *The Velvet Prison: Artists
Under State Socialism*. Written in the late seventies and early eighties,
during the final decade of János Kádár's administration, the book, which
was published clandestinely in its author's homeland some three years
after it first appeared elsewhere, reveals the mental barriers that a lifetime
of writing within strict political constraints throws up. To Haraszti, the
choice of whether to be a dissident writer or not is non-existent in a
country such as his because 'the only freedom within the socialist system
is that of participation' and 'there is no space for nondirected culture'.
As a result, he writes, 'the choice available to me is not between honest
and lying art, not even between good and bad art, but between art and
non-art . . . between the artists' retreat and the labour camp'.

In the somewhat less strict milieu of the late Kádár era – during
which writers, according to Haraszti, had internalised the constraints
they wrote under and policed their own work almost as a matter of

course – the limitations the ruling bodies placed on artists almost seemed to be a spur to creativity. Whereas traditional censorship presupposes the inherent opposition of creators and censors, 'the new censorship strives to eliminate this antagonism. The artist and the censor – the two faces of official culture – diligently and cheerfully cultivate the gardens of art together.' Celebrated and garlanded with honours in the midst of a booming art scene, with money lavished on sending them on creative retreats, Kádár's writers had, on the face of it, little to complain about. 'The persecuted artist is, on closer inspection, just not that unhappy,' observes Haraszti. 'True, artistic inspiration is not free from constraints, but is it free anywhere?'

He goes on to build an intriguing case, drawing parallels between the state artist and the creative professional employed by a big firm in the West. Working to a brief, a corporate writer will necessarily modify his or her style and approach to serve the interests of the employer. Under such conditions, Haraszti writes:

> Creative freedom has undergone a subtle change: the more successfully the artist has identified himself and his ideas with the interests of management, the more creative freedom he can retain. He has become a directed artist. He has become a company artist . . . How is this different from socialism? Only to the extent that, under capitalism, the artist is free to resign and go to another company.

When I read his words it was hard for a moment to disagree. I found myself wavering, as I so often do in my encounters with texts from elsewhere: on the face of it, how were writers working to briefs or under editorial direction in the West different to the man writing these words? Often following directions as to what to leave out, what to put in and the style and tone to aim for, how were we any more free?

Luckily, Haraszti gives us the key to our own liberty. It is there in the weariness and despair of his words, in the darkness of sentences such as 'Autonomy is a self-annihilating idea, like a bonfire on the moon' and in the blind walls of the 'closed world' that the authorial voice runs up against repeatedly. And if there is any room for doubt, he destroys it for good and all in the Afterword, which moves to quell the tide of mistrust that his enslaved words seemed to have sent surging through many minds:

> I intended the very existence of this book to be a denial of its own deliberate exaggerations. I hope that its publication is a proof that refutes the despair that darkens its sentences.
>
> . . .
>
> For this reason, I chose to speak mostly in the third person, in the voice of a state artist, rather than joining the chorus of my own natural compatriots in the ghetto of romantic individualism. Like a ventriloquist, I adopted this voice in order to deliver the verdict that directed culture confers on the independent spirit. But I hope that the sentence is rendered invalid by the very fact that it has been pronounced publicly by me, and by the fact that you, dear reader, hold this pessimistic book in your hands.

Darker than a mere pastiche, Haraszti's essay ventures so far into the false arguments and traps it exposes that it drags the reader with it, forcing us to wander in a hall of mirrors where we and the world we know appear distorted and strange, and nothing can be trusted – a place where we begin to see, think and read as a paid-up state writer might. It's only when we emerge, blinking, into the harsh glare of the After-word that the illusion is revealed. On paper the difference between a commissioned author and a state artist might appear slight – and might even seem to be done away with altogether by sophistry – but it is still there. It is in the optimism with which we contemplate what to read or write next. And in the spark of excitement as ideas fizz and fuse freely in our brains. It exists in the silent negotiation between any would-be writer and the blank page, untrammelled by a particular kind of fear.

And it is in the freedom to refuse ideas, to reject certain accounts and to throw books down and walk away. The fact that the door is open – even just a touch, far behind us – as we write and as we read matters. Because beyond it is the whole world.

*

Governments might be the chief culprits when it comes to trying to control the spread of ideas and information, but they are only part of the equation. To some extent, we all police what we allow words to say or do to us: censorship can be in the eye of the reader too.

A striking example of this arose when I set about trying to find a book from North Korea. I'd been fascinated by life in the country commonly billed as the world's most secretive state (although it loses out to Eritrea for the wooden spoon in Reporters Without Borders' Press Freedom Index) since reading *Los Angeles Times* journalist Barbara Demick's *Nothing to Envy* a few years previously. Still struck by Demick's portrait of a land that has plummeted out of the developed world – a place where tarmacked roads lie cracked and weed-strewn, and pylons hold up the casing for electric cables from which the copper has long since been stolen to barter for food – I anticipated that I would seek out some hard-hitting first-person narratives by people who'd managed to get out. In fact, when I started to prepare for the project, several people suggested that I contact the South Korean embassy in London to see if they knew of dissident literature by North Korean escapees that I could read. I was on the point of doing so when it occurred to me that, while this might well yield some fascinating texts, it would bring me no closer to knowing anything about literature inside the sixty-seven-year-old totalitarian state itself. What did people in Pyongyang read? What tales were household classics in the land of the then-Dear Leader? And what stories did North Korea tell about itself?

My opening gambit was to send the nation an email through the official website of the Democratic People's Republic of Korea and the Korean Friendship Association, set up in 2000 by Spanish-born Alejandro Cao de

Benós. As special delegate for the DPRK's Committee for Cultural Relations for Foreign Countries, Cao de Benós is the first foreigner to be allowed to work for the government and possibly the only non-national to ask for citizenship – although he is not the only outsider to have lived in North Korea for an extended period. Others include US Army deserter Charles Robert Jenkins, who stumbled into the country from the Demilitarized Zone after a drinking binge in 1965, hoping to be sent home by way of Russia, but was then forced to spend years studying the Juche philosophy of Kim Il Sung. He finally got out in 2004. Then there was South Korean film director Shin Sang-ok and his wife Choe Eun-hui, who were kidnapped by Kim Jong-il's special agents in Hong Kong in 1978 and brought to Pyongyang to make films commissioned by the Dear Leader. They only managed to give him the slip in 1986 on their first trip outside the country to a film festival in Vienna, where they convinced their driver to take them to the US embassy. (Believing them to have been abducted, Kim Jong-il subsequently sent them a message offering to help them escape the Americans and come home to Pyongyang.)

If Cao de Benós is something of an exception in his apparent enthusiasm for his adopted country (a place he has wanted to live in and work for since he was a teenager), his website is cut from the same cloth. In contrast to the satirical, damning and even hysterical reports that make up the vast majority of the English-language coverage of North Korea, korea-dpr.com proclaims its mission to be 'building international ties in the fields of culture, friendship, diplomacy and business'. The Korean Friendship Association may have come in for dubious press since its inception – most notably in the extraordinary 2006 film *Friends of Kim*, which documents the disastrous visit of an international group of Kim Jong-il supporters – nevertheless, the website is still there, cautiously soliciting approaches from interested parties around the world.

When I contacted the KFA for suggestions of what I might read from the DPRK, a message came back from none other than Cao de Benós himself. He regretted that most books that had been translated into English were tourism, politics or army-related, but said he would recommend one book, *Kye Wol Hyang*, which was based in historical events that took place in 1953 and demonstrated loyalty, honour and self-sacrifice for the motherland. These principles, he claimed, were reflected in all North Korean literature.

Curious to see what else Cao de Benós might be able to recommend, I replied that I was particularly keen to get hold of examples of contemporary adult fiction and would even consider getting a story translated myself, if need be. After a few days of waiting, a response came back. The special delegate for the DPRK's Committee for Cultural Relations for Foreign Countries was sorry but he was not aware of any adult fiction produced in the entire seven-decade history of the republic. Being a socialist country, the nation only allowed politically oriented works to be published. Books, films or cartoons in North Korea all had to contain the morals and Juche ideology of the Kim regime. In fact, he was certain that there was no such thing as adult fiction in the DPRK because everything that made it into print was either poetry or narratives based in historical facts and imbued with the principles he had described.

This puzzled me, particularly as I knew that Words without Borders had published its *Literature from the Axis of Evil* anthology in 2006, showcasing several politically orientated short stories from North Korea, which largely reflected the ideological stance Cao de Benós described. In addition, I had read in Article 19's 1988 *World Report* that, at least as recently as the late eighties, there were thought to be some 350 writers in the DPRK's Union of Writers and Artists, churning out around twenty novels and up to 500 short stories each year. Something wasn't adding up.

I thought about it for a while. Then it struck me that perhaps the word 'fiction' was the problem. If you understood it in its negative sense, meaning 'fabrication' or 'lies', then there was clearly no room for it in a country where all literature is believed to be 'based in historical facts'.

I redefined my terms and cited the names of the writers featured in the *Axis of Evil* anthology. My timing was unfortunate, however: shortly after I sent the email, Kim Jong-il died, whipping up a whirlwind of very public acts of grieving and making any communication with North Korea very difficult indeed. By the time it had subsided, the moment had long passed and I suspected Cao de Benós was unlikely to be drawn any further into a discussion of semantics in what was, in all likelihood, his third language. If there was some fundamental chasm of understanding between the meaning we ascribed to various words, my tentative messages didn't stand much chance of bridging it. All I could do was teeter on the brink.

In the interim, however, I heard from Nicholas Mercury in Canada, and what he said intrigued me. He had been prompted to get into North Korean literature and subsequently start his business selling books in English from the DPRK after reading *My Life and Faith*, a memoir by Korean Army war correspondent and ardent DPRK patriot Ri In Mo. He commended it to me as a text that contained 'a point of view completely unknown in the West . . . that of utter love and devotion and sacrifice for a country, political system, and especially leadership, that (most) of the rest of the world prefers to despise and hate'.

It was not fiction, but it certainly sounded like the sort of story I was after. I decided to give it a try and was delighted when the Pyongyang-published book arrived from an address in Beijing accompanied by a DVD featuring subtitled extracts from DPRK films, military displays, dances and marching songs.

The surprises didn't end there. Telling the story of Ri's early affinity with the DPRK's ideology, his capture in 1952, his thirty-four years of imprisonment and alleged torture in South Korea 'in blatant violation of the Geneva Convention', and triumphal return to his homeland in 1993, *My Life and Faith* provided me with more food for thought than I had anticipated. At times extremely gripping, with overtones of jail literature by the likes of Albie Sachs and Nelson Mandela – to whom Ri is compared in the Introduction – the book presents an intriguing view of national identity and Western attitudes to the regime. 'It is not until they take off the colour glasses of "anti-communism" that they understand it,' writes Ri. Examples of this apparently distorted perspective – given alongside plaudits for the Kims, laudatory poems about the Motherland, triumphal photographs and accounts of miracles connected to the ruling clan – include allegations of South Korean historians conveniently omitting or twisting facts, 'lies' from UN representatives, pro-Western propaganda in films and books, and a fascinating account of Ri's interactions with the world's media after his release in South Korea. Once again, this hinted at a barrier shored up partly by semantics:

> While talking with them, I found that there were differences in the way they expressed my ideas, and they seemed to take great effort to alter my words. When I said 'people' by habit, they changed it to 'the masses' . . . While altering my words in this way, the young journalists expressed the regrets [*sic*], 'If the words used in north Korea are used, readers may find fault with them, so they should be altered somewhat. I'm sorry [they said].
>
> . . .
>
> 'Many journalists with newspapers, radio and the foreign press visited me. They seemed to have not understood me well. There were instances of seriously distorted information.'

That pulled me up short. I thought of the ludicrous figure of Kim Jong-il in *Team America: World Police*, at whom I had laughed so hard, and the outlandish news reports of treacherous relatives of the ruling dynasty being obliterated by missiles or fed to wild dogs – or was it pigs? – stories that go viral on social media every few months. Such freakish accounts are eagerly, almost greedily, taken as fact, sometimes with little regard as to the credibility of the sources. Even as we express our abhorrence of what the regime stands for, we seem to want – to need – these bizarre things to be true, as though they somehow confirm for us that we are good and right by contrast to the wacky wickedness enacted in this 'other' place.

It's as though the outlandish stories are a shield between us and the bitter reality. We seem to prefer to swap cartoonish anecdotes than engage with the cruel facts: the malnourishment that means teenage boys fleeing the country in the last decade are on average five inches shorter than those growing up in South Korea; the UN reports of crimes against humanity committed on a scale unparalleled in the modern world; the network of secret prison camps, or *kwan-li-so*, in which as many as 120,000 people are held; and the horrifying testimonies of thousands of defectors – even if some of these turn out to have elements of omission or fabrication, as Blaine Harden found when he worked with prison-camp escapee Shin Dong-hyuk to write the compelling *Escape from Camp 14*.

Knowing these truths, what shocked me about the book I read was not its lies or its heartlessness or its absurdity, but the fact that it was able to appeal to me nonetheless. Even though it had been prepared, perhaps by a committee of propagandists, with a view to influencing Westerners – its publication in English and the reference to Nelson Mandela, a figure unknown to the average North Korean, made this clear, however fondly I might have liked to imagine I was getting a glimpse into DPRK literature – I had not expected to be taken in by it. The fact that it succeeded in touching me and making me think was, to some extent, a sobering lesson. It showed me the seductive whirlpool that words can create – which has some people baying for censorship when unwelcome ideas receive airtime – but it taught me something else too. In light of the glimmers of recognition that shone through parts of the narrative – the references to Ri's wife sitting next to him and laughing at his old-fashioned Korean, and the reminiscences, jokes and observations that caught me unawares – I found myself realising that I had been in the habit of thinking of the people behind the book as somehow lesser. Having grown up with two-dimensional satire and alarmist news stories about North Korea, I had come to picture those within its administration as crude and stupid. I had judged them incapable of subtlety or finer feeling or putting together anything that might have the power to move or intrigue me. I had underestimated them – perhaps because it was more comforting to think of them as less than human than to recognise both their humanity and their regime's heinous deeds. I could never condone the suffering and torture the Kims had built on Juche ideology, but neither could I condone the North Korea that the rest of the world (or at least the world I lived in) seemed bent on perpetuating: a place of slapstick set pieces and outlandish horror stories. By banishing its rulers to the realm of the inhuman, by ensuring there can be no common ground between us and no basis for dialogue, by using ridicule to insulate ourselves from outrages committed by fellow human beings, we seem to be doing our bit to ensure that things never change.

It was an attitude I found myself encountering directly not long after I read Ri In Mo's book. A few weeks after I published my thoughts on *My Life and Faith*, a comment appeared on the blog. Attacking my account of the mental labyrinth reading the book had taken me through, it rejected any attempt to engage with or weigh up words sanctioned by the authorities in North Korea and insisted there was 'nothing worth knowing' in its propagandised literature. I was struck by the sentiments expressed. They involved the same conviction that it is possible for some people always to be right (and therefore valuable) and some people always wrong (and therefore worthless) that seems to underlie most of the regimes that send writers fleeing for their lives, sanity and craft around the world. Such cast-iron confidence in the ability to write off every publication in a nation as trash is formidable. And a little frightening, too.

8

Broadening the mind

empathy and politics in literature

Ever since Aristotle outlined his thoughts on catharsis in his *Poetics* back in the fourth century BCE – and probably well before that – people have been fascinated by the power of stories to make us feel things. From Hamlet's passionate outburst at an actor's portrayal of the murder of King Priam to Anne Shirley's fascination with Tennyson's 'The Lady of Shalott', literature is full of characters who exhibit a range of strong reactions to the imaginary experiences of others. In recent years the emphasis has been less on the carthartic properties of books, and more on the question of empathy and the capacity that literature may have to take us into the experiences of other people and thereby influence how we act. At stake is the question of whether reading books – commentators have tended to focus on fiction, but I would extend the question to non-fiction stories too – might actually make us better people (no small matter in this age of arts funding cuts, when creative types are often required to justify the value of their craft).

At first glance, the evidence looks promising. After centuries of insistence from bibliophiles like French philosopher and Resistance fighter Roger Garaudy that 'a good book . . . is a force, a tool, a weapon to make the dreams of today become the reality of tomorrow', numerous researchers seem to be demonstrating the ability of stories to boost our emotional intelligence. The Dutch scholar Jèmeljan Hakemulder investigated how reading literature affected people's empathy with those in socially marginalised groups in his 2000 book *The Moral Laboratory*, concluding that the resultant 'enhancement of insight into human thoughts and emotions may bridge individual as well as cultural differences'. More recently, a study by David Comer Kidd and Emanuele Castano at the New School for Social Research in New York suggested that reading literary fiction enhances people's ability to gauge the emotions of their fellow human beings. Testing 1,000 participants' Theory of Mind (ability to attribute mental states, beliefs, desires, intents and knowledge to others), the duo found that those who had been given literary texts to peruse at the start of the session consistently scored higher than those who had been given other works. They attributed this to the fact that the process of gap-filling required by literature brings the same psychological processes into play as we use when negotiating real-life relationships. 'Fiction is not just a simulator of a social experience, it is a social experience,' claims Kidd. Meanwhile, some researchers have shown that the ability to empathise is an important indicator of how well someone is likely to be able to read in the first place. Southeastern Louisiana University psychologist Dr Tammy Bourg, for example, has done work with children which demonstrates that the ability to intuit others' feelings at the age of eight can be used as an indicator of what their reading ability is likely to be when they are ten or eleven, with those scoring highest in the first tests doing better later.

The increased capacity for recognising and entering into the feelings of others that literature seems to foster and depend on must, many claim, have a positive influence on the way we live our lives. The American philosopher Richard Rorty suggested that certain texts – particularly those by writers such as Nabokov and Orwell – help us become less cruel. This idea was also expressed by the academic Martha Nussbaum, who has argued extensively for fiction's potential for moral influence.

Yet while few people dispute the idea that literature has the power to move us, some are unconvinced that it will always have a positive effect. Though emotion might be a 'call to action', as neuroscientist Joseph LeDoux describes it, there's no guarantee that the action that results will always be desirable. Indeed, to a sadist or someone with dubious political motives, the ability to recognise when someone else is happy, frightened or in pain may be a tool for causing harm. The more intuitive the torturer, the worse things are for the poor sod at the sharp end of things. And the emotional manipulation that texts have the power to effect might well be a tool for radicalising, indoctrinating or hoodwinking – as I had discovered during my encounter with Ri In Mo's memoir, *My Life and Faith*.

In any case, there's no guarantee that the emotions a reader feels or believes characters to be feeling will be those the writer intended, or be shared by others encountering the same text. Cultural differences might lead people to ascribe false reactions to characters based on what they themselves might feel in a given situation, regardless of accuracy. Many people reading about mourners shouting abuse at a corpse during a funeral might feel shock and disgust, but some Malagasy readers would see only a traditional way of honouring the dead.

Even where there is no such barrier, readers may respond very differently. Oscar Wilde purportedly found the death of Little Nell hilarious, while thousands saw only tragedy. One American editor rejected Orwell's *Animal Farm* because there was no market for animal stories, apparently untouched by the allegory. And where some readers regard the suicide of the children in Hardy's *Jude the Obscure* – 'Done because we are too menny' – as one of the most devastating episodes of late Victorian literature, others see a sick joke. As Alberto Manguel puts it, 'one reader can despair and another can laugh at exactly the same page'.

What's more, if readers do have the expected response, there's no guarantee that they will do anything other than feel. As Suzanne Keen points out in *Empathy and the Novel*, the evidence that reading promotes positive social action is more than a little scanty. 'Empathy is easy to feel, but like all fleeting emotions, it passes and relatively few altruistic actions (or even simple helping) can be securely linked in a causal chain to our empathetic feelings.' And as Michael Hanne observes in his book on *The Power of the Story*, the Western reviewer's favourite adjective, 'powerful', is generally accepted to mean 'little more than approval of the novel's capacity to involve and move the individual reader emotionally'. The question of whether a novel or memoir might prompt us to get up from our armchairs and do something to address the real-world situations that might correlate to the long-past or imaginary wrongs or happiness that has affected us simply doesn't come into it. On the face of it, the emotion we feel when we read is an end in itself, an absorbing indulgence in sensation. There might even be something rather distasteful about it – a kind of voyeuristic revelling in feeling through texts that, as Shu-mei Shih has put it, transform 'harrowing human experience into literary spectacle waiting to be turned into film'. Seen in this light, reading matter – particularly books from elsewhere – is merely fodder for privileged people whose lives are too comfortable to offer them the full palette of emotions first-hand. Nothing more.

*

Deep down, it's another story. Books seem to persist in making things happen. They can be ugly things, like the stabbing of novelist Naguib Mahfouz and of Hitoshi Igarashi, the Japanese translator of *The Satanic Verses*. They can be incidental things, like the misconceptions about sex that A.S. Byatt claims D.H. Lawrence bequeathed to an entire generation of women. And they can be inspiring things, such as the unprecedented queues one Ukrainian fan wrote to Aleksandr Solzhenitsyn to report when *One Day in the Life of Ivan Denisovich* came out. Noting that standing one in front of the other was almost a way of life in Kharkhov, where people were habituated to waiting for hours for anything from entry to see the film *Tarzan* to the chance to buy products such as women's underwear, chicken giblets and horse-meat sausage, the correspondent observed he had nonetheless never seen anything like the line of people that formed when the book arrived in the public libraries.

Whether it can be empirically proven or not, we persist in our conviction that books make a difference, and we will often go out of our way to press those we believe in most strongly on others. During my year of reading the world, I decided to include a book from an extra territory that wasn't represented on my list of 196 countries. To help me choose this wild-card entry I ran a poll on the blog. The response was surprising, with input from hundreds of people who were clearly motivated by concerns other than simply helping me choose the best piece of literature from what became known as the Rest of the World. (A tweet from BBC Radio 3 presenter Sara Mohr-Pietsch, for instance, saw a surge in votes for Jaume Cabré's *Winter Journey*, a trend that puzzled me until I realised that listeners to her classical music programmes were most likely driven by the fact that the short-story collection was inspired by Schubert's *Winterreise* song cycle, rather than the desire to see Catalan literature more widely read.) As the deadline approached, campaigning grew fierce among supporters of the titles from the two most hotly contested places on the shortlist: Catalonia and Kurdistan. In the end, some especially vigorous tub-thumping using the hashtag 'Twitterkurds' sealed the victory for Jalal Barzanji's *The Man in Blue Pyjamas*, but it was a close-run thing.

This belief in the power of books to influence people seems to be one of the few things pretty much all readers agree on. Almost everyone, from the hardest of hard-line dictators to the woolliest of woolly liberals acts as if stories are a force to be reckoned with – whether they're banning them and locking writers up, or travelling West Africa distributing books and hugs from the back of a Volkswagen camper van.

So what's really going on? If empathy is every bit as unreliable and flimsy a means for motivating us as Suzanne Keen suggests, how come books retain their hold over us? Why do companies and governments spend huge amounts of money stimulating or halting the spread of stories? Why do people risk their freedom for the sake of the written word? What's it all about?

Oddly enough, the key to the puzzle may lie in an experiment run by Keen herself. Presenting her students at Washington and Lee University with three documents – a 419 scam email, a handwritten letter purporting to be from a schoolgirl in Uganda, and a first-person story-within-a-story taken from Alexander McCall Smith's Botswana-set *Morality for Beautiful Girls* – and details of their provenance, she asked the class to write down their reactions to each text and what they would be likely to do in response to it in real life. The answers were varied, but the trend that emerged was that the participants looked more favourably on the fictional character and tended to buy into her story more. One even went so far as to claim that 'After reading the book, [she had] a new perspective on Africa/Botswana. The country seems more innately "good" whereas before [she] only knew of the negative things about it.' By contrast, the first two appeals set the students' alarm bells ringing, with many of them claiming that they would delete the email and also throw the letter away, even though they thought it had a chance of being genuine. Where there was a possibility of a (truthful or otherwise) real-life person wanting something directly from them in response to their reading, the students kept their guard up and were unmoved. To Keen's mind, this contrast 'dramatizes fiction's freedom to evoke feeling and readers' option to feel without following through with action'.

In other words, it is perhaps as much what stories allow us not to feel as what they make us feel that explains their power. Freeing us from the obligation to get involved, fiction (and, I would argue, memoirs, which usually reach us long after the events described are past) allows us to enter wholeheartedly into the events described. We are, as Keen puts it, in a 'safe zone'. These are not charity adverts crafted to manipulate our emotions with a view to making us take specific action. We do not have to watch our back or prepare our excuses in the thick of a story. No chugger will leap out at us when we close the final page, demanding that we sign up to a lifetime of circulars and guilt-by-post. No one will want to come and stay with us or borrow our car or make us sponsor them or demand that we listen to their woes. And no one will judge us for failing to do any of those things, because the people and situations we have been reading about do not (or no longer) exist. With the best will in the world, there is nothing we can do to change them – however much we might like to go and retrieve the letter from under Angel Clare's carpet, or give Vronsky a piece of our mind, or chuck Fantine a bob or two. We cannot even begin to try.

Obligation to do the right thing isn't the only encumbrance we get to shrug off at the start of chapter one. As the German literary scholar Wolfgang Iser wrote, 'with reading there is no face-to-face situation'; we have the luxury of getting rid of our faces too. We don't have to be ourselves, with all the logistical, financial and emotional complications that our lives entail. We don't really have to be anyone at all. And while we might never lose ourselves completely because we are, after all, the organism that brings the story to life at that moment, we can unclasp quite a lot of the inhibitions and worries that buckle us into who we are. Paradoxically, at the same time as being able to be more self-indulgent by escaping into a world where no one can reasonably expect us to do anything, we have the luxury of putting ourselves and our needs, wants and fears aside for a while; by being more selfish in a book, we become less self-ish.

The advantages of this became clear to me a few years ago when, with the long-suffering Steve, I found myself in the hill station of Kalimpong in north India. The plan was to stay and relax for a few days, and it seemed as though there could be few places better suited to this than the sleepy village wrapped in swirling mists, which cleared every so often to afford sweeping views over the jungle-clad foothills of the Himalayas. The lodge we were staying at was an orchid nursery, Gompu's café in town served delicious momos (Nepali dumplings), and you could get a beer for a very few rupees. After the heat and chaos of Kolkata, it seemed like paradise – until, that was, I got chatting to a local man.

Despite its peaceful appearance, he told me, Kalimpong was the scene of growing unrest. The ethnic Nepali Gorkhas in the region were agitating once more for the creation of a separate state called Gorkhaland and the attendant outbreaks of violence, protests and strikes had brought the area to its knees several times during the preceding months, with roads and businesses ordered to close on pain of attack, police opening fire on demonstrators, and tourists evacuated. A year before, the leader of one of the local political parties had been hacked to death at a public meeting in nearby Darjeeling by a mob who tried to decapitate him after he criticised the main pro-Gorkhaland party's methods. With an election approaching, many locals feared they might see a return to the violence of 1986, when scores of townspeople were shot dead and severed heads were hung up on the main street. The trouble was, everyone was too scared to speak out about what was happening. If only there were an independent journalist who could present the story to the wider world.

I couldn't help myself. Casting aside all thoughts of a break, I plunged into researching the Gorkhaland issue and before I knew it, my contact had arranged interviews for me with key players on all sides of the argument, as well as jeeps to ferry me to assignations up and down the mountain roads. Dragging Steve along as my 'photographer' on the basis that if I got kidnapped it would be better to have him there, I set off with all the enthusiasm of the rookie journalist, determined to get to the bottom of things. Over the days that followed I spoke to representatives of local tribes, regional politicians, journalists, campaigners, protesters and innocent bystanders. Some of the people I met were too frightened to give their names. Others posed proudly for Steve's shots – among them retired Indian army Major S.P. Warner, the chairman of the Gorkhaland Personnel, a uniformed organisation of some 18,000 sixteen- to twenty-one-year-olds who were equipped with batons and drilled in martial arts by ex-commandos, and could be mobilised within forty-eight hours. Their role, the major told me without a hint of a smile, was to direct the traffic in the event of an emergency, but if violence happened to break out . . . well, what could he do? Young people were so hard to control these days.

I followed the story as closely as possible, recording everything and asking all the questions I could think of. But even though I knew I'd done everything in my power, I couldn't help but feel conscious of a barrier between me and the people I'd met. For all my searching questions and hastily acquired knowledge of regional politics, I was an outsider. I was a privileged person with access to education and opportunities that most of the people I'd encountered there couldn't even imagine. I was one of life's lucky ones, with the freedom to go where I liked and inquire into whatever struck me as interesting. And precisely because of this, I was wary too. Conscious of my isolation in this remote outpost where messages could take several days to trickle down to the bustling plains, I had to keep my wits about me. I was not there on an assignment. No newspaper would start to ask questions if I failed to keep in contact. Gung-ho though I might have been at the start of the adventure, I couldn't help but feel a flash of intimidation as I walked into the major's compound and saw him stand up and stroll towards me while a group of his associates looked on. And rich though I was in comparison to most of the people of Kalimpong, I could not afford to forget myself.

A month or so later, back in the UK, I read Kiran Desai's *The Inheritance of Loss*. Set in the 1980s, the novel was woven around the first campaign for Gorkhaland, featuring the bloody events of July 1986 that were still so fresh in the memory of many locals. Its description of the pitched battle the day the state government started firing on people, soaking the high street with blood and strewing bodies over the steps of the police station I had passed so many times, was particularly striking. And in a funny sort of way, it took me into the heart of the Gorkhaland dispute as no amount of interviews with local people had been able to do – at least, not interviews by me. Thanks to Desai's imaginings, I could shuck off my anxiety and self-consciousness and wrap myself instead in her narrative. I could wander in between the panicking policemen with impunity. I could creep through the jungle with the insurgents and I could witness acts of intimidation, abuse and even murder without fearing for my safety or surreptitiously checking for a signal on my mobile phone. Reading that book, I was much less a British visitor – with all the advantages and limitations that go along with that – than a sentient presence, a spirit let loose to walk among events and make of them what I would. While my knowledge of the village no doubt made the novel all the more enjoyable by affording me the pleasure of recognition, the experience of the story was purer than it had been when I was really there – much less tainted by my own preconceptions and concerns, or by my sense of obligation to my contact and desire to repay his efforts by telling the story as widely and well as I could.

*

The space that stories grant us, by allowing us to bail out some of the emotional and logistical paraphernalia we carry with us in the real world, makes extraordinary things possible. With our minds free of everyday concerns and the volume turned down on our interior mono-logues, we have the scope to engage in creative activity of our own, as our imaginations construct the fictional worlds sketched out by the words before our eyes.

This can have a transformative effect. Because books cast us in a creative role they enrich and broaden who we are. As Joseph Conrad noted in a letter to Cunninghame Graham in 1897, 'One writes only half the book; the other half is with the reader', or as psychologist David Comer Kidd observed in the wake of his study into the effects of reading more than a century later, 'What great writers do is to turn you [the reader] into the writer'. Immersing ourselves in images that we ourselves generate in response to words, we seem to inhabit differ-ent realities, such that, as Henry James described it, the act of reading 'makes it appear to us for the time that we have lived another life – that we have had a miraculous enlargement of experience'.

As co-architects of a book's imaginary universe, we do not merely register the events of a story: we create and feel them too. They are ours even as they are the author's, and without us they would not exist exactly as they are. This emotion is what makes us feel connected to readers of the same book. It explains the bond we share with strangers when we hear them express something we have also felt about a particular character, scene or sentence. It reveals the power of reading groups and book-blogging communities. And it sheds light on the generosity of the many people who went out of their way to help me read the world and from whom I still hear more than two years after the project finished: Cristina and her husband Razvan, whom I met for coffee when they came to London and who spent an hour telling me about journalism in their home country, Romania, and about the challenges facing the nation as it moves from being a society that used to accept international aid to one that sends support out to others; Jason Cooper in Wyoming, whose persistence sparked the whole project off in the first place, and whose book and film recommendations continue to challenge and intrigue me; Suneetha Balakrishnan, whose timely observation about the anglocentric nature of the recommendations on my blog list for her nation prompted me to venture into translated Indian fiction and discover the delights of Malayalam writer M.T. Vasudevan Nair, and who went on to interview me for *The Hindu* as a result; and many, many more.

As visitors to the same imaginary territory, we seem to have a connection. We have felt comparable things, our thoughts have travelled along similar tracks, and we have shared an experience that goes far beyond the events of the narrative. This is because, as well as having constructed and inhabited an alternative reality using the same plans, we have been inhabited too. As Belgian literary critic Georges Poulet reveals in his reflection on the process of reading, texts are not simply objects upon which our imaginations act, but also vehicles of influence with the power to infiltrate and control: 'Because of the strange invasion of my person by the thoughts of another, I am a self who is granted the experience of thinking thoughts foreign to him. I am the subject of thoughts other than my own. My consciousness behaves as though it were the consciousness of another.'

Texts act upon us every bit as much as we act upon them. They work, grab the reader, tug at the heartstrings and call forth the emotions. They thrill, delight, surprise and devastate us. And when we give ourselves over to a story, shrugging off many of the defensive mechanisms that protect but also isolate us from one another in the real world, we embrace the possibility of our ideas being recalibrated. Like subjects giving ourselves over into the hands of a skilled hypnotist, we submit to having our thoughts tampered with when we read.

As a result, books don't simply have the potential to transform our thinking; they can restructure our brains. Brown University professor Paul B. Armstrong found this to be the case a few years ago, when he struck out from his usual discipline of English literature to research the neuroscience behind the processes that make reading happen. Through surveying the findings of a range of experiments conducted to monitor brain activity during the reading of literary texts, he realised that the experiences of harmony and dissonance to which stories – along with art and music – expose us 'facilitate the brain's ability to form and dissolve assemblies of neurons, establishing the patterns that through repeated firing become our habitual ways of engaging the world, while also combating their tendency to rigidify and promoting the possibility of new cortical connections'. The results Armstrong studied are, in effect, scientific evidence of the assertions of figures such as nineteenth-century French psychologist Léon Dumont, who wrote that 'Flowing water hollows out a channel for itself which grows broader and deeper, and when it later flows again, it follows the path traced by itself before. Just so, the impressions of outer objects fashion for themselves more and more appropriate paths in the nervous system.' What we now know as Hebbian learning – simplistically explained as brain cells firing and wiring together in response to stimuli – takes place as we read and has the potential to develop new patterns in our thinking. As adult brains retain a degree of plasticity throughout life, this means that, within certain limits, books have the power to shape us. Stories can make us who we are.

The implications are huge. If our brains can be changed by what we read, this provides support for the grand claims made by champions of literature in previous generations about the improving power of books. There may in fact be physical evidence to back up statements such as critic Hans Robert Jauss' assertion in his 1967 lecture 'Literary History as a Challenge to Literary Theory' that 'the experience of reading can liberate one from adaptations, prejudices and predicaments of a lived praxis in that it compels one to a new perception of things' and that this in turn might advance 'the emancipation of mankind from its natural, religious and social bonds'. Rather than simply filling our minds' eyes with marvellous and strange images, it's possible that the mere act of concocting the images themselves increases our brains' capacities to imagine things that would otherwise be alien or unknowable to us. Stories, it seems, truly can be life changing.

But before you throw this book aside and run for the fiction aisle in an effort to reimagine yourself as wisely and well as your still-malleable brain will allow, it's worth bearing a few things in mind. Just as texts appear to have power to formulate new pathways in our brains, so they can equally reinforce and shore up what is already there. Prejudices and ideologies can be bolstered by stories that flatter them and the boundaries of the worlds we live in can be hammered all the more firmly into place by books that simply replay familiar accounts of who and what we are. The American critic Nicholas Dames, for example, argues in *The Physiology of the Novel* that 'the Victorian novel was a training ground for industrial consciousness, not a refuge from it'. Whether or not that's true, it's likely that much of the reading material with which we are surrounded works by reassuring rather than challenging us, using accepted formulas communicated to us before we even open the first page. We know, for example, what to expect when we pick up a Marian Keyes, Patricia Cornwell or James Patterson. In fact, that's part of these writers' enormous success. We feel safe in their hands and their stories are a welcome haven in lives that can often shock, disappoint and break faith with us. We don't pick up a Helen Fielding to be reconstructed; we read her novels to be entertained and feel better about who we are.

Even if we do consume a variety of challenging texts, there's no guarantee that they will work towards the same end. They might establish contrasting neurological firing patterns, overwriting each other in turn, like children scrawling and then kicking over patterns in a sandpit. As Paul Armstrong puts it, 'a lifetime of reading a variety of texts will push and pull readers in many different directions'. Indeed, to Armstrong's mind, the substantial cerebral changes that may result from reading would require – if not a lifetime – then certainly a good while to make themselves felt. 'It usually takes a long time for neural structures to get established, and a single reading of one particular book is unlikely to transform them,' he writes. Alain de Botton may be correct that Proust's *À la recherche du temps perdu* can change your life – but it will take considerably more than one go. And if you do have a road-to-Damascus moment while reading a book it's likely that other factors will have laid the foundations for this over the preceding weeks and months.

*

Understanding the effects of reading in terms of gradual, structural changes in our make-up explains why those looking for direct causality between reading a book and doing good (or breaking bad) usually struggle to find examples. By and large, this is not the way stories work. They are companions rather than evangelists, and their authors are usually more interested in building a connection with you as you are, than in transforming you into something else. If anything, it is the repeated process of connection with a variety of texts over a long period that can make a difference, instead of what one story can do on its own.

This potential should not be underestimated, however. As I discovered during my project, the cumulative attrition of a tide of texts from elsewhere on your consciousness can be profound. While 200-odd books is certainly not equivalent to a lifetime's reading for many people (although a recent Book Trust survey found that this is the number of titles owned by the average Brit), it is a considerable helping of words to consume in a year. Just ask Steve, who had to watch the shelf he built bow under the weight of the 144 volumes and manuscripts (plus fifty-three ebooks) I read over the course of 2012, prompting a flurry of comments from blog visitors anxious – and occasionally, I suspect, a little bit mischievously hopeful – that it might break. Spending an average of three or four hours a day immersed in this weighty matter (along with some three or four hours researching and blogging, and eight hours at work five days a week) had a tangible effect on my life. Everything non-essential (and a good deal that was essential) fell by the wayside and I became adept at reading while walking, using my peripheral vision to steer, and picking out the corner of the Tube carriage where tinny headphone seepage was unlikely to interfere with the stream of words flowing into my brain.

As the months went by, I found this stream of words began to carve out contours of its own in my mind. Much in the manner Léon Dumont anticipated some 150 years ago, the external, literary objects I held before my eyes began to erode and reshape the pathways in my brain. I started to be aware of difference in a way that I hadn't been before, despite having grown up in London and having celebrated Diwali, Eid, Chanukah, Christmas and Chinese New Year with gusto at primary school. Somehow the richness of human variety had never been as real to me as it became that year. Although I might have known about the importance and value of diversity, in the same way that I know $E = mc^2$, reading such a deluge of different stories took me into the workings behind the equation, as though Einstein himself were leading me through the steps in its formulation and kindling in me the delight of discovery. Having inhabited a sample of tales told from perspectives other than the default Anglo-American platform from which I was used to seeing the world, I began to look at life from fresh angles. Reading as widely and intensely as I did that year made me more sensitive to the complexity and uniqueness of the people around me. It provided an inoculation against the reductionism that British literary critic John Carey has identified as our standard response to many situations. 'Given the multitudes by which the individual is surrounded,' he writes, 'it is virtually impossible to regard everyone else as having an individuality equivalent to one's own. The mass, as a reductive and dismissive concept, is invented to ease this difficulty.' Books, it seemed, could go some way to counteract this, stimulating and maintaining more complex thought patterns.

In addition, things that I had lived with unthinkingly because they were widespread took on a new strangeness, and terms that made up part of the basic trappings of conversation started to chafe. I began to feel as never before how limiting catch-all labels for different groups in society are – labels that have often grown out of injustice and restrictions on opportunities, rather than positive statements of identity. Words such as 'black' and 'white' felt cramped and inadequate as a means of talking about ethnicity, suggesting, as they did, that I must have more in common with an Albanian donkey farmer than with the Zimbabwean-British family living down the hallway from me. Such distinctions seemed to deplete the individualism of all of us and make us poorer, more two-dimensional people. And while they express certain truths about abuses of power and experiences (whether of privilege or discrimination) broadly common to certain ethnic groups in many societies – things that, as one Angolan woman I met through the blog put it, 'need to be healed' – these labels are also a capitulation to what Tanzanian writer Abdulrazak Gurnah calls 'uttering the lie with increasing ease, conceding the sameness of our difference, deferring to a deadening vision of a racialised world'. Having been inundated with visions of the world as seen through a wide range of other eyes, I found such sweeping categories mind-numbing. They seemed liable to encourage complacency and to dull brains that might otherwise engage in finding more valuable ways of expressing identity and difference.

The same thing held true for some of the terms I had been used to framing the world with. Words like 'developed' and 'developing' – bandied around so earnestly at many of the media organisations I had worked at over the years – suddenly revealed themselves as Trojan horses packed with assumptions. 'We've got it right!' they seemed to crow. 'Everyone else is just catching up. After all, who wouldn't want traffic jams and pollution and Type 2 diabetes and loneliness and depression? Inconceivable that anyone wouldn't choose to be like us!' As I made my way through books built on other foundations, page by page, the stories seemed to be uncovering the complacency packed into many of the things I had been thinking and saying, revealing the impoverishing effects of such mental habits.

Perhaps the most dramatic shift, however, came in terms of the world itself and that long list of books and countries that dictated my schedule for twelve months. Volume by volume, the entries on that cold, rather faceless register of place names that I had begun the year with started to take on character and richness in my eyes. Page by page, these regions ceased to be mysterious blanks or dead bundles of facts and figures and became living, breathing entities, as if their stories had made them real. As if by tacit agreement, the works were waging war on my assumptions about the boundaries printed on the world maps I'd grown up seeing on classroom walls. Lines that once seemed every bit as definite and decisive as the coastline around Great Britain were beginning to blur. If I thought the main issue consisted in establishing what counted as a country and drawing up the borders, I could think again.

This growing sense of the world's reality changed how I looked at the project and my role in it. Instead of a dispassionate observer looking down on the world and all its curiosities for interest's sake, I began to feel intimately connected to it. Rather than being removed, I was part of the global community and my choices and decisions affected it – albeit in a very small way. As I worked my way through the titles, I found myself developing what leading Spanish-language translator Edith Grossman has called the kind of reading-induced perception that 'keeps expanding until it spills over into ordinary, concrete life'. In my case, this insight spilling into action manifested itself in the controversial decision to change the list – and hence my world – some six months into the project.

The issue centred around Palestine. While getting books from many countries required hours of research, correspondence and luck, I'd been inundated with recommendations for tempting-sounding Palestinian reads almost from the launch of the project. People had left comments with lists of titles, many of them assuming that the Arab nation would be included as a matter of course. I'd even been lobbied by Cairo-based book blogger M. Lynx Qualey, who, in the post she wrote recommending Arabic titles in translation, appealed: 'politics aside, the literature of Palestinians is un-missable. Really, Ann, you'd be doing yourself a disservice.'

At first, I shrugged off these comments. I would personally have been very happy to read a book from Palestine, but I didn't see that there was a lot that I could do about it. The nation wasn't on the list of 195 sovereign states plus Taiwan that I'd been working from and that was that. If I'd thought about it before I launched the project, I might well have added it in too, but what with all the toing and froing over what counted as a country in the first place, I hadn't had time to give much thought to individual nations' cases. Besides, I wanted to steer clear of politics. I was looking for a list to make these difficult decisions for me and I'd got one. It was too late to go changing things now.

However, as the months went by I began to have doubts. Little by little, I found my complacency crumbling in the face of thousands of tiny chisels that chipped away at it every day: the words in the books I was reading. The challenges came in a host of guises. They included novels where characters found themselves at the mercy of agreements made by foreign bureaucrats thousands of miles away, as in Jamil Ahmad's *The Wandering Falcon* – set during the fixing of the border between Afghanistan and Pakistan – and stories about people wrestling with a disdain for their own cultural identities inculcated by decades of colonial rule. The common thread, however, seemed to be this: what much of the world declares about political situations in other parts of the planet often bears very little relation to the experience of the people living there.

Of course, some of these ideas were not new to me. I'd seen enough reports from grim-faced, khaki-clad journalists to know that the world was a conflicted place and that the impact of decisions made in the centres of power was often only felt by those unable to advocate for themselves thousands of miles away. But to be taken into the thick of these situations by writers freed by their imaginations and spurred on by a deep affinity for and knowledge of a place and the people who live there was a new and humbling experience. This was not saccharine sentimentalism, reaching for the heartstrings with the slickness of a charity appeal; nor was it explorer's obsession, tripping over itself in its eagerness to analyse and explain. No – at its best, literature revealed a love forged and tempered by years of living in and absorbing a region in all its beauty, brokenness, brutality and brilliance. It brought home the reality of leading a life shaped by a foreign power's story of who or what you are. Chapter by chapter, it transformed that list of countries stretching down the screen on my blog from an intellectual puzzle into a vital creed: a set of statements of belief about the world and those in it that had the power to make or destroy people's happiness, peace and lives. Nation by nation, these writers' works were enabling me to create and inhabit their homes anew.

So whose story was I following, then? Which reading of the world had produced the list of 195 sovereign states – with its single addition of Kosovo to the list of UN-recognised nations – that I was using as the basis for my project? Where did it come from, this strange register of country names, so ubiquitous that, in spite of all my research into the fraught question of nationhood, I had blithely taken as a universal yardstick?

I retraced my virtual steps. There was the mysterious 195 on Wikipedia. And there it was again in a series of articles on authoritative-sounding platforms, sometimes with the addition of Taiwan taking it to 196. It cropped up on information sites and in chatrooms, and in response to questions on forums all over the world. Apart from the occasional expression of doubt, the number seemed to be taken as gospel, Torah or Bhagavad Gita truth by the majority of the English-speaking online community, who quoted it and passed it on without the slightest qualm. So categorical and universal did it appear to be, that it was almost as though some independent, pan-global body had debated the issue and reached an official consensus, placing it on a par with such universal truths as death, or toast always landing butter-side down.

And then in amongst the landslide of parroted and regurgitated information, in between the virtual piles of 1s, 9s, 5s and 6s, I found an innocuous-looking list of 'Independent States in the World' on the US government website. It consisted of the names of 195 countries – the UN-recognised states plus Kosovo – oh, and there was an extra mention of Taiwan under the title 'Other' at the bottom. The truth hit me: despite all my efforts to establish an objective list of countries at the start of the year, I had succumbed to that most twenty-first century of maladies, *data infecta*. I had allowed my thinking to be contaminated by a piece of incomplete information that had mutated away from its context and then multiplied all over the internet like some sort of superbug. I had been reading the American world all along. Just as a map that put Europe at the centre had the effect of shaping the world's view of itself for 400 years, so the politics of the planet's most powerful country – and the anglophone nation with the highest number of internet users – had shaped, whether by design or by chance, my picture of the global community. (Incidentally, the American list of sovereign states may tally pretty nearly with the British one, for all I know – when I phoned up the Foreign and Commonwealth Office media department to check which countries the UK recognises, I was told there was no list they could share because it was a 'very political' issue.)

After the initial phase of fist-biting and forehead-slapping over my own stupidity subsided, I started to think about what to do. One thing was certain: I couldn't continue with the list as it was. My aim for the project had always been, as far as possible, to adopt a politically neutral stance and give voices from all the countries involved equal weight. Reading books from a list of states drawn up according to the political agenda of one nation undermined the whole principle. The project was political, whether I liked it or not, and in this conflicted, contrary world of ours there was no room for sitting on the fence.

But there was the problem of the number 196. The whole quest was built around it. It was splashed across the banner and around the growing number of blogs and articles referring to the venture. Six months in, it was too late to go tinkering around with that. Somehow or other, I needed to come up with a non-partisan, global list of 196 countries that I could continue reading books from. And I needed to do it fast.

After a couple of sleepless nights, and a weekend in which not much was consumed other than my own fingernails as I sat squinting at a range of involved and contradictory articles about sovereignty around the world, the solution came to me. The answer lay in my somewhat erratic decision to include Taiwan on the original list despite the fact that the country lost its UN membership in 1971.

If my justification for including Taiwan on the original list was that it had once been a UN member and so had had a degree of UN recognition at one stage in its history, there was another nation that merited inclusion on those grounds: Palestine. Although the nation's attempts to achieve full UN membership around the time I was preparing to undertake my project had failed, it already had a degree of acknowledgement as a 'non-member entity'. This meant that it, along with the only 'non-member state', Vatican City (or more precisely the Holy See), was allowed to observe UN conventions. If my new yardstick was to be UN recognition (not itself entirely neutral, given the weight of certain key players, as discussed in chapter two), then shifting from an

190

American to a global perspective could simply be a matter of bringing Palestine in to replace the only country on the list of 196 with no degree of UN recognition at any time in its history: Kosovo. In fact, when you looked at the question of acknowledgement on a country-by-country basis, Palestine was way ahead of Kosovo, with official recognition by more than 130 UN members as compared with Kosovo's 91. The Arab state might not have fitted with the agenda of certain Western nations, but it existed without question in the minds of much of the rest of the globe.

The decision was made. Having amended my explanation of the criteria for including countries in the project, I clicked the list open and changed the world – or at least my version of it. Henceforward, the story I was reading included Palestine.

In the event, it proved to be a timely decision. On 29 November 2012, the UN passed a resolution to upgrade Palestine's status to that of 'non-member state' in response to a campaign led by Palestinian president Mahmoud Abbas.

The world was changing. And its books were changing me.

9

Dealing with culture shock
when books and readers clash

In the 1950s, when psychologists began to analyse the growing numbers of international students making their way to the UK, a trend emerged. People coming from elsewhere, it was found, frequently had trouble adjusting to life in Britain. They were often disorientated, bewildered and overwhelmed. Many of them struggled to integrate into the host society and failed to comply with its mores and rules. They were irritable, overly afraid of being robbed or cheated, and disproportionately friendly with people who reminded them of where they had come from. Some studies demonstrated a higher incidence of mental illness among those who had made the transition from home to abroad. Even in best-case scenarios, it seemed, people relocating to another culture for a considerable length of time could expect to experience a sequence of emotions including excitement, exhilaration, disorientation, homesickness and even disintegration, before finally achieving a sense of pride and independence as they began to find their feet and carve out their own existence in their new home. Seen in this light, the etymological link between the word 'travel' and 'travail' was not such a stretch.

In 1960, anthropologist Kalervo Oberg borrowed a term that had first been used in 1951 by one of his peers, Cora Du Bois, to account for the effect that exposure to an unfamiliar environment has on human beings. 'Culture shock', Oberg wrote:

> is precipitated by the anxiety that results from losing all our familiar signs and symbols of social intercourse. These signs are

the thousand and one ways in which we orient ourselves to the situations of daily life: when to shake hands and what to say when we meet people, when and how to give tips, how to give orders to servants, how to make purchases, when to accept and when to refuse invitations, when to take statements seriously and when not. These cues, which may be words, gestures, facial expressions, customs, or norms are acquired by all of us in the course of growing up and are as much a part of our culture as the language we speak or the beliefs we accept. All of us depend for our peace of mind and our efficiency on hundreds of these cues, most of which are unconsciously learned.

Being cut adrift from such cultural moorings isn't always a bad thing. Indeed, some psychologists have pointed out that, in mild doses, the disorientation that comes from stepping outside the familiar environments most of us operate in most of the time can be beneficial when it comes to developing self-awareness. There is also evidence to suggest that certain scenarios lead to positive cultural exchange, whereby both the host society and the visitor stand to gain insight and richness from their interaction. Nevertheless, as the negative connotations of the term 'shock' imply, the majority of researchers treat the process of relocation as primarily disruptive and problematic, and focus their attention on ways people can assimilate and move beyond the experience as efficiently as possible. While some talk in terms of immigrants and long-term visitors having to go through a period of 'adjustment' in order to be able to live successfully in a new society, others favour the more neutral description of 'culture learning' because, as Adrian Furnham and Stephen Bochner explain in their survey of *Culture Shock: Psychological reaction to unfamiliar environments*, '"adjusting" a person to a new culture has connotations of cultural chauvinism, the implication being that the newcomer should abandon the culture of origin'.

Yet while psychologists quibble over the terminology, they are in agreement about one thing: the issue of integrating into a new milieu, particularly permanently, involves more than simply learning whether to hold a door open or when to make eye contact. It comes down to beliefs about what is important – values relating to power, prestige, the role of religion, the status and rights of the individual, sexual identities and gender roles. Put simply, moving to a society that lives by codes and morals you don't share is likely to be stressful. Much as they may demur from the term 'adjustment', Furnham and Bochner appear to have no doubt that 'a poor fit between person and the environment may lead to distress and anxiety until the values of the new society are understood and internalized'. For better for worse, getting the most out of life in a new country involves a degree of personal recalibration.

It's a theme that fiction writers have explored to great effect for a long time. Indeed, centuries before the term 'culture shock' came into play, many of the world's best stories revolved around journeys to distant places and the success – or otherwise – of the protagonists in fitting in there. Wallowing in the Slough of Despond, John Bunyan's pilgrim Christian was arguably having a touch of the traveller's blues, while Gulliver, pegged down in Lilliput, might have made much more headway had he known it was illegal to 'make water' in the capital. In recent decades, as travel has become increasingly common, more and more novels have made disorientation and cultural alienation a central theme. Sometimes this is done humorously, as in the case of Srđan Valjarević's comic masterpiece *Lake Como*, a rare English translation of which was brought back from Belgrade for me by a Serbian colleague during my quest; it follows an alcoholic would-be novelist who manages to bag a residency at an exclusive retreat in northern Italy and journeys there from his war-torn homeland determined to make the most of the free food and booze. In other cases, cultural alienation is a magnifying lens through which we can examine the minutiae of something we might otherwise take for granted. In Hungarian writer Ferenc Karinthy's *Metropole*, for example, the workings and uses of language come under scrutiny when polyglot linguist Bubai gets on a flight to the wrong destination and finds himself stranded in an unknown country where he cannot make sense of anything – and cannot make himself under-stood. There are touching *Bildungsroman* accounts of youthful jaunts turned sour, as in J.M. Coetzee's memorable *Youth*, in which the South African would-be poet protagonist and his hapless Indian colleague Ganapathy atrophy in soulless computer-programming jobs under louring London skies. And there are wholesale demolition jobs, such as Tayeb Salih's towering classic *Season of Migration to the North* – voted the 'most important Arabic novel of the twentieth century' by the Damascus-based Arab Literary Academy in 2001 – in which the enigmatic Mustafa Sa'eed plays British culture off against Sudanese exoticism and finally gets caught and crushed between the two. Though they may have rather different ways of expressing it, on this science and art seem to agree: when people find themselves in unfamiliar environ-ments they – and sometimes the world – will change.

*

As readers, we don't travel. In fact, for many of us that's precisely the point: we open books to experience ideas and places we don't have the budget, time or stomach to go through in real life. All the same, the burgeoning number of travel-related metaphors attached to reading these days seems to imply that we inhabit something of the migrant's mindset when we venture into stories from elsewhere. Whether you're a bookpacker, literary nomad, armchair traveller or biblioglobe (yes, I've heard that one too), it seems likely that you'll know something of the experience of striking out into the unknown when you set off in the company of a new narratological guide. And if you venture some distance off the paths and tracks you've followed before, you may go through some form of culture shock.

The reasons for this become clear when you dig into the ways we make sense of the words before us on the page. Just like the thousand social mores Kalervo Oberg wrote that we acquire when growing up in a particular time and place, so the texts that we read shape our expecta-tions and habits; our literary manners, as it were. Those of us brought up on Hans Christian Andersen know that the phrase 'Once upon a time . . .' will lead us into a world of mermaids and witches and poisoned apples. In this context, we wouldn't dream of scoffing at the notion of people sleeping for 100 years or living in kingdoms under the sea, because this is a dimension where the laws of physics operate somewhat differently from our own. We understand the rules. But if a shabby detective turned up and started laying down the law to the wicked stepmother, we might feel more than a little bewildered. By the same token, if you're familiar with the West African Anansi stories, you'll know that 'A story, a story, let it come, let it go . . .' heralds the start of a yarn about the ingenious spider – and you'd be baffled by being plunged into an office romance about a shy guy with a stammer and the girl next door. However, you might struggle to know where you are with a tale that starts 'The Old Ones told me . . .' unless you've encountered Native American stories before. Similarly, for many of us, a legend that purports to take place in the Dreamtime that forms the setting for many indigenous Australian myths would keep us guessing as to what sort of imaginary universe to expect.

Having stored up and honed our literary mores since the first stories were read to us as children, our brains are adept at analysing cues and priming our expectations accordingly. The hairs start to rise on the backs of our necks as soon as the lone woman enters the dark alleyway. The warm, schmaltzy – or perhaps nauseated and cynical, depending on your preferences – feeling floods through us as soon as the heroine catches sight of the handsome stranger. The Camusian angst wells up with any mention of Mother dying on anything other than a very clearly specified day. Indeed, far from simply floating along on the currents of a given narrative, our brains are often far out in front, tugging the story along. As the German philosopher Martin Heidegger put it, understanding involves anticipation, the creation of a '*Vorstruktur*' (forestructure) based on how we think things are going to play out; or in Professor Paul B. Armstrong's words, 'we are always ahead of ourselves when we understand, especially (but not only) when we read'.

This business of anticipating what's going to happen next can make reading a very soothing experience. You only have to scan the bestsellers chart to see that we like tried-and-tested formulas that play out as we expect them to with certain, safe margins for surprise and variation built in. It's probably part of the reason that sports and game shows are so popular: watching action unfold along familiar lines, yet with variation inside understood limits, is satisfying. It reassures us that the world remains as we believe it to be: ordered according to a set of well-known rules, still with the potential to surprise and delight us, but not too much.

But it can also be boring. Too little variation sees us rolling our eyes and drumming our fingers on the arms of our chairs. At a certain point – no doubt different from person to person – familiarity breeds contempt. This impatience stems from what neural scientists Irving Biederman and Edward Vessel have described as 'the human preference for experiences that are both novel and richly interpretable'. We want to be challenged and intrigued, and our brains need the chance to grapple with ambiguity and develop and restructure themselves in the process, but this has to be on our terms. Differences and surprises have to play out within the range our brains are equipped to operate in – again calibrated according to what we have been exposed to previously – or else we struggle. When it comes to books, as Armstrong puts it, this means that the most satisfying stories walk a tightrope whereby they at once 'manipulate contingent, cultural conventions, and in doing so . . . teach us to read in new ways (what was unnatural can become recognizable and familiar)' but without falling into the trap of undertaking too many 'experiments with form [that] may simply be too much for the brain to handle smoothly and routinely'.

Looked at this way, it's easy to understand the popularity of works that mediate between cultures and stories by writers with hyphenated nationalities. The Stieg Larsson novels that took second place on the global bestsellers list in 2008 meld the conventions of crime fiction with what was then a refreshing Swedish setting. They are at once familiar and different; their strangeness is recognisable and digestible to us; they are, in Donald Rumsfeld's memorable phrase, 'known unknowns'. Western-style books that offer glimpses into closed worlds through the medium of narratives shaped by Western sensibilities and norms – as Afghan-American Khaled Hosseini's *The Kite Runner* does – walk a similar line of harmony and dissonance. In the company of a storyteller guide who understands our preoccupations and blind spots, we can be shepherded into the little-discussed arena of homosexual rape under the Taliban regime, confident that, while we may be challenged, the book is unlikely to do anything to make us nervous. Pitched correctly, techniques like this can make a writer's career. According to the Austrian author Anna Kim, the potential rewards of striking the balance accurately are enough to make it a consideration for almost anyone keen to make a comfortable living from words: 'of course, there is the small matter of foreign licences and translations: if one's work is too regional, it might not be interesting enough for a foreign audience, but if it is too general, it might not be interesting either. The right amount of foreignness – or should I say regional-ness – seems to be crucial to being a successful (modern) writer.'

Some authors, however, have no intention of making life easy for us in the worlds they portray. The situations they describe are so extreme that no one is supposed to feel at home in them. The Vietnamese jungle battlefield in Bao Ninh's *The Sorrow of War*, the torture chambers in Jérôme Ferrari's *Where I Left My Soul* and the lawless wastes of Ahmadou Kourouma's *Allah is Not Obliged* are no man's lands – and that's the point. No human being could feel comfortable there. We might find the writing compelling, but we are supposed to be sickened, disgusted and troubled by the situations described. We are meant to stand outside them every bit as surely as Brecht could have intended when in 1936 he coined the term *Verfremdungseffekt* (alienation effect) to describe a distancing technique used to stop audiences from losing themselves in a piece of theatre. Indeed, some descriptions are so extreme that they even succeed in making our own society strange or even repugnant to us. The indifference of the West can sometimes be chilling, as in Egyptian writer Radwa Ashour's novel *Spectres* when an announcer on CNN compares Baghdad under fire in 1991 to 'a huge Christmas tree . . . "It's a magical, thrilling sight!"' – words that echo comments made by an American fighter pilot during the real-life conflict. It is also deeply uncomfortable for those of us reading the book in English translation.

Such disorientation isn't confined to stories from geographically distant societies. Books from or about different eras often have comparable effects; as L.P. Hartley's *The Go-Between* famously has it, 'The past is a foreign country: they do things differently there.' Chinese author Han Dong would no doubt agree: he felt that the events he described in his novel *Banished!*, which portrays the forced relocation of a writer and his family to a remote, rural area during the Cultural Revolution of the late 1960s and early 1970s, would be so alien to readers in his home country that he even created a glossary to help them decode the jargon of the era. According to his anonymous narrator, the time was so strange that it is likely to be equally bewildering to readers everywhere:

> I can only sincerely apologize to my young readers or those from another world. The world I describe here was, after all, a peculiar and transitory one, constructed of language that enshrouded and permeated it with what Buddhists call *anitya*, a mysterious impermanence.

Whether geographical or temporal, wherever distance exists between the audience and the milieu described, writers have the opportunity to show readers their societies from an outsider's perspective. It's a technique that Djiboutian writer Abdourahman Waberi uses to striking effect in his novel, *In the United States of Africa*. In that book, Waberi makes the West and all its processes strange by turning the world on its head, transforming Africa into the superpower tasked with finding solutions for the wars, famines and epidemics that are afflicting Europe and North America and sending streams of Caucasian refugees to its shores in search of relief. The opening section, 'in which the author gives a brief account of the origins of our prosperity and the reasons why the Caucasians were thrown onto the paths of exile,' is a consideration of a Swiss refugee in the Gambian capital Banjul, and it sets the tone for a demolition job on Western complacency:

> Let's call him Yacuba, first to protect his identity and second because he has an impossible family name. He was born outside Zurich in an unhealthy favela, where infant mortality and the rate of infection by the AIDS virus remain the highest in the world today.
>
> . . .
>
> The cream of international diplomacy also meets in Banjul; they are supposedly settling the fate of millions of Caucasian refugees of various ethnic groups (Austrian, Canadian, American, Norwegian, Belgian, Bulgarian, Hungarian, British, Icelandic, Swedish, Portuguese . . .) not to mention the skeletal boat people from the northern Mediterranean, at the end of their rope from dodging all the mortar shells and missiles that darken the unfortunate lands of Euramerica.
>
> . . .
>
> These warlike tribes with their barbaric customs and deceitful, uncontrollable moves keep raiding the scorched lands of the Auvergne, Tuscany or Flanders, when they're not shedding the blood of their atavistic enemies – Teutons, Gascons, or backward Iberians – for the slightest little thing, for rifles or trifles, because they recognize a prisoner or because they don't. They're all waiting for a peace that has yet to come.

It's funny and it's shaming. And it works because Waberi, who has lived in France for most of his adult life, knows precisely what we are about as Western readers. He is familiar with the assumptions upon which our readings of the world rest and knows precisely what to do to pull them out from under us. In his hands, literary culture shock becomes a tool that can make us look at our own society with disbelieving eyes.

*

Intentional alienation is one thing, but it's by no means the only experience of being *dépaysé* that you are likely to undergo while reading narratives from other cultures. Venture away from the works carefully modulated to interpret one group of people to another and you'll quickly find yourself grappling with all sorts of dilemmas that stem largely from the fact that you are not where the author imagined you to be when he or she sat down to commit a story to the page. Writers of books of this sort won't hesitate to stray from Western storytelling conventions and will make references likely to bamboozle an anglophone reader, and there's no earthly reason why they shouldn't. They're not being rude or wilfully exclusive (well, most of them aren't), it's just that, in the nicest possible way, we're not their target audience. Rather than deliberately shutting us out, these tales simply weren't written with us in mind. They were directed at people with different religious references and historical frameworks and a raft of other proverbs, mannerisms and in-jokes. As with so many stories, they were created for people like their authors, a point deftly captured by *A Clockwork Orange* author Anthony Burgess when he observed that 'the ideal reader of my novels is a lapsed Catholic and a failed musician, short-sighted, colour-blind, auditorily biased, who has read the books that I have read. He should also be about my age.' The writers of the notoriously difficult ancient Mesopotamian *Epic of Gilgamesh* weren't setting out to be obscure. The world in which they and their audience operated was just markedly different to our own – and they had no reason to suppose, or care, that thousands of years later their texts might be the subject of scrutiny by literary historians who would have been only too glad of an explicatory footnote or two.

Sometimes these cultural difficulties will be headed off at the pass by the editors and translators through whose hands stories pass on the way to new audiences. Footnotes will be added. Tone will be tweaked. Passages of contextual information will be shoehorned into the narrative in an effort to give readers the tools they need to appreciate the story in the spirit in which it was meant. There are even situations in which references are changed altogether. In the case of the BBC hit comedy *Fawlty Towers*, the inept Spanish waiter Manuel switches nationality depending on where the programme is shown: he becomes a citizen of the Basque region when he appears in Italy, and Mexican when the show airs in Spain. For all our differences, it seems none of us likes to be the butt of someone else's joke.

When it comes to books, however, the problems can start before we've even opened the first page. Creatures of habit that we are, we tend to operate with very fixed ideas about how stories should look. Even though books as we know them have only been around in their current form for a few hundred years – less than that, when you reflect that paperbacks were first produced by firms like Routledge & Sons, Simms & McIntyre and Ward Lock & Co. in the early- to mid-nineteenth century – we treat them as sacred and immutable things. The advent of e-readers threw many into a frenzy, sending streams of vitriol coursing through the letters pages and, oddly enough, comments sections of online newspaper articles that dared to express anything other than grave concern at the thought of reading in any form other than that which God intended. As Alberto Manguel puts it: 'at different times and in different places I have come to expect certain books to look a certain way, and, as in all fashions, these changing features fix a precise quality onto a book's definition. I judge a book by its cover; I judge a book by its shape.'

As such, anything that fails to conform to the shifting but narrow range of expectations we associate with the concept of 'story' in our culture has a high chance of throwing us into a spin. Whether it's books that fail to reflect the distinctions between poetry and prose that many of us are used to, hopscotching in and out of verse as the author sees fit, or stories written in multilingual environments where switching between tongues is a form of changing registers and slipping out of the starched shirt of official, standard English into the baggy housecoat of the local creole is a necessary statement of intimacy and identity, literary works that function along lines different to what we're used to can make us reticent and sullen (you only have to look at the faces of students in a seminar on James Joyce's *Ulysses* to see that). And when it comes to the question of books with pictures, we find ourselves far outside our comfort zone. Although graphic novels are a respected form in many parts of the world – take Japanese manga works, for example – they are relegated to a niche in mainstream anglophone culture. Many regard such works with suspicion and disdain – and do their best to inculcate their feelings in others, as Sarah Mkhonza recalls in her memoir of life at a British-style boarding school in Swaziland, *Weeding the Flowerbeds*:

> Sometimes when we were bored, we would read picture dramas like *Chunkie* and other cartoons. Our teacher would be furious with us. 'Never read these picture things. Even an illiterate can read these. Bring this here. I don't want to see it,' she would say as she confiscated our picture dramas.

Even when books look as we would expect, reading foreign texts written for an audience from another culture may be a testing experience. At any moment, you are likely to be plunged into a situation where your literary, social and moral compasses are all to cock and you have no idea how you are expected to react; without having the due north of what passes for normality in a particular genre or setting to steer by, you are left to navigate the narratological wilds on your own. This sense of disorientation might come by way of unfamiliar rituals and social situations, such as polygamous marriages or the violent wedding-night rites and battles of sorcery between husband and wife depicted in some West African narratives. It can also arise in the form of previously unknown set pieces. Newcomers to Nepalese folk tales, for example, may find the frequency with which coins are stuffed into animals' rectums in the hope of making them appear to excrete gold disconcerting, but it seems to be a standard trick in the fictional Himalayan japester's armoury, and narrators have no need to explain it. Similarly, historical events that are central to others' understanding of who and what they are can come as a jarring shock when you've not been used to hearing about them. Descriptions of the early twentieth-century Armenian massacres, which have historically been drowned out in Western ears by the guns of the First World War trenches, are stark and disconcerting. The same goes for the sufferings of many citizens of the Baltic states under Soviet rule – in circumstances so appalling that the Nazis were welcomed as liberators when they invaded Latvia in 1941. To read about atrocities of such magnitude with very little background knowledge of events is unsettling. It is to discover that the world is a different place to the one you believed it to be; and that it has secrets that you have blithely been living alongside your whole life.

Without the context to understand the significance of these events, we are left faltering, wrong-footed, unsure how to respond. Should we feel pity for the wife who is forced to submit at knifepoint or treat this as part of a ritualised performance enacted to formalise marriage? Are we supposed to laugh at the gold-stuffed donkey or disapprove of the owner for being cruel? Can we take what we read at face value or is there unknown contextual information that might temper these accounts? Like newly arrived international students at a university meet-and-greet, we stare hesitantly at the things on offer, unsure where to start and what is expected of us, afraid of committing a faux pas.

In the absence of anything else, we tend to draw on our own experience to make the best of things as we go along. Because reading is an active process in which, as Wolfgang Iser has it, we participate by 'filling in the gaps left by the text', we search for things to plug the interpretative holes crying out for our attention. We look for equivalencies between what we are engaged in imagining and what we have encountered before – just as in real life we might reach for a comparison to help others picture a place that they have never been, dubbing Montreal the Paris of the West, for instance, or Udaipur the Venice of the East. When I read Libyan writer Ibrahim Al-Koni's *The Bleeding of the Stone* during my project, I found myself repeatedly drawn to make comparisons between the novel's poetic evocation of the age-old practices of the Bedouin and the mournful homage to the rural traditions in the works of Thomas Hardy. The parallel may have some truth to it – both writers have negative things to say about the effect of progress on people who live off, and steward, the land – but it is also distorting, because expectations based on Hardy have no place in Al-Koni's novel. If I were to give in to the temptation to read the novel in Hardy's terms, I would find the gory denouement – in which the lone Bedouin protagonist Asouf is crucified – inexplicable and nonsensical. The jolt between what I anticipate and what comes would be too violent and I would have no option but to reject the story as absurd.

However, while unfamiliar references and historical context can act as stumbling blocks, the real sources of friction have a yet more fundamental source. The crunch comes over issues of morality, freedom, right and wrong. As in real life, so with reading: the most extreme cases of literary culture shock occur when you find yourself in a story that operates inside a value system markedly different to your own.

Take gay rights. Few issues have caused more division in the international community in recent years. From calls to boycott the 2014 Sochi Winter Games because of Russia's persecution of its homosexual population to protests against legislation making same-sex relationships punishable by imprisonment or even death in some parts of the world, it seems few things are likely to cause intercultural friction than the rights or otherwise of adults to love whom they choose. In print, things are no different. With homosexual acts illegal in seventy-seven countries at the time of writing, sexual orientation is one of the topics most likely to prove contentious for readers of texts from elsewhere.

The problem is not so much stories that openly attack and vilify gay people; though these no doubt exist, few contemporary publishers have been foolhardy enough to attempt to bring them to the West. Instead, the challenge comes in the shape of stories suffused with the assumption that same-sex unions are wrong. Papuan writer Regis Tove Stella's novel *Mata Sara* (*Crooked Eyes*) is a case in point. On the face of it, the book is the story of several young Papuans' experiences as students in Sydney. We travel with them and see the Western metropolis through their eyes, encountering it as a visitor would. In the grand tradition of many such books, the story sparks in the places where two cultures collide and difference is tested. For the Papuans, homosexuality is one such area. Coming from a country where same-sex relationships are outlawed, they cannot help but be challenged by the public displays of affection they witness between gay people in the Australian capital. On one level, this can be read as an instance of the 'Crooked Eyes' of Stella's title – a Papuan phrase which, he takes pains to explain in the novel, refers to skewed vision and a mistaken way of looking at the world, something he portrays Westerners as being as guilty of in relation to Papua New Guinea as the students are with regard to Australia. The problem is, however, that the casual homophobic slurs that pepper the narrative and the increasingly outlandish plot – which comes close to conflating homosexuality with paedophilia when a child abuse ring is exposed in the final chapters – make giving the novel the benefit of the doubt difficult. While it might be possible to dismiss isolated instances in the book as characterisation, the cumulative effect of them is problematic. It dawns on us slowly that Stella expects us to share his protagonists' prejudices, and the result is uncomfortable.

It's a similar story with Liberian writer and gynaecologist Dr Mardia Stone's *Konkai: Living between two worlds*, an account of her homosexual half-brother's diagnosis and struggle with AIDS in the late eighties and early nineties. Though written as an honest attempt to promote understanding and tolerance, and tackle the taboo surrounding homosexuality in Stone's home country because 'Africans themselves are not writing their stories, everyone else is writing for them', the book is hemmed in by the very fears and misconceptions it seeks to challenge. In particular, its speculation about the role of an episode of child abuse in shaping the author's brother's sexual preferences gets into muddy water. Indeed, the implications of the narrative as a whole made the publisher uncomfortable enough to insert, at the front of the book, a disclaimer that the work 'is not a pronouncement on any debates about the nature of sexual orientation'.

The problem with reading such stories from a liberal Western standpoint is not that they present arguments with which we would disagree, but that they assume feelings and beliefs that we cannot share. Instead of involving us in a debate about the rights and wrongs of differences in sexual orientation, they require us to be complicit in constructing a world on foundations in which we can put little faith. Yet because they draw us in and treat us as a trusted confidant who is bound to share their outlook, they are difficult to challenge. They put us in an awkward position, as Michael Hanne observes on the subject of racist anecdotes:

> The significance of the seductive nature of narrative is that the point of a story is established, indeed imposed on the narratee, in terms of the story's whole narrative form and development. So, for instance, it is much harder to counter a racist story (whether it purports to be a factual record of personal experience or a simple joke) than it is to demonstrate the nastiness and inaccuracy of more direct forms of racist statement.
>
> . . .
>
> It is usually impossible to invalidate such a story by pointing out logical faults or statistical errors as one can with more abstract observations about, for example, the unwillingness of a particular racial group to do hard work. To counter the racist point of a story, it is necessary to combat the story in its totality. In fact listeners are often caught up in a story before it becomes entirely obvious that its point is racist or sexist.

207

When the story comes not in the form of a distasteful anecdote, but as a 300-page book, the difficulty is amplified. We can choose to remove ourselves from the narrative, we can hurl the copy across the room, but the story remains intact – and those of us who value free speech would probably argue that it should. Yet the world that the words require us to construct is one that we cannot inhabit with any degree of comfort. Because, as Vladimir Nabokov wrote, 'the good, the admirable reader identifies himself not with the boy or the girl in the book, but with the mind that conceived and composed that book', stories built on value systems and beliefs that we cannot share force us into the position of being lesser readers. Unable to internalise the values necessary to overcome literary culture shock and integrate successfully into the society of the story – blocked from adopting the text's outlook as our own – we have no choice but to remain relative outsiders in these imaginary communities. Although we might identify with parts of them, the gulf between who we are and who the writer expects us to be prevents us from being absorbed completely in such works. Like troubled immigrants, we can only loiter on the fringes, ill at ease, conflicted, and impatient for the time when we can return home.

*

When the Sherlock Holmes stories began to appear in China in the late nineteenth and early twentieth century, a series of curious incidents occurred. Instead of reproducing the titles of Arthur Conan Doyle's detective classics exactly as they had been in the English versions, the Chinese translators changed many of them to give away the twist at the end of the story before the narrative began. 'The Adventure of the Blue Carbuncle', for example – which turns upon a thief feeding a goose a stolen gemstone to escape arrest – became 'The Case of the Sapphire in the Belly of the Goose', and 'The Gemstone Swallowed by a Goose' in another rendering. Another title was blunter still, morphing into 'The Case of the Jealous Woman Murdering Her Husband'. Indeed, when Eva Hung, an academic at the Chinese University of Hong Kong, surveyed the translations of Conan Doyle's stories undertaken during the late Qing and early Republican periods, she found that fifteen stories had been given new titles that contained the answers to the mysteries. 'It would seem that the translators were not concerned about giving the story away, and did not expect their readers to be upset by this translation approach,' she observes.

At first glance, from a Western perspective, such an attitude is hard to understand. Suspense is such a key component of crime stories as we know them – indeed of many genres, as well as much literary fiction – that it seems incredible that it shouldn't be a factor in a reader's enjoyment of a work. We read to find out what happens. We gripe at reviewers thoughtless enough to include spoilers in their evaluations of the latest blockbuster. If we are unlucky enough to miss an episode of whatever TV drama currently has us hooked, we assiduously avoid social media and hold up our hands in panic when the topic crops up at work or social gatherings, terrified that someone might spill the beans before we've had a chance to watch it for ourselves. The idea that someone might not care that they are finding out what happens prematurely – more, that it might not even occur to them to regard this as significant – seems inexplicable and strange.

When we look into the background to these translations, however, the conundrum starts to unravel. The dog that didn't bark turns out to be the reason for importing the stories in the first place. Far from being selected for their commercial potential by publishers keen to profit from high sales, the Sherlock Holmes adventures – along with a raft of other Western literature translated into Chinese around the turn of the twentieth century – were introduced into the country for their educational value. A series of upheavals and reforms among the ruling elite from the 1890s onwards led to a new interest in exploiting literature's potential to convey knowledge to the general population. 'In this context,' writes Eva Hung, 'the literary merit of individual works was of . . . less importance. None of the famous proposals for making fiction – particularly translated fiction – serve utilitarian purposes showed any concern for importing or building up a body of canonical literature.' Instead, 'works of fiction were a source for knowledge current in the West'. A notice about the publication of translated fiction, which was issued by a Chinese Military Defence Circuit Intendant and appeared in all editions of a fiction series launched by the writer Xiaoshuo Lin in 1905, makes the intentions behind the sudden surge in translations plain:

> Those who strive for the same goal have grouped together and collected a sum of money, to be used for the purpose of selecting Western fiction which is novel in ideas and upright in principle, to be translated and published in book form. This will serve to broaden our countrymen's knowledge, supplementing areas in which school education is deficient.

In the case of the Sherlock Holmes stories, the incisiveness of the hero's logic and his deployment of much-admired Western investigation techniques proved a powerful draw for those keen to boost their knowledge. According to Hung, 'the Holmes stories were repeatedly recommended as texts to be studied by detectives in order for them to acquire superior methods of investigation'. Whether or not the readers were gripped by the plot was neither here nor there – the point was that those in the law-enforcement game might be able to improve their working practices by taking a leaf out of Sherlock Holmes' book.

With no direct precedents to work from – the rich, 3,000-year Chinese literary tradition having been devoid of detective fiction, much as the English tradition was until Wilkie Collins' *The Moonstone* – those charged with converting Conan Doyle's mysteries into language their compatriots could understand and profit from had to muddle through as best they could. Like all readers venturing into uncharted territory, whether consciously or not, they reached for equivalencies in works they did know; in this case, the *gong'an* (court case) tradition. Thought to have originated in the puppetry and oral performances of the Song dynasty and developed to revolve around the figure of Judge Bao (a real-life magistrate) during the thirteenth- and fourteenth-century Yuan dynasty, *gong'an* stories and novels describe how a judge resolves knotty legal cases. The emphasis is on the process of the investigation and the analysis of the evidence rather than the solving of a mystery – indeed, the perpetrator is usually known from the very first page. Rather than 'whodunnit', the central question is more like 'whaddyagonna-doaboudit'; a sentiment, incidentally, which still seems to have a place in contemporary fiction such as Chinese-American author Yiyun Li's *Kinder Than Solitude*, of which one reviewer wrote, 'the whodunit is less mysterious than [the characters'] interconnected fates'.

With the legalistic *gong'an* stories shaping their expectations of how crime should be dealt with in fiction, many of the Chinese Holmes translators saw no issue with giving the twist away because in their minds it wasn't the point of the story. The interest of most of the crime-related narratives they had encountered before lay in the weighing up of competing claims and moral and legal concerns – the method was the point. Given that they were working to make a whole raft of other culturally specific things intelligible to their contemporaries – not least restructuring narratives to avoid confusing readers unused to the nest of flashbacks so favoured by Conan Doyle, as well as adapting his descriptions to conform with Chinese conceptions of decorum and female beauty – it must have been a relief to lean on something familiar once in a while.

Interestingly, the early translators' inadvertent spoilers seem to have done nothing to hinder the popularity of Sherlock Holmes in China. Throughout the twentieth century, the adventures of Curly Fu and Peanut (the national nicknames for Holmes and Watson because they sound like the Chinese versions of their names) have drawn millions of fans inside the country. The stories have been imitated and copied, with several Shanghai-based spin-offs hitting the bookshelves. Even the Maoists couldn't fault them, claiming Holmes as one of their own because he battled evil brought about by capitalist greed and injustice. In addition, as the literary character to appear in more films than any other in the world, Holmes has made the transition to Chinese cinema and television screens smoothly, cropping up in several adaptations. The enthusiasm for him in all his guises is such that the BBC struck a deal with video-hosting service Youku to license it to broadcast the latest British version of *Sherlock*. This goes out with Chinese subtitles just a few hours after the series airs in the UK – soon enough to pre-empt the pirates, but with enough delay for the censors to check it first.

Sherlock Holmes isn't the only survivor from the early days of modern translated fiction in China. The era's utilitarian approach to storytelling seems to have stuck to some extent too. In 2008, for example, an article about the forthcoming publication of a list of China's 300 most influential books of the last thirty years featured the following quote from Nie Zhenning, president of the China Publishing Group Corporation:

> These 300 books provide a broad, deep, and true record of the magnificent surge of history over the 30 Years of Reform and Opening Up [an economic policy introduced by Chinese leader Deng Xiaoping in the 1970s]. They . . . explore 30 years of Sino-Marxist historical progress and fully reflect the deep changes that Chinese society and the Chinese people have gone through over the past 30 years under the leadership of the Chinese Communist Party. They proclaim the achievements of the 30 Years of Reform and Opening Up and the contributions which China has made to the development and progress of human society, thereby provid-ing readers with rich resources regarding the history of the 30 Years of Reform and Opening Up, and adding one more priceless jewel to the cultural treasure-stores of the Chinese nationality.[1]

Such words do not seem a million miles away from the pronouncements of Mao Zedong in his talks on literature and art at the Yan'an Forum in

---

1 Translated by Eric Abrahamsen on paper-republic.org

May 1942. In particular, they recall his assertion that the Chinese people 'must take over all the fine things in our [China's] literary and artistic heritage, critically assimilate whatever is beneficial, and use them as examples when we create works out of the literary and artistic raw materials in the life of the people of our own time and place'. The notion of stories as a utilitarian tool is threaded through China's recent past and seems unlikely to be dispensed with any time soon.

This may be one of the reasons why so little of the nation's literature makes it on to anglophone bookshelves – or indeed the bookshelves of most other language groups. The end-of-year roll call from China-based translation collective Paper Republic, which includes all prose and poetry translated into and published in English anywhere in the world, tells the story succinctly: in 2012 a grand total of twenty Chinese works made it across the language divide, with fourteen following suit in 2013. More are slated for the years to come, but the figures still represent a minuscule proportion of the output of writers in the world's most populous country.

According to translator Nicky Harman, who compiles the register, the didactic element that is still evident in much genre fiction – although not in literary works – often presents a cultural barrier. As a result, publishers who go looking for crime blockbusters by Chinese writers are frequently disappointed. 'Western publishers always think they're going to strike the goldmine,' says Harman. 'They think they're going to find the next Scandi fiction in China and they never do.'

Among the few such novelists to have made it into English is law professor He Jiahong – and his approach is rather different to the David Baldaccis of this world. Explicitly didactic in his approach, the author makes no secret of his desire to teach his readers about evidential law, as he told Harman. Instead of the tortured, world-weary investigators who trudge through the pages of Western contemporary crime fiction, often battling self-doubt, alcoholism, depression or relationship break-downs as well as criminal masterminds, He Jiahong's heroes are relatively faceless. They tend not to get emotionally involved in the

213

cases they deal with, and the crimes rarely present them with moral dilemmas but are instead forensic puzzles to be solved.

The situation is similar with fantasy novels – in which hackneyed scenarios and antediluvian gender stereotypes often jostle with didactic messages – and children's fiction. The latter presents the added challenge of being at once graphically violent and strangely naïve, making pitching it for the correct age group among anglophone readers very difficult. And when it comes to romantic fiction, the moralism hits new heights. Martial arts fiction is the one bright spot, at least as far as genre novels are concerned. Unparalleled in Western literature, these stories involve readers in fast-paced plots packed with monks, assassins, cops and bad guys, and are punctuated with vicious yet balletic fight scenes. Several are slated for publication in Britain, opening up the possibility for a reversal in the one-way transmission of genres that has characterised the relationship of Chinese and anglophone literature over the last hundred years. Who knows? A century from now, a book not so different from this one might be written by a Chinese reader, commenting on the strange mutations of martial arts fiction to be found in the British literary stable and picking out works executed by authors with a peculiarly English take on how the genre functions and what it is for.

*

If differing ideas about what stories are make for some intriguing cultural barriers, things move on to a whole other level when it comes to dealings with the reader in books from elsewhere – especially when we find ourselves faced with books that deliberately set out to tease, bamboozle or confuse. If you thought the works of Thomas Pynchon, Donald Barthelme or Robert Coover were tough to get your head round, try taking on their North African counterparts; they plunge you into a world where you are the butt of jokes you can only guess at because, in addition to the deliberate obfuscation at play in the narrative, your cultural sense is at odds with the world of the story, leaving you flailing for something to grip on to. In these books, the reader is not an esteemed personage sitting in judgement on the narratives – not 'an extension of the author, . . . the higher court that receives the case already prepared by the lower court', in the words of the eighteenth-century German writer Novalis – but rather a miserable stooge bumbling from one misunderstanding to the next without the local savvy to avoid even the most elementary of pitfalls. We are, to quote Ricky Gervais and Stephen Merchant, 'an idiot abroad'.

I first ran up against this in Abdelwahab Meddeb's *Talismano*, a novel built around the narrator's imagined return to Tunis, Fez and the other cities of his youth. Peppered with references to everything from Dante, Hesse and Joyce to the Koran and ancient Egyptian theology, the story, which unfolds over a period of roughly twenty-four hours against a backdrop of streets built half from memory and half from fantasy, makes for a bewildering read. Its complex web of allusions and meandering, labyrinthine plot are particularly tough to deal with – you find yourself confused and angry, and wondering repeatedly whether you are missing something. You feel inadequate and parochial – and if you are new to Tunisian literature you must endure the nagging worry that you don't understand simply because of your ignorance of what is commonplace to people in the nation. Only in the Epilogue does it all finally make sense, when Meddeb, appearing to eschew even grammatical conventions, rounds off the novel's series of knowing commentaries on the author's craft with the most telling piece of all:

> We have confided through writing, but without giving you a foothold, have strained your eyes with our arabesque of words, have recommended the circuits of our journey, have warned you of the fissure in all that meets the eye, have unsettled you on high moral grounds, have ruined you among the most robust constitutions, have dusted myself off, vanished into thin air, have found my way inside you through the least perceptible slit.

It's a sentiment echoed to an almost uncanny extent in Moroccan writer Tahar Ben Jelloun's novel, *The Sand Child*, when, towards the end of the similarly bewildering narrative, the Blind Troubadour says, 'Besides, a book – at least that's how I see it – is a labyrinth created on purpose to confuse men, with the intention of ruining them and bringing them back to the narrow limits of their ambitions.' Here, at last, after nearly 200 pages, foreign readers can reassure themselves that the fiendish difficulty of trying to extract coherent meaning from the narrative is deliberate and not merely a function of their own ignorance of local references. We are meant to be bemused. Just like many postmodern Western works, these stories are spoiling for a fight, bristling in the red corner, just waiting for us to make the mistake of trying to pin them down. They want to break us; to ruin us, no less. It's simply that, coming to the arena without the padding of regional awareness, we are punier and more vulnerable than most.

This cultural defencelessness can make for rather uncomfortable reading when it comes to texts that use confusion like a weapon. Cast in the role of ignorant fools in need of punishment and correction through a sort of literary boot camp designed to shatter assumptions and create a blank foundation on which more lucid thinking can be built, many readers from elsewhere are apt to feel indignant, defeated and ashamed when the efforts of the narratives to wrong-foot them are compounded by their lack of local knowledge. It can be a shocking and enraging experience. As the author sends you off on a twelve-mile hike through dense undergrowth, with only the dull knife of your wit to use to cut your way through, you feel every bit as indignant and defensive as the grumpiest teenager on an outward-bound weekend. This was not what you signed up for when you bought the novel. You are not used to carrying your own body weight in metaphors you can't begin to understand while being deliberately sent down the wrong path. You thought you were broadening your horizons and doing your bit for cross-cultural understanding when you decided to read a story from another country. Doesn't the book know who you are?

However – provided you resist the temptation to abandon the stories altogether – as the pages turn, things begin to look rather different. Wading through their chilly tide of impenetrable allusions, feints and false starts, you may be surprised by the connections and recognitions that flash from them like gems buried in the shifting sand of the seabed. The frustration you feel at not knowing exactly where you are and how the world you are moving through works gives way to a pleasant sense of discovery. Not being able to define, categorise or explain everything is, in a way, liberating: without the need to make sense of it all, you are free to see what strikes you, wandering among the scenes and images of the narratives like a visitor at a bustling bazaar, stopping every now and then to admire a rare treasure mixed in among the knick-knacks on a trader's stall. Much like a traveller coming out of the most acute disorientation/disintegration phase of culture shock, you begin to find your way and adapt to these unfamiliar narratological structures. You learn new manners and that confusion can have a value in its own right, that it is not always something to be apologised for, done away with and hidden as quickly as possible, as we in the Western tradition tend to do. It can be a brave, enriching and fulfilling thing. And, for all the discomfort, jostling and frustration these masters of misdirection put you through, when you reach the end of the road and look back along the route you've travelled, you get one hell of a view.

10

Finding myself

representations of the West in books around the world

'You British always pride yourselves on playing cricket and being fair. But deep down, you're all racists to the bone.'

The words stood out starkly on the page, like a warning. I tried to fence them back into the safe 'not-real' space of the story, but they would not be contained. They waited there, as if for a response, as if, of all the words written on the 300 pages or so of that book, they had found the wormhole through from make-believe to real. They bothered me and I wanted to work out why.

In many ways, the sentiment was not a surprise in the context of Suchen Christine Lim's novel, *Fistful of Colours*. Tracing the British colonial legacy and the impact of waves of Chinese, Malaysian and Indian immigrants on Singapore over the last few centuries, the book buzzed with questions of identity, justice, prejudice and influence. I'd smiled in recognition and even chuckled at some of the jibes at the failings of my compatriots in other parts of the narrative – references to the 'patronising asses from the British Council', for example, and the generations of 'English-educated malcontents' churned out by Western-style schools. All the same, this was different. I couldn't laugh this off. There was something too direct about the statement. Even if the words were a vehicle for protagonist Suwen's frustration at her perpetually stalled love affair with Scottish colleague Mark, there was a bitterness and anger behind them that seemed to make them throb on the page. They wanted my attention. They refused to be ignored. No doubt I was being paranoid, but I couldn't help wondering if Rafidah, the woman who had chosen the book and posted it to me from the other side of the world, had picked it out on the strength of these two lines, as if to send me a direct message. It was most unsettling.

My brain began to perform a series of awkward manoeuvres. Unable to consign the statement to the witticism and irony drawer outright, I set about attempting a series of contortions whereby I could read the sentences in the context of the story and yet get round having to deal with their implications. All right, so Suwen had claimed to be referring to 'all' British people, but she surely couldn't mean that. Not all. All was a very broad statement. In fact, thinking about it, wasn't 'all' somewhat racist in itself? Precisely the sort of generalisation that had riled Suwen in the first place. It was a slip of the keyboard; it had to be. Perhaps Lim, an English-language author, had meant to write 'many of you' – admittedly not as rhythmically compelling, but surely nearer the mark. Maybe she meant football hooligans. Or BNP supporters. Or the people who stalked around in bovver boots with St George's crosses tattooed on their bald heads. Now she might well be on to something there. That sort of British person could probably very safely be lumped in the 'racist' category (except for the ones who weren't, of course. Because the whole point about not being racist was that you didn't judge a book by its cover – even when it was coming at you, belching the National Anthem, with 'HATE' inked on its fists). At any rate, Suwen couldn't seriously mean 'all' Brits were racist. Not the cultured ones, surely? Not people who read widely enough to access Lim's book in the first place. Not . . . me.

*

Those of us who were born into and grew up in Western Europe and North America's majority communities have, from a young age, been surrounded by powerful stories about who we are, and how the rest of the world fits in with that. These narratives, which come to us, often unchallenged, by way of the news stories we hear, the advertising campaigns we consume and – yes – many of the books we read, have varying degrees of Western bias, but, as Palestinian-American critic

Edward Said argued in his influential book *Culture and Imperialism*, they work collectively to reinforce 'the belief that European [and by extension US] pre-eminence is natural'. And these stories have deep foundations. For centuries, Western European writers and thinkers have been asserting their nations' role in and right to international governance. In 1910, erstwhile British prime minister Arthur James Balfour pronounced to the Houses of Parliament that it was better that the UK ruled Egypt because 'Western nations as soon as they emerge into history show the beginnings of those capacities for self-government . . . having merits of their own', whereas 'you may look through the whole history of the Orientals in what is called, broadly speaking, the East, and you never find traces of self-government' (perhaps he was in the school sanatorium the day they studied the Pharaohs). The same year as Balfour set out his stall for keeping the Egyptians in their place, the French explorer, diplomat and doctor Jules Harmand put forward his view that 'there is a hierarchy of races and civilizations, and that we belong to the superior race and civilization', a fact that, he claimed, 'underlies our right to direct the rest of humanity'. Even that nineteenth-century champion of Jeremy Bentham's utilitarian ideal of the greatest happiness for the greatest number, John Stuart Mill, saw no issue with exploiting people in faraway places for national gain, as he explained in his 1848 book, *Principles of Political Economy*:

> These [territories] are hardly to be looked upon as countries . . . but more properly as outlying agricultural or manufacturing estates belonging to a larger community. Our West Indian colonies, for example, cannot be regarded as countries with a productive capital of their own [. . . but are rather] the place where England finds it convenient to carry on the production of sugar, coffee and a few other tropical commodities.

The reasons these men of influence thought so little of the people unlucky enough to live in the territories upon which they had designs become clear when you look at the information they had to go on. According to many of the accounts circulating in the heyday of empire, following the European nations' 'scramble for Africa' in the late nineteenth century, the occupants of distant territories were a disreputable bunch. Sometime governor of Hong Kong, John Bowring, for example, painted a picture as ludicrous as it is dubious of the sort of character you might run into in the colonies, in his 1859 account of *A Visit to the Philippine Islands*:

> It has been said of the Indian that he is more of a quadruped than a biped. His hands are large, and the toes of his feet pliant, being exercised in climbing trees, and divers other active functions. He is almost amphibious, spending much of his time in the water. He is insensible alike to the burning sun and the drenching rain. The impressions made upon him are transitory, and he retains a feeble memory of passing or past events. Ask him his age, he will not be able to answer: who were his ancestors? he neither knows nor cares. He receives no favours and cannot, therefore, be ungrateful; has little ambition, and therefore little disquiet; few wants, and hence is neither jealous nor envious; does not concern himself with the affairs of his neighbour, nor indeed does he pay much regard to his own. His master vice is idleness, which is his felicity. The labour that necessity demands he gives grudgingly.

Poor, dear, ugly, bumbling locals, anyone without first-hand experience or access to contrasting accounts of the people in question may well have been inclined to think. They were practically animals, by the sound of it. Thank goodness they had sharp-minded Europeans to make decisions for them and lick them into shape. Just as well the earth's colonial masters were there to keep them in check. Otherwise heaven knows what they might get up to.

And keep them in check the Europeans did. So persuasive and pervasive was the rhetoric surrounding those in the northern hemisphere's right to rule, that by 1914 European empires accounted for around

85 per cent of the earth's territory. For Britain, it was the culmination of a tradition of managing the affairs of others that stretched over some 800 years, back through the colonisation of the Americas to the 1150s, when Ireland was ceded to King Henry II by the Pope. Britain and some of its European neighbours could rule the world because they had done so for so long that it was as if they had always been in charge. Empire was simply the way things were done. And because it was the way things were done, it had to be the way things were supposed to be. 'Hail happy Britain! Highly favoured isle,/ And Heaven's peculiar care!' wrote William Somerville in 1735, in his most famous poem, 'The Chace'. The implication was clear: Britain was in charge of things because God ordained it so. 'We shall run the world's business whether the world likes it or not. The world can't help it and neither can we, I guess,' as Holroyd, the American financier who backs British mine owner Charles Gould in Joseph Conrad's *Nostromo* (1904), puts it. In other words, the West produced born rulers. It was their place to be in charge just as it was others' place to be subordinate. It was their right – nay, their duty – to show the rest of the world the way.

In possession of the divine mandate to govern and many other 'honest prejudices which naturally cleave to the heart of a true English-man', in the words of the *Spectator* founder Joseph Addison, Britain and her European peers wasted no time in disposing of their colonial posses-sions as they saw fit. Just like Adam in the Garden of Eden, given the power to express his dominion over the animal kingdom by naming the beasts, the world's rulers set out to define, describe and categorise their territories and subjects – subjects who, by virtue of being subordinate, could never be the equals of those in charge. They sent back reams of observations and data, and books on everything, from the twenty-year-long *Description de l'Égypte* series, featuring the findings of around 160 scholars and scientists who accompanied Napoleon's expedition to Egypt, to Flaubert's historical novel *Salammbô* and Richard Burton's *Personal Narrative of a Pilgrimage to Al-Madinah and Meccah*. Though many of these were written with the honest intention of delineating and sharing knowledge about hitherto unknown parts of the world – and some did so admirably – they couldn't help but be influenced and directed by the prevailing rhetoric of European supremacy and non-white subjection. As in Bowring's account, many of them employed zoological descriptions and animal comparisons when it came to writing about the inhabitants of other parts of the world, and all were built on the belief that these societies could not be nearly as rich, complex or successful as those back home. For British historian Basil Davidson, who conducted a survey of writing on Africa up until the mid-twentieth century, the observation behind such accounts was, without exception, 'circumscribed within a cramping limit' – and that limit was the belief that it was the prerogative of one group of people to rule everyone else.

Even writers who stayed at home worked to shore up this narrative. As Edward Said showed in *Culture and Imperialism*, many of the great British novelists of the nineteenth and early twentieth century reflect the tenets of domination whether they appear to be writing about the empire or not. From Sir Thomas Bertram's Antiguan plantations in *Mansfield Park* to the violently insane Bertha Rochester from Spanish Town, Jamaica, the colonies presented an abundant stock of shadowy, two-dimensional and often less-than-human figures and situations that authors could plunder for plot twists, without appearing to think anything of it. In fact, as Said wrote, one of the 'difficult truths' he encountered in his research was how few of the British and French artists he admired took issue with the notion of 'subject' or 'inferior' races in their work. Even those, like Conrad, who tackled the subject directly, were unable to step far enough outside their own heads to imagine a workable alternative to the status quo:

He writes as a man whose *Western* view of the non-Western world is so ingrained as to blind him to other histories, other cultures, other aspirations. All Conrad can see is a world totally dominated by the Atlantic West, in which every opposition to the West only confirms the West's wicked power. What Conrad cannot see is an alternative to this cruel tautology. He could neither understand that India, Africa and South America also had lives and cultures with integrities not totally controlled by the gringo imperialists and reformers of this world, nor allow himself to believe that anti-imperialist independence movements were not all corrupt and in the pay of puppet-masters in London or Washington.

This blinkered attitude to the issue of domination did not, in Said's view, undermine the 'massive strengths' of the novels, but their 'inherent limitations' did reveal something of the mechanisms by which power imbalances are established and maintained because, traditionally, 'representation itself has been characterized as keeping the subordinate subordinate, the inferior inferior'. The cumulative effect of book after book of flat, marginal, vagrant, voiceless characters from mysterious, distant lands can be every bit as powerful as the most compelling bit of oratory. Such stories can inculcate in us the habit of thinking of others as less than ourselves, and therefore deserving, or perhaps in need of, our control. Even in the wake of two decades' more scholarship into world literature, Said's observations are a warning against the complacency of conflating books by Western writers 'set' in countries with literature 'from' particular places, as many of those engaged in round-the-world reading adventures sometimes do in the absence of anything more *echt* in the bookshops. Fascinating and gripping though such works might be – packed with insights into human life as many of them are – they are the latest in a long line of stories that have imagined reality elsewhere in Western terms. They are the youngest generation of books working to make not just one little room but one little world – our world – an everywhere. And they need to be read as such.

However, lest we think that tackling works by writers from other countries might on its own be enough to counteract the 'misleading self-satisfaction' that a diet rich in such narratives might nurture, it's worth remembering that imperialism can lurk in the act of reading too.

Speaking to the Houses of Parliament in September 1909, for instance, Viceroy of India Lord Curzon, who is recognised for championing social reform and justice in the subcontinent, advocated the study of Eastern art, history, traditions and religion because, as he saw it, this was 'the sole basis upon which we are likely to be able to maintain in the future the position we have won'. It was a subject he returned to five years later when the establishment of what was to become the University of London's School of Oriental and African Studies came up in a debate at Mansion House:

> In my view the creation of a school like this in London is part of the necessary furniture of Empire. Those of us who, in one way or another, have spent a number of years in the East, who regard that as the happiest portion of our lives, and who think that the work we did there, be it great or small, was the highest responsibility that can be placed upon the shoulders of Englishmen, feel that there is a gap in our national equipment which ought emphatically to be filled, and that those in the City of London who, by financial support or by any other form of active and practical assistance, take their part in filling that gap, will be rendering a patriotic duty to the Empire and promoting the cause and goodwill among mankind.

For a certain breed of imperialist, it seems, reading the world can itself be a means of keeping it under control. And who's to say that this book and the project behind it aren't a continuation of that tradition every bit as much as they are an attempt to continue the global conversation advocated by Goethe some eighty years before Curzon's statements? Undertaken in the same spirit as the expeditions of the nineteenth-century explorers my quest was arguably an attempt not just to understand the world, but also to make it mine.

*

When Helga Schneider received a letter in 1998 asking her to visit her ninety-year-old mother, Traudi, before she died, she was thrown into a quandary. Not having seen the woman for twenty-seven years, she wasn't sure she could face making the trip to the old people's home Traudi lived in near Vienna. There was a good reason for Schneider's reluctance: the last time she had seen her, her mother had asked her to try on her old SS uniform and had attempted to give her a handful of gold stolen from the Jewish victims she had been responsible for gassing at Auschwitz-Birkenau. What followed on from the letter was an extraordinary and chilling encounter that formed the subject of Schneider's best-selling book *Let Me Go: My Mother and the SS*. In it, the writer describes her visit to see Traudi and the chess game of denial and horrifying revelations that ensued as she talked to the by turns steely, vulnerable and confused elderly woman about the past and watched her 'trying to explain the inexplicable'.

Although she hadn't been brought up by her mother (Traudi left to join Heinrich Himmler's organisation when her daughter was four and the pair did not see each other again until thirty years later when Traudi was in her sixties), Schneider found her life marked by being 'the ex-Nazi's daughter'. In the book she describes being confronted by a concentration camp survivor, for whom she was a symbol of hate. Such was the weight of her mother's past – for which Traudi served several years in prison – that Schneider did everything she could to distance herself from it, moving to Italy and 'denying [her] mother tongue' so that her German became halting and rusty with disuse. Written largely in the second person and addressed to Traudi, even the narrative seems to want to deny itself: 'I look at you, mother, and I feel a terrible, lacerating rift within me – between the instinctive attraction for my own blood and the irrevocable rejection of what you have been, of what you still are.' The genetic bond compels her to stay, however, and, driven by what she describes as a 'demon', Schneider asks her mother question after question about her life as an extermination camp guard until the horrible details of her role are laid bare: they included separating women from children too young to work, cremating gas chamber victims, some of whom may still have been alive, and readying human guinea pigs for medical experiments. Over the course of the conversation, we see the effects of the Nazis' dehumanisation training in full force, as Traudi explains how it is possible to hate to order 'if you are convinced of the reasons' and resolutely insists that the Final Solution was right because the Jews were guilty 'of everything. Of Germany's defeat in the First World War, of constant defeatism towards Germany, of international conspiracies to unleash fresh conflict.' In the closing moments of their encounter, the frail woman sums up her motivation for the crimes she committed: 'I believed in Germany's mission: to free Europe from that . . . from that repugnant race.'

Shocking though Schneider's account is, it is by no means unique. In the decades since the end of the Second World War, bookshelves have groaned under the weight of novels and memoirs dedicated to portraying and processing the atrocities that took place in the name of National Socialism. From stories of underground resistance work, such as Jan Petersen's *Our Street*, to soul-searching explorations of guilt by association like Schneider's, the body of German work relating to the events of the Holocaust is formidable. It continues to inform conceptions of German identity today – so much so that in 2008, *New York Times* journalist Joseph Berger wrote a feature about a programme run by the German School in White Plains, New York, designed to help its pupils face up to the legacy of their forebears without their having 'to go through life ashamed of being German'. Indeed, the notion of war-related guilt is so widespread and familiar that it has even become a joke – with examples including Basil Fawlty's paranoia about referring to the Second World War and figures such as Harry Enfield's 1990s comic character Jürgen the German, who feels he must apologise for his country's behaviour everywhere he goes.

Comparing the British Empire to the Third Reich might seem more than a bit of a stretch to many of us; after all, the liberal driving principle, articulated in 1766 by member of parliament and philosopher Edmund Burke, that 'the British Empire must be governed on a plan of freedom, for it will be governed by no other' is a far cry from Hitler's Nazi ideology.

Nevertheless, this is a parallel that commentators in other parts of the planet have reached for in relation to some aspects of the world's largest-ever empire. In 1964, for example, an announcer on Accra's home service in English stated that 'Western imperialists . . . are the economic next-of-kin to Hitler'. Three years earlier, the leading revolutionary writer and psychiatrist Frantz Fanon had made a similar point in his rallying cry to the world's colonised peoples, *The Wretched of the Earth*:

> Not long ago Nazism transformed the whole of Europe into a veritable colony. The governments of the various European nations called for reparations and demanded the restitution in kind and money of the wealth which had been stolen from them . . . There was only one slogan in the mouths of Europeans on the morrow of the 1945 V-day: 'Germany must pay.' . . .
>
> In the same way we may say that the imperialist states would make a great mistake and commit an unspeakable injustice if they contented themselves with withdrawing from our soil the military cohorts, and the administrative and managerial services whose function it was to discover the wealth of the country, to extract it and send it off to the mother countries. We are not blinded by the moral reparation of national independence; nor are we fed by it. The wealth of the imperial countries is our wealth too . . . From all these continents, under whose eyes Europe today raises up her tower of opulence, there has flowed out for centuries towards that same Europe diamonds and oil, silk and cotton, wood and exotic products. Europe is literally the creation of the Third World.

It's a sentiment that Guinea-Bissauan independence campaigner Amílcar Cabral illustrated neatly when he observed in his 1960 essay on 'The Facts About Portugal's African Colonies' that 'the setting up of each European family costs Angola one million escudos. For an African peasant family to earn that much money, it would have to live for a thousand years and work every year without stopping.'

Though the ostensible aims of Europe's global empires were nowhere near as stark as those that motivated Helga Schneider's mother and her fellow Nazis – and the technological, legal and social reforms and innovations Western Europeans introduced to much of the world no doubt brought some benefits – their consequences shared more than a passing resemblance in the eyes of many of the people who had to live through them. To Fanon and the many activists who drew inspiration from his words, their erstwhile rulers were 'like nothing more than war criminals', who had created a Manichean 'world cut in two', and who, in order for humanity to move forward, 'must first decide to wake up and shake themselves, use their brains, and stop playing the stupid game of Sleeping Beauty'. This, as Jean-Paul Sartre put it in his Foreword to Fanon's book, involves accepting that to be a European 'is to be an accomplice of colonialism, since all of us without exception have profited by colonial exploitation'. 'You, who are so liberal and humane,' wrote the philosopher, seeming to lean out from the text to take us by the shoulders and do some of Fanon's shaking in advance, 'who have such an exaggerated adoration of culture that it verges on affectation, you pretend to forget that you own colonies and that in them men are massacred in your name.'

In the more than fifty years since *The Wretched of the Earth* came out, however, there has been precious little sifting of the colonial experience in Western literature. By contrast to the reams of German reflections on the Holocaust, the bestseller racks in the UK have little to offer when it comes to accounts of the darker side of Britain's world domination. The children or grandchildren of the men who opened fire on the crowd during the Amritsar Massacre of 1919 have written few memoirs trying to reconcile their abhorrence at the slaughter of unarmed people with their sense of family loyalty. We don't find haunting, morally conflicted novels about Churchill's decision to refuse shipping to transport rice from Burma to India, thereby condemning more than a million Bengalis to starve in the famine of 1943. There are no troubled fictional accounts of young soldiers forced to oversee the mutilation and murder of Kikuyu detainees in the British concentration camps during the Mau Mau Uprising of the 1950s – indeed the UK government only got around to paying compensation to survivors of the torture in 2013. For those of us in the UK, it is as though, because these terrible acts took place far away from British soil, they were committed by other people, different sorts of Britons with whom we can't be lumped together. Not us. Not me.

If anything, rather than being ashamed of some of the things that have been done in the name of our nation, some seem to be rather wistful for the days of empire. As Said stated in *Culture and Imperialism*, 'many people in England probably feel a certain remorse or regret about their nation's Indian experience, but there are also many people who miss the good old days'. He's not wrong. When the subject of the British Empire came up at a social gathering I attended recently, I found myself collared by a rather indignant, self-dubbed 'empire boy' – who was only a decade or so older than me, but whose father and grandfather had served in Hong Kong until its sovereignty was transferred to China in 1997. He informed me that the administration had been excellent, that criticism of the empire was out of proportion to the facts, and that whenever he and his relatives visited the ex-colony they were beset by people asking them when Britain was going to take it back. Perhaps he is right in the case of Hong Kong, where officials did much to end foot-binding and infanticide. Perhaps his relatives were some of the many individuals who reportedly forged meaningful friendships and brought about positive change over the centuries of Britain's rule around the world. Or perhaps politeness, humour, irony or sarcasm don't translate very easily. At any rate, as I reassured him that I could well believe that his grandfather and father were very good at their no doubt useful and well-intentioned jobs, I couldn't help wondering at his unwillingness to acknowledge what British academic Piers Brendon has described as the 'chaotic mixture of black and red' on the moral balance sheet of the British Empire – a balance sheet Brendon ultimately declares as being 'in grave moral deficit' because, regardless of the good it did, in the words of eighteenth-century historian Edward Gibbon, 'a more unjust and absurd constitution cannot be devised than that which condemns the natives of a country to perpetual servitude, under the arbitrary dominion of strangers'. I was also struck by my interlocutor's certainty that what he saw as an endorsement of British rule wasn't simply an expression of regret at Hong Kong's current circumstances. Here, surely, was an example of what Said identified as 'that weighty, almost philosophical sense of imperial mission that one finds in Britain'.

These days, one finds it on the other side of the Atlantic too. The empires may have largely dissolved and the flags been packed away, but the sense of entitlement to direct the affairs of the rest of the globe seems to remain in many Western hearts and minds. With America having assumed the role of world superpower in the mid-twentieth century, it's the US that leads the charge, as Institute for Policy Studies co-founder Richard Barnet explained in his 1972 book *Roots of War*:

> Thus the United States sets rules for Soviet behavior in Cuba, Brazilian behavior in Brazil, Vietnamese behavior in Vietnam . . . Cicero's definition of the early Roman empire was remarkably similar. It was the domain over which Rome enjoyed the legal right to enforce the law. Today, America's self-appointed writ runs throughout the world . . . The United States, uniquely blessed with surpassing riches and an exceptional history, stands above the international system, not within it. Supreme among nations, she stands ready to be the bearer of the Law.

This sense of entitlement to rule is evident in the repeated interventions that America, Britain and their allies have made in nations around the globe – actions that took place in some form every year from 1945, according to Barnet, until he gave up counting in 1967. More recently, it has been shown by the highfalutin speeches about foxholes and smoking people out that characterised the George W. Bush administration, and in the filmic news reports of the Iraqi and Afghan invasions:

'Showdown Iraq,' proclaimed the TV news banners when I was in the US the year after September 11, as though the conflict would be a tale of goodies versus baddies as satisfying as any classic Western. At the other end of the scale, the construction and maintenance of the image of the Anglo-American ruler-hero also feeds on the perceived weakness and neediness of those in different parts of the world – as represented by the simplistic charity appeals and news reports that so often reduce people in other places to pitiful, two-dimensional portraits of need.

Easy though it is to pick holes, none of us stands outside this way of thinking. Even when we try consciously to free ourselves of colonial bias, it can creep into our words, betraying our prejudices as we deny them. The 2008 Lionel Gelber Prize-winning book *The Bottom Billion* by Paul Collier, Oxford University professor of economics and former director of development research at the World Bank, is a case in point. Written to address the question of why people in fifty or so of the world's states remain poor while the rest of the globe gets richer, it sets out to identify the causes of and solutions to the problem. Collier, who reveals in his Preface that his interest in such issues began when the 'colonial connections' of some of his friends at university in the 1960s 'rubbed off' on him, insists that 'change is going to have to come from within the societies of the bottom billion' and states his intention to take the reader 'beyond the images' of deprived societies that clog our media reports and fetter our thought processes. Yet, time and again his words turn against his intentions. Take this sentence for example:

> We cannot make poverty history unless the countries of the bottom billion start to grow, and they will not grow by turning them into Cuba.

All of a sudden, in the closing words of the statement, an agent emerges from the undergrowth. The inclusive, global 'we' of the start of the sentence shatters and the countries Collier insists must take ownership of their future shrink once more and become passive in the face of an external force with the power to turn them into Cuba if it chooses (or not). It's a small thing and yet the story of why any of us thinks the way we do is made up of the drip, drip exposure of our minds to unconscious habits of thought. Such unexamined semantic shapes carve out the paths along which our thoughts run. They go a long way to explain why whoever wrote the blurb for *The Bottom Billion* felt justified in hurling the question, 'Why do these states defy all attempts to help them?' into its first paragraph: in his or her mind these nations were still, on some level, recalcitrant children huddled under the skirts of Mother Empire, in need of guidance and correction.

In the face of such a bulwark of assumptions stretching throughout Western culture and discourse, it has often been left to writers from elsewhere to assert their identity and humanity and that of their compatriots in the space that independence cleared. This may come in the form of devastating portraits of cruelty, such as writer Jorge Icaza's *Huasipungo*, which depicts the exploitation of Ecuador's indigenous population by the white descendants of the Spanish administration that relinquished its hold on the nation in the nineteenth century. It may take the shape of portraits of psychological breakdown as protagonists internalise the political struggles gripping their nation, as in Donato Ndongo's *Shadows of Your Black Memory*, a book set during the year before independence in Equatorial Guinea, and the first novel from the country to be made commercially available in English. In the case of narratives from nations that have emerged from British rule in the last 100 years, education often provides a key theme or backdrop. Gheysika Adombire Agambila's *Journey* and John Saunana's *The Alternative*, for example, use the setting of English-style boarding schools to play out the impact of the imperial legacy on their characters, capturing the conflict that sees them at once coveting and despising the administration that has shaped their societies irrevocably – in Saunana's work, the protagonist Maduru even unionises his fellow pupils at a school dubbed the 'Eton of the Pacific' to get a teacher removed, enacting the national drama facing the Solomon Islands on a smaller stage. Such novels are

233

interesting because they reflect the somewhat paternalistic rhetoric often used by British politicians during the age of empire that was indicative of the underlying assumption that, in the words of the British controller-general in Egypt, Lord Cromer, 'these people . . . are all, nationally speaking, more or less *in statu pupillari*'. At once using the former rulers' favoured metaphor of the teacher–pupil relationship against them, and yet colluding in and perpetuating it too, these narratives encapsulate the effect of decades of control by outsiders whose power rested on diminishing those they subjugated.

For other writers, Western narratives themselves become the prism through which to diffract the rays of imperialism. Joseph Conrad's famous and problematic *Heart of Darkness* has been the vehicle for several retellings that seek to redraw the relationship of ruled and ruler on the world map: novels such as Ngũgĩ wa Thiong'o's *The River Between* and Tayeb Salih's *Season of Migration to the North*, the central character of which, Mustafa Sa'eed, is a 'mirror image' of Conrad's Kurtz, according to Edward Said. There are also books that reverse the polarisation process, turning Westerners into the same ominous, two-dimensional 'Other' that lurks in the margins of much European writing. In Jordanian-born Abdelrahman Munif's *Cities of Salt*, the American oil prospectors who arrive with a host of unknown practices, machines and mores remain sinister, distant and sometimes ridiculous figures throughout – insensitive and inscrutable beings who strip off and perform strange physical jerks in the sun regardless of propriety, and rip up trees and houses that stand in their way without pause or reflection.

In some books, particularly those aimed at a global audience, authors temper their discussion of the ills of imperialism with the presence of a go-between. Often a disaffected young Westerner (perhaps in the mould of the malcontents Suwen describes as being churned out by the English education system in Suchen Christine Lim's *Fistful of Colours*), this character acts as a processing centre for some of the negative experiences portrayed, usually learning any lessons the author hopes his or her reader might glean from the book. Examples include Martin Pearce, a nineteenth-century English explorer and self-confessed aspiring 'Orientalist' who stumbles out of the desert in Abdulrazak Gurnah's *Desertion*. He is cared for by a shopkeeper in Mombasa until the hard-hearted district officer Frederick Turner appears, to accuse 'these dark unfamiliar people that he felt inexplicably angry with' of robbing the man and bears Pearce off to his comfortable home. The state-of-the-empire conversations that ensue between Turner, Pearce and local estate manager Burton – who believes that the future for British terri-tories in Africa is the 'gradual decline and disappearance of the African population, and its replacement by European settlers' – allow Gurnah scope to air the racist ideology that drives the officials without falling into the trap of tarring all Englishmen with the same brush, by virtue of Pearce's, albeit restrained, dissent. 'I think in time we'll come to see what we're doing in places like these less heroically,' says Pearce, when pressed for a view by the others. 'I think we'll come to see ourselves less charmingly. I think in time we'll come to be ashamed of some of the things we have done.' Although it seems doubtful that most people would dare to articulate even such mild reservations in the context in question, figures such as Pearce are by no means mere fanciful devices. In addition to sweetening the pill of the bitter realities portrayed in these narratives for Western readers, they represent the bubbling dissent that lay just below the surface for many of those working the levers of the colonial machine. As George Orwell points out in *The Road to Wigan Pier*, the fact of the UK's relatively benign dominion over nearly a quarter of the earth was not enough to quell the pangs of conscience for some of those charged with enforcing its rule:

> All over India there are Englishmen who secretly loathe the system of which they are a part; and just occasionally, when they are quite certain of being in the right company, their hidden bitterness overflows. I remember a night I spent on a train with a man in the Educational Service, a stranger to myself whose name I never discovered. It was too hot to sleep and we spent

the night talking. Half an hour's cautious questioning decided each of us that the other was 'safe'; and then for hours, while the train jolted slowly through the pitch-black night, sitting up in our bunks with bottles of beer handy, we damned the British Empire – damned it from the inside, intelligently and intimately. It did us both good. But we had spoken forbidden things, and in the haggard morning light when the train crawled into Mandalay, we parted as guiltily as any adulterous couple.

Yet although such illicit dissent may have been present in the hearts of a number of colonial officials, it was by no means the rule. Indeed, for some writers around the planet, the desire to present events in an even-handed – and Western-reader-friendly – manner can lead to a softening of people and circumstances beyond the scope of historical fact. Such was the situation that Abdulaziz Al Mahmoud found himself faced with when he began work on his novel *The Corsair*. Prompted by his chance discovery of *Coast of Pirates*, a book by a nineteenth-century British officer about efforts to protect the trade routes in the Persian Gulf and the enigmatic pirate leader Erhama bin Jaber, Al Mahmoud, a former engineer and erstwhile editor of aljazeera.net, Alsharq and *The Peninsula*, began to research the region's history. Having worked his way through many of the English-language documents relating to the period as well as Arabic records, including a number held in a private library in Saudi Arabia, he decided to write a novel to share his findings with his compatriots and set about constructing a complex plot moving between characters in Plymouth, Bombay, Bahrain, Qatar, Madeira and many places in between.

To achieve a compelling story, Al Mahmoud found that he had to play around with some of the details. This was especially true in the case of the character Major George Sadleir, who is sent to the Gulf to safeguard the transport of British cargo by diplomacy or military action. Although none of the parties in the novel is innocent of corruption and underhand dealing, the British officers emerge as among the worst – welshing on deals, commissioning murder, and executing local informants when they are no longer useful. Sadleir is the exception to this, looking on his compatriots' cruelty with sadness and forming a nascent friendship with Erhama bin Jaber's son, Bashir, who strikes at the root of the conflict in the novel when he tells Sadleir, 'You would think differently if this land was your land and if these people were your people.'

In reality, Sadleir was nowhere near as likeable as he is made to seem by Al Mahmoud, who purposefully wrote the novel in simple Arabic with an eye to translation – a strategy which paid off when, in 2012, *The Corsair* became the first Qatari novel to be translated into English. On his return from the Arabian Peninsula, the real-life Sadleir published his *Diary of a Journey Across Arabia* (1819), in which he expressed hatred for and disgust at the people he had encountered on his travels.

'I made him sympathetic because I couldn't make everyone bad,' Al Mahmoud told me. 'In real life he was so bad, really. But just imagine: put yourself in his shoes. How do you deal with people you think are dirty and barbaric?'

For Al Mahmoud, this question is not purely academic. While working as an engineer for the Qatar Emiri Air Force, he attended a number of training courses at airbases in the UK. These usually involved him learning alongside British personnel, an experience that gave him an insight into some of those in the military. One encounter, during an exercise involving army officers at RAF Cranwell, stuck in his mind. Having offered a tissue to a soldier who sneezed, Al Mahmoud was greeted with a surprising response. 'He said: "Thank you very much. You know, my people hate you, but I won't do that anymore." Really! I swear to God! I laughed.'

For all Al Mahmoud's amusement at the memory, however, I found it hard to laugh with him. Mortified at my compatriot's words, I hurried to express my shock and outrage at the anecdote and launched into a tirade against the evils of the British Empire, some of which Al Mahmoud had depicted so deftly in his book.

The author, however, was unimpressed by my attempts to cast my nation as the villain of the world – and of his stories. Only the day before we spoke he had signed a contract for his second novel, another historical work, this time focusing on the period in the early sixteenth century when the Portuguese invaded Bahrain and embarked on numerous battles in the Persian Gulf. His research had turned up some striking material: 'I found out that the Portuguese committed so many atrocities. I took that from their own archive. And the way they described the atrocities, as if they were doing it for the sake of God – it's unbelievable! If you compare them with the British, the British didn't disrupt people's lives. They normally dealt with the tribal leaders of this region. They wanted to protect the trade route. It's just the opposite of what the Portuguese were trying to do. So the British were not looked at as real enemies that needed to be fought. It was not that positive. But not as bad as the Portuguese – or the Dutch!'

Neither saviour nor arch-villain, Britain is just one of many influences Al Mahmoud marshals to create his stories. The key point is not that 'in the past we [the Western world] made history and now it is being made of us', as Sartre wrote in his Foreword to *The Wretched of the Earth*, but that history is being made of other things entirely – events in which we may not figure at all. Narratives that are coming into our orbit are recasting the roles and adjusting the lighting and direction. The account of the world as English-language speakers can access it is shifting ground: the powerful play is going on, and it is no longer all about us.

*

In the 1986 global hit film *Crocodile Dundee*, bushman Mick Dundee leaves Australia for the first time to visit New York as part of research for a series of articles by American reporter Sue Charlton. Showing him around his luxurious suite in Manhattan, Charlton points out the television in the corner. Dundee, however, is unimpressed: when he switches on the machine, it is playing a repeat of the black-and-white classic American sitcom *I Love Lucy*, the same programme he saw when someone showed him television years before in Australia.

Popular culture is so ubiquitous and homogeneous that it's a joke. From Alice Springs to Zanzibar, you can get hold of a lot of the same music, TV and books. As a result, one of the issues frequently aired when the subject of globalisation comes up is the concern that with increased cultural exchange – particularly Western culture, as discussed in chapter five – across national borders, we will lose our individuality. Instead of being a series of distinct and interesting communities, we will become indistinguishable as our differences shrink with every passing year until at last we inhabit a single, quasi-American hybrid world with about as much character as a bus station. As Edward Said wrote in his 2003 Preface to *Orientalism*, the fear is that 'we may be approaching the kind of standardization and homogeneity that Goethe's ideas were specifically formulated to prevent'. And at its most extreme, the pervasiveness of Western culture can even seem to be an extension of the imperial control wielded by previous generations, a way of colonising and shaping the 'empires of the mind' that Churchill predicted would loom large in our lives.

It's a worry that many writers around the planet seem to share, with numerous recent novels featuring nightmarish, globalised characters who move from place to place without ever seeming to engage or connect with specific situations – and who often leave a trail of havoc in their wake. There are the NGO workers in Sunethra Rajakarunanayake's 2008 novel *Metta*, for example, who spend their lives travelling from disaster zone to disaster zone, inoculated against the grief they witness by virtue of their peripatetic existences. 'They don't feel the pain of our injuries because they have already seen too much pain in the places they have been,' muses a Sri Lankan character, Sasha, before urging one of the young women not to remain in her job too long because she'll 'never be able to return to a normal life'. Yet more damningly, there are characters like the beautiful Victoria de Winter (very possibly a literary relation of du Maurier's dark creation) in French novelist Éric Reinhardt's *The Victoria System*. As head of HR for a massive multinational company, Victoria compartmentalises her jet-set life to such an extent that it ends up destroying her and those who believe they have her love, as described by the novel's narrator, serial adulterer David Kolski:

By moving around, you're able to hedge your bets. You can forget things more easily, erasing from your mind any evil you've committed or any promises you've made. If the people who ran the world were not always moving so fast (whether geographically or mentally), they would see the stark truth of what they were doing, and they wouldn't be able to bear it.

Yet, while the pervasiveness of Anglo-American culture is undeniable in most parts of the globe, it is by no means true that this is forcing all writers to standardise – or that the influence is working in one direction only. Though lack of translation opportunities has prompted some authors to try to play Westerners at their own game by writing in English and aping popular genres, the ubiquity of anglophone culture has generally had much more varied effects. In many places, far from being the gold standard, English-language cultural products are more like bric-a-brac for writers to appropriate for their own ends. Instead of being inexorable forces riding roughshod over local distinctiveness, Western influences can become fair game for authors to manipulate and twist at will. The Kinks, *Reservoir Dogs*, Elvis Presley, Daniel Defoe, J.D. Salinger and Shakespeare (along with many others) are playthings for Bulgarian writer Georgi Gospodinov in his book *Natural Novel*, often with startling results. It is as though, by virtue of its ubiquity, Anglo-American culture has become a sort of debased currency, available by the wheelbarrow-load for anyone to use for what it's worth. In the words of Seneca, tutor and adviser to Nero, ruler of one of the world's other once-great empires, 'Everywhere is nowhere. When a person spends all his time in foreign travel, he ends by having many acquaintances, but no friends.'

The same could be said of cultural products. A case in point is *Sex and the City*, probably one of the most widely watched programmes in the world of recent years (it was the most-cited Western creation in the books I read during my project, along with IKEA). It is sometimes represented as a surprising symbol of emancipation for women in repressive societies; however, the flip side of its popularity is that it and the myriad other Anglo-American works swilling around the world's online stores, stalls, shops and black markets are culturally adrift objects for the imaginations of others to act upon and appropriate as they see fit. Broadcast everywhere, our culture could end up representing nowhere. As the world reflects back its own readings of who and what we are, we may find that, instead of our culture altering the habits of others, the identity most subject to change and fragmentation is our own.

Though the fetters of empire still constrain many minds in former ruling and subject nations alike, the tables are starting to turn. As the colonial era begins to drift to the limits of living memory, the stories of the states that oversaw it are gradually becoming putty in the hands of the world's writers, who increasingly have the mental freedom and distance to interpret and mould them as they choose. The process is much the same as the one that generations of Western European and American writers put into practice in the past, cherry-picking what interested them from the waves of immigrants flooding to their nations and from journeys and expeditions to the rest of the world, and fitting it to their own perspectives and concerns. Indeed, it is a process that stretches back a long way, as far as the Roman translations of Greek classics just before the start of the Common Era, when poets such as Horace and Propertius remade the works of writers from the previous leading empire, Alcaeus, Archilochus and Philetas among them, to their own taste. And with the opening up of several writing awards it's likely that this literary magpieing will grow even more common among the planet's writers as cultural exchange becomes ever easier; 2014, for example, saw the extension of the Man Booker Prize to encompass all works written in English and published in the UK rather than just those by writers from Commonwealth countries, Ireland and Zimbabwe. But while recent trends may seem to point towards standardisation, it does not necessarily follow that a more closely linked global culture wouldn't be every bit as creative and varied as what we have now in the long term, as Montserrat Guibernau argues in *The Identity of Nations*:

241

After having an initial homogenizing effect, I expect that the rise of a global culture, if this were to emerge, would result in the proliferation of novel forms of cultural diversification.

. . .

How could such a culture be created? A cosmopolitan culture . . . would be formed by a mixture of elements originating from various national, ethnic and other cultures, to be selected according to whether or not each specific element complies with cosmopolitan values. In this respect, a cosmopolitan culture could be defined as a hybrid and moral culture destined to overcome ethnocentrism and ready to defend the principles of ethical cosmopolitanism when applied to cultural elements and practices.

It sounds rather clinical, as though a global culture might be the creation of a team of cultural scientists pipetting imagery and narratological structures into Petri dishes and leaving them to grow inside a laminar flow cabinet, but the point stands: cross-fertilisation between cultures, albeit largely through the dominant strain in the world at the moment, need not produce uniform results. In fact, to assume that it would is rather to underestimate the creativity of writers. To presuppose that the process of globalisation leads to an inexorable drift towards standardised, faceless, quasi-American verbiage is to think of those producing stories in other cultures as fragile, weak-willed and easily swayed. It is to imagine them as lesser artists, cowering in the presence of the cultural wonders of the world superpower, rather than as imaginative, subversive, independent agents with command of their own talent and the freedom to appropriate, subvert, reject, ignore or respond to material as they choose. It is to keep peddling the imperial narrative in a world where the story is changing.

11

Crossing the language barrier

translation

There can have been few more dangerous jobs going in recent years than those done by the local interpreters who assisted the foreign forces after the 2003 US-led invasion of Iraq. Incurring the wrath and suspicion of many of their compatriots, these men and women risked their lives to help their largely monolingual employers gain control of volatile situations. The importance of their work was indisputable: without an interpreter, Captain Zach Iscol told a Senate hearing in 2007, his marines were as good as deaf and dumb during combat. By many accounts, the 'terps', as they were known, should have been feted as heroes.

In reality, however, things were rather different. Although treated as soldiers in so far as uniforms and salaries were concerned, the interpreters were the only team members to be searched inside the military bases. They were not allowed many of the luxuries that sustained their Western colleagues throughout tours of duty: mobile phones, email, satellite TV, computers, cameras, video games and CD players were proscribed. Even the swimming pools and weights rooms were out of bounds to them. In addition, they reportedly endured regular racist slurs from some of the people whose safety depended on their skills.

At the root of it all lay a nagging sense of unease. 'We'd be nowhere without them,' US Army staff sergeant Paul Volino told *Christian Science Monitor* correspondent Charles Levinson in 2006. 'We'd be lost. But you always have this fear that they might be leaking op-sec

243

[operational security] stuff. You want to trust them but you're still reserved.'

Such institutionalised 'reserve' led to a rather uncomfortable existence for many terps. Although they were prime targets for attack by local insurgents, they were not allowed to carry weapons or armour when they left the base. As one Iraqi interpreter going by the name of 'Roger' explained to Levinson: 'If you look at our situation, it's really risky and kind of horrible. Outside the wire, everyone looks at us like we are back-stabbers, like we betrayed our country and our religion, and then inside the wire they look at us like we might be terrorists.'

For many, things did not end well. By 2013, some 1,000 interpreters were thought to have been killed in Iraq. In many cases, the influence they wielded made them vulnerable. As University of Washington history professor Vincente L. Rafael wrote of the situation in his 2009 essay 'Translation, American English and the National Insecurities of Empire', the danger for all concerned stemmed from the fact that 'in dealing with an interpreter, one is addressed in one's own language – Arabic or English – by an other who also has access to an idiom and culture [that are] alien because unavailable to one.'

Away from the battlefield, some of the same suspicions often colour the way those of us who are monoglots look at those who work with words. Though literary translators – at least those not working on *The Satanic Verses* – rarely face death threats, theirs is, in the words of Spanish-language translator Edith Grossman, 'a much-maligned activity that is often either discounted as menial hackwork or reviled as nothing short of criminal'. A glance back over the written discussions about world literature produced in the last few centuries reveals a trail of quibbles, jibes and opprobrium, with commentators such as the Danish critic Georg Brandes blasting the practice as 'a pitiful expedient' that 'eliminate[s] the literary artistry precisely by which the author should validate himself' and produces poor, botched, patched scraps of text that 'are not even replicas'. In the same vein, lexicographer Francis Gose dubbed practitioners 'sellers of old mended shoes and boots, between cobblers and shoemakers' and Robert Frost famously claimed that poetry is what gets lost in translation. Indeed, it seems no collection of essays on the topic will make it to press without some mention of the age-old Italian pun '*traduttore, traditore*' ('translator, traitor') – a phrase of which many of those Arabic, Kurdish and other-language speakers stationed in military bases in Iraq during the first decade of this century would no doubt appreciate the significance.

A strain of unease not dissimilar to that felt by the US soldiers is no doubt part of the thinking behind many of these surly statements. Though the stakes might not be as high as on the battlefield – a mangled sentence in a manga story is, after all, unlikely to get us killed, unless the book comes with a very unusual set of accessories – the nature of translation requires us to put a lot of trust in a stranger. As Maria Tymoczko, a professor of comparative literature at the University of Massachusetts, has observed: 'Translation always entails large ethical issues. A central question pertains to affiliation: where do one's allegiances lie?' And while translators may settle this question for themselves, we as readers are not usually privy to the answer.

Depending on a third person to bring us something from a place we are unable to venture to on our own is an act of faith. It is as though, having put in our order for the story, we have to rely on someone else to go and copy it down for us. They may do a good job, but who's to say they won't get distracted or take it into their heads to cut bits out, twist the words or add in things that were never there, safe in the knowledge that we are unable to check the original and so will be none the wiser? Indeed, can we always be sure that they are competent to do the job? With translation still not a 'regulated profession' under European Commission Professional Qualifications Directive 2005/36/EC, there is to date very little to stop an unqualified person from working as a translator in Europe; except, strangely enough, in Slovakia, where they have to hold certain certifications by law. Everywhere else, anyone with a grasp of two or more tongues can theoretically have a go at pouring meaning from one language-shaped jar into another. And if they spill a pint or two or mix in other ingredients during the process . . . well, we'll probably never know.

In certain cases, readers are right to be wary. Society for Promoting Christian Knowledge member George Sale's 1734 translation of *The Koran: Commonly Called the Alkoran of Mohammed*, for example – carried out 'at leisure times only, and amidst the necessary avocations of [his] troublesome profession' as a solicitor – does not inspire confidence. Despite being the first translation of the religious work directly from Arabic into English, and although Sale was driven by his professed desire to 'do the original impartial justice', it is clear from the first sentences of his Foreword 'To the Reader' that its creator would have been hard pressed to look at the text with an objective eye:

> I imagine it almost needless either to make an apology for publishing the following translation, or to go about to prove it a work of use as well as curiosity. They must have a mean opinion of the Christian religion, or be but ill grounded therein, who can apprehend any danger from so manifest a forgery.

If further proof of his own bias were needed, Sale then goes on to suggest several rules for those who want to attempt the conversion of Muslims to Christianity, based on his experiences. These include the observation that would-be evangelists should 'avoid teaching doctrines against common sense; the Mohammedans not being such fools (whatever we may think of them) as to be gained over in this case'. Even given Sale's avowal that he has done his best 'to keep somewhat scrupulously close to the text' and his acknowledgement that his work can by no means 'pass as free from faults', it seems inevitable that his belief that the source document 'pretends to be the Word of God' will have coloured his choices, tilting the narrative in favour of his agenda by degrees, as some commentators have claimed. For those who don't reject the concept of translating the Qur'an outright because of the inherent sacredness of the original text – a belief held by the many Muslims who study Arabic expressly to read the scriptures as God intended and without human intervention – Sale's comments act like a warning sign near a cliff edge. 'Beware! Unstable ground!' they seem to proclaim. 'Proceed with caution!' What was written to draw eighteenth-century readers into the text and win their trust by reflecting their prejudices and concerns has the effect of pushing twenty-first-century lectors away.

Sale is by no means the only translator to have risked letting his world view get between a text and reader. As Jorge Luis Borges discovered when he came to assess some of the earliest English-language renderings of the classic *One Thousand and One Nights*, the preoccupations of the men who worked on them crept into and shaped the texts on both the conscious and unconscious level. Borges found the efforts of Victorian Orientalist Edward Lane particularly telling, and labelled Lane's version an 'encyclopaedia of evasion' for its slew of cuts and revisions. His reworkings include recasting a hermaphrodite fish as one of mixed species and replacing the detail that a polygamous king kept his wives happy by sleeping with them on alternate nights with the rather chilly assertion that he treated them 'with impartiality'. In cases where events strike Lane as too lewd to mention, he chops them out completely, contenting himself with recording the excision in a volume of supplementary notes, replete with such gems as 'I shall overlook an episode of the most reprehensible sort', 'I must of necessity suppress the other anecdote', and 'Here, the story of the slave Bujait, wholly inappropriate for translation.' As Borges put it, 'the most oblique and fleeting reference to carnal matters is enough to make Lane forget his honor in a profusion of convolutions and occultations'. His desperation to avoid letting the side down makes for rather amusing reading at nearly two centuries' remove. Interestingly, however, the translator's rampant sense of propriety is not enough to compromise his work beyond merit in Borges' eyes. 'There is no other fault in him,' the great author goes on to write, and 'when free of the peculiar contact of this temptation, Lane is of admirable veracity'. In fact, he proceeds to praise the version, in contrast to some other less faithful renderings, claiming that Lane's 'scandalous decorum . . . is not an unpardonable sin in the sight of the Lord when the primary aim is to emphasize the atmosphere of magic'.

For readers of translations, this is rather unsettling. That so bowdlerised a work as Edward Lane's *One Thousand and One Nights* can nevertheless receive a commendation from one of the world's leading literary figures presents a problem. If a translation can be both reprehensible and laudable – if it can simultaneously cheat us out of some aspects of the primary text and serve our interests by presenting a faithful picture of much of the original – where does that leave us? Without the skills to go back to the first version and sift the wheat from the chaff, we have no way of knowing where a writer's work ends and a translator's influence begins. We cannot vet the cuts and inclusions and the myriad choices relating to tone, register and grammatical constructions on every page to decide whether we approve and whether we would have made the same call. Though we might suspect that an ulterior agenda is operating in a text when we read a foreword such as Sale's or because of extraneous information about the controversy surrounding the production of a book, we have no means of verifying whether or how it has affected the work we hold in our hands. Like children, we can only trust that the decisions being made on our behalf are taken with good intentions and that those in a position of authority have our best interests at heart. We are vulnerable when we read translations. We leave ourselves open to deception and betrayal. The contracted go-between could be feeding us a pack of lies and half-truths about the movements of a story's insurgents; they could be encouraging us to believe all sorts of things that don't serve our purposes, and we wouldn't have a clue.

*

Monolingual readers aren't the only ones for whom the concept of translation is problematic. Almost since the practice of converting text from one language to another began, those in the field have struggled to express and define exactly how it should be done. Indeed, differing opinions on the duties of those who work with words in this way have made for a number of awkward situations, as St Jerome found in the fourth century CE, when an informal translation he had made of one of Pope Epiphanius' letters got into public circulation. Outraged that he had not converted the text word for word, as translators were expected to do, Jerome's detractors accused him of deliberately distorting the document. Jerome addressed their charges in his indignant 'Letter to Pammachius', in which he defends his practice of translating text 'not word for word, but sense for sense'. To support his claims, he cites Cicero's prologue to his translation of the orations of Aeschines and Demosthenes, in which Cicero claims that he has presented the work 'as an orator, keeping the same meanings but with their forms – their figures, so to speak – in words adapted to our idiom'. Warming to his theme, Jerome goes on to quote several of his own prefaces, and refers to the example of Hilary the Confessor who, in turning numerous homilies and commentaries from Greek into Latin, 'did not camp near the soporific letter nor contort himself with a foul translation characteristic of rustics, but by right of victory carried the meaning as if captive into his own language'. In the theologian's eyes, it seems, literal translation was not merely unsatisfactory but slavish, contemptible and demeaning. True art lay in not merely apprehending sense but in mastering it and, by observing their manners and mores, making the work speak fluently to those in another language group.

In the centuries since Jerome set out his stall for something more sensitive than the mere word-for-word conversion of texts, numerous voices have been raised in support of the idea that translators should strive to capture something of the spirit rather than just the letter of the documents they reproduce in altered form. 'One must take heed that an Author's grace not be lost through too much scrupulousness, and that the fear of being unfaithful to him in some one thing not result in infidelity to the whole,' cautions Nicolas Perrot d'Ablancourt in his 'Preface to Tacitus', while John Dryden protests that 'since every language is so full of its own proprieties, that what is Beautiful in one is often Barbarous, nay sometimes Nonsense in another, it would be unreasonable to limit a Translator to the narrow compass of his Authours words: 'tis enough if he choose out some Expression which does not vitiate the sense'. It is a sentiment that the twentieth-century German literary critic and translator Walter Benjamin echoes when, in his essay on 'The Task of the Translator', he observes that 'a literal rendering of the syntax casts the reproduction of meaning entirely to the winds and threatens to lead directly to incomprehensibility'.

These days, numerous online translation tools both demonstrate and test the truth of Benjamin's claim. Primed to convert words on a pretty much unit-by-unit basis, sites like Google Translate produce texts that may convey the rudimentary significance of parts of whatever has been inputted but often collapse into nonsense, sometimes with unintentionally humorous consequences. During my project, I found myself relying on the technology to get the gist of some of the comments and articles sent to me by readers in other languages. As a primary sifting tool it had its merits – having run something through the site, I could usually glean enough to know whether the message was anything to worry about and whether I should get someone with the necessary language skills to unpack it further for me – but there were plenty of slips along the way. When a Romanian website did a post about my project, I found myself stumped and entertained in equal measure by the sentence 'Well, I feel frustrated man can not live with the trouser on the walls all day and read,' which, Google Translate assured me, featured in the otherwise fairly intelligible piece. It wasn't until a Romanian friend looked at the original for me that the mystery was cleared up. The phrase in question was a variation on '*sa-ti pui picioarele pe perete*', which means literally 'to put up your legs' or, in idiomatic English, 'to put your feet up'. As the blogger had used a slang word for *picior/picioare* (leg/legs) – '*crac/craci*', which can be translated literally as 'trouser leg(s)' – the machine had been thrown off its stroke. It had also mysteriously defaulted to making the female writer's sentence masculine from the genderless Romanian, which started a debate about the potential misogyny of

Google Translate. 'Why not "I feel frustrated woman can not live with the trouser on the walls"?' as my friend very sensibly said.

The interesting thing about the products of tools such as Google Translate, however, is that they do make an odd kind of sense. Far from being incomprehensible, as Benjamin's words suggest they should be, they contain cracked significance, reflecting glimmers of the original meaning as well as rogue beams shining from elsewhere. By virtue of their uncompromising, inhuman approach to words, they show us something of the indefinable *je ne sais quoi* that living, breathing translators work into their creations to make them speak convincingly. This was an idea that Taiwanese poet Hsia Yü explored when she worked on *Pink Noise*, a collection of poems built from phrases siphoned from English-language blogs, articles and other sources and then run through the Chinese computer translation tool 'Sherlock'. Having tested the technology with work by Shakespeare, Poe and Pushkin, she found herself looking at a series of bizarre translations in 'the most unimaginable Chinese, so queer and uncanny that it left [her] speechless' and made her 'feel like a foreigner in [her] own language'. Intrigued to explore its potential, Hsia Yü embarked on a programme of 'linguistic assassination', splicing together phrases that, although often vacuous in their original context, were rendered strange and even beautiful by the machine. 'One day the translations are going to be so fluent, these cybernetic Sherlocks will turn into mediocre poets,' Hsia Yü told Steve Bradbury. In the meantime, however, she found in the weird fragments a kind of radical deconstruction, 'albeit entirely unconscious, for [Sherlock] feels accountable only for providing a word-for-word equivalence without regard for any underlying meaning or significance. That's why he produces so many wonderful discrepancies. All that, and just that, is poetry to me.'

Hsia Yü is not alone in her enjoyment of discrepancy. For some translators, the linguistic and cultural jolts and jarrings as two languages grind against each other are to be celebrated and showcased, attesting as they do to the inherent foreignness of a work. Far from agreeing that, as American Bible translator Edgar J. Goodspeed put it, 'the best translation is . . . one that makes the reader forget that it is a translation at all and makes him feel that he is looking into the ancient writer's mind, as he would into that of a contemporary', practitioners such as Vladimir Nabokov maintain that the distance between original writer and new reader should be preserved. Translations should read like translations, he argues, and the best way to achieve this is by taking a literal approach to the text and refusing to polish the finished result to make it shine in the new language. He tackled Pushkin's *Eugene Onegin* in this way, refusing to keep within the iambic verse structure where he felt the words did not allow it, so that the text veers in and out of prose. The results make for hard reading. Indeed, the critic Edmund Wilson found the rendering so terrible that he suggested Nabokov had gone out of his way to make it ugly: 'One suspects that his perversity here has been exercised in curbing his brilliance; that – with his sado-masochistic Dostoevskian tendencies so acutely noted by Sartre – he seeks to torture both the reader and himself by flattening Pushkin out and denying to his own powers the scope for their full play.'

Mind-boggling experiments and awkward texts aren't purely the preserve of those who espouse literalism over sense. At the other end of the scale, where translation crumbles into adaptation, those who take a very free hand with a source text often produce equally outlandish results. One of the most striking recent examples is *Multiples: 12 Stories in 18 Languages by 61 Authors*, edited by British novelist and critic Adam Thirlwell. A sort of literary Chinese Whispers, the collection grew out of a series of relay translations (where works pass from one language to the next and on to the next, instead of each version working from the source text) created by writers with varying degrees of language skill and translation experience: 'The truth is, I'm useless at English,' confesses Yannick Haenel in a commentary on his conversion of Dutch writer A.L. Snijders' 'Geluk' (Happiness) from English into French. 'Even at school I was bad . . . The English I believe I understand, the English I have inflicted on you in order to translate the superb text in this anthology, is an approximate language that I was taught by Johnny Rotten.' Invited to 'come on strongly', in the words of Hungarian writer Péter Esterházy, another contributor, the authors set about making the stories their own. Characters appear and disappear. Section divisions come and go. Subtitles pop up unannounced. Plots change shape and sometimes play out entirely differently. And as the texts crisscross back and forth into and out of English, meaning starts to migrate, so that the stories seem like unstable radioactive elements registering different half-lives with each reading. 'I behave as though I were one of Vila-Matas's own more wilful and self-involved characters,' writes Irish novelist Colm Tóibín of his rendering of Enrique Vila-Matas' 'Los de abajo'. 'I tried to make it read as though I had written it on a bad day and it needed root and branch work.' No doubt the most extreme form of transmutation in the collection is Sjón Atvik's conversion of 'Geluk' from English into Icelandic. The resulting text runs to less than half the length of the Jeffrey Eugenides translation he was working from – a shortfall that Atvik's brief note on the translation goes a fair way to explain:

> Flóki Sigurjónsson, my thirteen-year-old son and a native Icelandic speaker, was given half an hour to memorize Jeffrey Eugenides's translation. I refrained from reading the source text. Three weeks after listening to Flóki's oral retelling of Jeffrey's 'Happenstance', I wrote it down from memory as 'Atvik'. I have not compared the two.

The idea is fascinating, and I only wish Thirlwell had commissioned another English translation so that anglophone readers could glean some deeper insight into the effect of Atvik's unorthodox methods. Nevertheless, his could hardly be a workable process for producing translations. As Julian Barnes observed in a discussion of the book shortly after it came out: 'would you really want Atvik translating your work like that?'

In practice of course, professional translators rarely venture to either extreme. Though few have much time for what Edith Grossman has called 'the literalist fallacy', most regard themselves as duty-bound to present a version that could be said to do justice to the original. As ever with translation, the challenge comes when you try to work out precisely what this means. Once again, the concepts of loyalty and betrayal loom large, with many translators talking of trying to achieve 'fidelity' to the source text. For a good number of practitioners and readers, this seems to have to do with conveying the original reading experience to the new audience as closely as possible. While 'we expect approximate truth in a translation', wrote critic Oliver Edwards in his 1957 *Talking of Books*, 'what we want to have is the truest possible *feel* of the original. The characters, the situations, the reflections must come to us as they were in the author's mind and heart, not necessarily precisely as he had them on his lips.' Five decades later, Taiwanese writer and translator Chen Li agrees: 'The translation that enables readers to fully feel what you have felt is a good translation,' he claims in his recent essay on 'Traveling Between Languages'.

Finding a way to capture and convey the experience of reading a text is no mean feat. It involves the translator calculating and balancing a wide array of considerations to do with our place in the world and how we understand it – not just in terms of the relationship of these to the text, but in terms of the likely reader-to-be's relationship to the work that will be produced. Gender, politics, religion, social mores, value systems and law can all have weight, as can the issue of whether to pitch a work in contemporary language, regional dialect or the vocabulary of its era; the question of when to use glossaries, footnotes and other external commentaries; and the problem of how much knowledge to assume in the new audience. And that's before you even begin to grapple with the nuts and bolts of the languages, the myriad idiosyncrasies and grammatical curiosities which mean that, as Eugene Nida puts it, 'there can be no fully exact translations', even between closely related tongues such as Spanish and Italian. In the words of Friedrich

Schleiermacher, for whom Google Translate's gender bias might not have been such an issue, anyone considering transforming a text into another language must ask himself whether he should 'really venture to take two men who are as far distant from one another as his country-man who speaks only his language and the writer himself, and to bring them together in so immediate a relationship as that between a writer and his original reader?'

Achieving such a rapprochement might seem tricky at the best of times – 'an utterly foolish undertaking', Schleiermacher goes so far as to call it, before going on to expound enthusiastically on his preferred methods of approaching it – but it's particularly difficult when the things described are completely outside the experience of the audience. Explorer Tété-Michel Kpomassie found this to be the case when he returned home to Togo after living in Greenland with the Inuit people for several years. Having run away as a teenager and travelled up through Africa and Europe to board a boat to the territory that had captured his imagination when he read about it in an evangelical book-shop in his local village, Kpomassie had much to tell – and indeed went on to recount his adventures in his excellent memoir *An African in Greenland*, which he wrote in French. But when he tried to put his experiences into words for his grandfather, he encountered a problem: the local language, Mina, had no terminology for snow. However hard he tried, the equipment was simply not there to communicate the full extent of what he had seen and done. Kpomassie could take his grand-father a certain distance on his travels, but when it came to Greenland's frozen wastes, he was on his own. It was an extreme example of what philosopher Bertrand Russell meant when he suggested that 'no one can understand the word "cheese" unless he has a non-linguistic acquaintance with cheese'; in this case, not only the real-world experi-ence but the term itself did not exist.

With so much to balance and exceptions to almost every rule, it's no surprise that, for all their linguistic skills, translators often struggle to articulate what they do and how others should go about it. 'The whole foundation, as we have found it over and over again in discussion of translation, is hopelessly vague,' writes George Steiner in his essay on 'The Hermeneutic Motion'. You only have to look at the welter of metaphors and similes applied to the art – or is it a science? – to see that things are far from clear. Some talk in terms of translation being an act of exceptionally close reading; others define practitioners as writers, an observation bolstered by the fact that, in many more multilingual cultures than ours, famous wordsmiths such as Baudelaire, Goethe, Chateaubriand, Murakami, Borges and Nabokov have turned their pens to recasting works in other languages. There are those, like Ralph Manheim, who describe translators as actors speaking the authors' lines as they would if they spoke the destination language, while some of their peers see themselves as painters, reproducing the scene before their eyes. Yet others move away from the sphere of art altogether, reaching for comparisons to mapping, mathematical translation and accountancy. George Steiner, for example, goes on to try and clear up the ambiguity around translation by likening it to a form of bookkeeping. 'A translation is, more than figuratively, an act of double-entry; both formally and morally the books must balance,' he writes. Figurative or not, there's no question that the issue of defining translation has called forth instances of extremely creative and sometimes beautiful writing. The translators' preface to the King James Bible of 1611 heaps lyrical image upon lyrical image in a passage worthy of the most expressive psalmist:

> Translation it is that openeth the window, to let in the light; that breaketh the shell, that we may eat the kernel; that putteth aside the curtain, that we may look into the most holy place; that removeth the cover of the well, that we may come by the water.

Whatever else it may be, translation is clearly slippery. It calls forth a rotating kaleidoscope of images that capture something but not everything of what it is about and seems to urge those who evoke them ever onwards in search of a metaphor that takes them nearer the mark.

Paradoxically, those engaged in the business of making sense cannot entirely explain themselves. They move in a zone that language does not quite reach. There is a gap between the act itself and the words used to describe it. Translation is as untranslatable a concept as they come.

*

While people familiar with the translation process might find it difficult to talk about what they do, it seems to be nigh on impossible for most of the rest of us. This is so universal that, as those working in the field so often lament, most reviews of works originally written in other languages barely mention the fact, with many even omitting the name of the translator. Publishers frequently don't help matters, as large numbers opt to banish the name of the person who wrote the words contained in the book from not only its cover but also sometimes its title page. A reader wandering into Waterstones on a wet Wednesday afternoon could be forgiven for thinking that many of the books he or she picks up from the shelves of the foreign language sections started life in English, so rarely are translators credited in such a way as to attract our notice.

The reasons for such omissions are the subject of much debate. Some see it as further evidence of the entrenched prejudices against and suspicion of foreign languages that seem to underscore much of anglophone culture. Others, like Belgian-American translation theorist André Lefevere, suggest reviewers' and literary theorists' reticence has to do with a widespread preoccupation with the Romantic 'assumption of the genius and originality of the author who creates *ex nihilo*' – a hang-up which does not seem to be an issue for other nations you might expect to share the legacy of Romanticism, such as France and Germany. There's also the possibility that those who espouse the Edgar Goodspeed school of thought that the best translation is one that 'makes the reader forget that it is a translation at all' have become victims of their own success. Perhaps by producing translations that read like British or American literary novels, some translators have lulled readers into complacency and written themselves out of the story.

The truth, however, is probably closer to the issue that translators themselves face when they come to discuss their work: many of us don't have the words. It's not usually – perhaps with the exception of the 'If English was good enough for Jesus Christ it's good enough for me' bumper-sticker brigade – that we're unaware that the book we're reading was written first in another language; it's simply that we don't know how to talk about this. Not being party to the process of bringing it into our language, we feel unsure of how we're expected to respond. If someone as knowledgeable as Lefevere freely admits that 'it is plain impossible to define, once and for all, what a "good" translation is', what hope is there for us? Without access to the original, after all, we're in no position to judge the fidelity of the text – if we were, we wouldn't need the translated book in our hands. Should we tie ourselves up in impossible knots by trying to crowbar the translator's name into every mention we make of the author's tone and style? Should we erase the original writer from our comments? Or is that equally unfair? Are we even allowed to mention such things as tone and style, given that we can't know at which point they crept into the piece? Every way we turn seems fraught with linguistic problems that make us afraid of saying foolish things. The correct formulations elude us. The words simply aren't there. And as Wittgenstein put it, '*Wovon man nicht sprechen kann, darüber muss man schweigen*' ('What you can't talk about, you have to leave unsaid' – my translation).

In this respect, translators sometimes don't help. When you're trying to talk about the work of people who make words their business, it's painfully easy to drop a clanger, as those brave or stupid enough to put their heads above the parapet and venture some sort of comment on translations often find to their cost. The justifiable indignation those in the field express at critics' lack of mention of their efforts pales into insignificance when it comes to evaluations they perceive as ham-fisted, ignorant or lazy. Here's Edith Grossman out-hatcheting the hatchet jobs:

Even if it is unrealistic to wish that every reviewer of a translated work were at least bilingual, it is not unreasonable to require a substantive and intelligent acknowledgement of the reality of the translation . . . So few of them have devised an intelligent way to review both the original and its translation within the space limitations imposed by the publication. It seems to me that their inability to do so is a product of intransigent dilettantism and tenacious amateurism, the menacing two-headed monster that runs rampant through the inhospitable landscape peopled by those who write reviews.

She's not the only one to feel aggrieved. Summoning the wit and energy that Edmund Wilson found wanting in his translation of *Eugene Onegin*, Nabokov launches a broadside on insipid reviews in his essay on 'Problems of Translation: *Onegin* in English':

I constantly find in reviews of verse translations the following kind of thing that sends me into spasms of helpless fury: 'Mr (or Miss) So-and-so's translation reads smoothly.' In other words, the reviewer of the 'translation', who neither has, nor would be able to have, without special study, any knowledge whatsoever of the original, praises as 'readable' an imitation only because the drudge or the rhymester has substituted easy platitudes for the breathtaking intricacies of the text. 'Readable', indeed! A schoolboy's boner is less of a mockery in regard to the ancient masterpiece than its commercial interpretation or poetization.

You can understand the frustration. It's the irritation of anyone who's had to submit to being told how to do their job by someone manifestly less qualified and less knowledgeable. It's the gritted teeth of the employees going through an inane health-and-safety inspection on how they use tools they've worked with for years. Seen in this light, it seems ludicrous that anyone who did not have extensive knowledge of the craft of translation could presume to advance an opinion about anything connected with it. Philosopher Jacques Derrida certainly seemed to feel the weight of this at the start of his lecture on 'What is a "Relevant" Translation?', delivered to the French Assises de la Traduction Littéraire à Arles in 1998:

'How dare I proceed before you, knowing myself to be at once rude and inexperienced in this domain, as someone who, from the very first moment, from his very first attempts (which I could recount to you, as the English saying goes, *off the record*), shunned the translator's métier, his beautiful and terrifying responsibility, his insolent duty and debt, without ceasing to tell himself "never ever again": "no, precisely, I would *never* dare, I should *never*, could *never*, would *never* manage to pull it off"?'

If the father of deconstruction worries that he is unequal to the task of doing justice to translation, just imagine how I feel writing this – I, whose practical experience of translation extends not much further than French and German A-level and a week's work experience at *Die Badische Zeitung*. I can almost sense a crowd of experts standing behind me, muttering furiously about amateurs and dilettantes. Faced with my unworthiness and ignorance and the possibility of making many glaring faux pas, it would seem much safer to avoid stepping into the minefield altogether and stick to the solid territory of what I know: discussing the good old English-language canon that, barring a smattering of Proust, Flaubert, Duras, Kafka, Brecht and Mann, did me very nicely, thank you, for much of my first three decades. After all, what could I possibly have of value to say about works written in other languages?

Such was the conclusion I nearly came to five months into my project. Well into a routine of reviewing and blogging about four books a week, I had posted up a piece on Katy Derbyshire's translation of Clemens Meyer's *All the Lights*, my German choice, when a comment from a PhD translation student going by the username Alua pulled me up short. Zeroing in on my statement that Meyer's minimalistic style had been 'rendered through Derbyshire's deft translation', she proceeded to warn me off expressing opinions on the quality of translations, particularly 'the language and everything that relates to it' as I could be in no position to judge this without reading the original work.

I had to hold my hands up here: 'rendered through Derbyshire's deft translation' was an asinine thing to write and I wasn't sure what I'd meant by it. I had fallen into the trap of unthinking, lazy reviewing where a desire to indicate an awareness of the text having been translated made me reach for something trite and meaningless in the absence of anything better to say. Essentially, I had wanted to show that I enjoyed reading the book and that I was conscious this wasn't down to Meyer's skill alone. But there seemed to be no way of saying this that didn't sound idiotic. Perhaps Alua was right and it really was best to leave well alone.

Something niggled, however. While she was correct that I was in no position to comment on the fidelity of the translation (just reading the text on the strength of my rusty German would have taken a good few weeks and a very large dictionary), Alua did not entirely convince me when she wrote that 'the language and everything that relates to it' were beyond my grasp as a reader of translations. Of course, I wouldn't know the decisions behind the words on the page and whether they stemmed from the original text or the translator's initiative, but I could evaluate the effect of the finished article. I could notice whether a passage engrossed or distanced me, and whether the voice was familiar, mannered or strange. I could identify the use of literary techniques and be delighted or exasperated by them. What's more, there were places where it was possible to recognise the hand of the translator at work. I could, for example, be impressed by Sarah Ardizzone's deployment of Jafaican, or Multicultural London English as it's more formally known, in her rendering of Faïza Guène's *Kiffe kiffe demain* (*Just Like Tomorrow*) and appreciate the lengths she must have gone to not only to find a linguistic setting to match the novel's gritty Parisian tower-block backdrop but also to make it fluent, lively and plausible throughout. Similarly, I could find myself unsettled when characters in rural Croatia popped up sporting Yorkshire accents and a cockney twang and know that this decision would have had nothing to do with the original author of the novel I was reading. And when the dialect word 'emmet' spoken by a peasant tripped me up in my edition of Tolstoy's *Anna Karenina*, I could ponder whether the problem lay with the translator trying too hard for rustic authenticity or with my own Cornish connections, which made me think of the word primarily as meaning 'outsider' rather than the more widespread definition 'ant'.

If the way I expressed these thoughts was clumsy and ill-focused, and gave the impression that I did not appreciate the efforts of the translator or understand that I was reading the work in a new incarnation, then that was a problem I had to address. I needed to be more mindful of the way I put things and do my best to fit my words to what was going on there on the page – even if it was hard and made me feel like a child fidgeting over my homework once more.

Yet it was important to do so. And it is important that critics as a whole establish and enlarge a vocabulary with which they can talk comfortably, accurately and perceptively about works originally written in languages other than English. Because when you stand back and consider the overall thrust and purpose of reviews, they are vital to the success or otherwise of the works they discuss. For better or worse, the inhospitable landscape of the books section is the nursery in which new talent is nurtured, trained or stamped out. It is the launch pad for many literary careers. And if reviewers feel reluctant to tackle translated works for fear of being lambasted or sounding like an idiot, you can be sure many readers will give such stories a wide berth too.

*

I am one of the few people in the world ever to have had a book translated specially for me to read. I mention this not to show off – well, all right, there's a bit of that – but, because of all the brushes with translation I've had so far in my life, this was the one that gave me the greatest insight into the business of changing a text from one language to another. And in so doing, it gave me a glimpse of the direction we might move in if we are to develop the vocabulary to get round the semantic impasse that cuts off many monolingual readers from meaningful discussion of works from other language worlds.

The process came about when I reached the end of the road after spending months trying to find something to read from the small, lusophone, African island nation of São Tomé and Principe. At Steve's suggestion, after the latest in a long line of linguists, translators, NGO workers, doctors on placement and gap-year students I'd contacted in growing desperation came back with the answer that they knew of nothing that I could read, I put out a call on Twitter and Facebook for people who might be willing to help translate something for me. I was doubtful that anyone would be prepared to give up their time and talents for so egocentric a project (forget vanity publishing, this was vanity reading), but my scepticism quickly turned to delight and then amazement when messages poured in from Portuguese-speakers in Europe and the US. As time was tight (this was towards the end of September) and because I had no idea who would be interested in helping, I accepted all credible offers as they came in, with the result that the nine volunteers who signed up within a week had hugely different levels of translation experience. They ranged from someone I knew from school, who had studied Portuguese for a year or two at university, to Margaret Jull Costa, translator of Nobel Prize winner José Saramago. Despite their varied expertise and backgrounds, however, the participants shared two qualities: generosity and reliability. Within a month of my sending them their allocated pieces from Santomean-born Olinda Beja's short-story collection *A casa do pastor* – one of the few Santomean works I could find with ten copies available to buy – all the translators had returned their sections of the book and the entire collection of short fiction set in Portugal's Altai mountain range was mine to read in English.

Along with their translations, many of the participants shared their thoughts on the writing and notes on some of the decisions behind their pieces. Denmark-based Angolan writer Yema Ferreira, for example, asked for my help in choosing how to handle the name of the title character 'Maria Giesta', because the surname denotes a relatively obscure flowering shrub which features in the story (we went for Maria Genista in the end, rather than Mary Genista, which Ferreira had initially considered). Meanwhile, Margaret Jull Costa took me through her treatment of a riddle she had to adjust so that it would make sense in English. And from Spain Robin Patterson, who was just starting out as a professional translator, sent me several pages of meticulous commentary explaining the reasons why he had plumped for particular words and phrases, including:

'fair' (*festa*) – I use 'festival' later on when the context is established, but I felt 'fair' here would help orientate an English reader and avoid a Glastonbury/Hay connotation of 'girl I met at a festival'. Later on I use 'fairground' for *terreiro da festa* – in both cases I think a gentle hint at festival/fair cultural translation is justified.

'toe-rag' (*borra botas*) – I think this strikes the right balance of earthy insult, put-down, somewhat ridiculous, archaic and yet not rude enough that a father couldn't say it to his son, or in front of his daughter (I had also considered 'pipsqueak' but that sounded a bit posh).

'he wasn't a man to mince his words or indeed honey his words' (*ele que não era de meias palavras nem de palavras meigas*) – I've repeated 'his words', to emphasise the narrator's rather clunky word-play (there are other examples in the story that are more difficult to transpose).

Given the range of the translators' experience, I had been prepared for the tone of the stories I read to vary considerably – which it did, no doubt partly because of the fluctuating style of the Portuguese text, which several of the volunteers told me was very mixed. What I hadn't been expecting was the wildly different reactions of those involved to the original. While some responded warmly to the simplicity of the storytelling, finding parallels with the work of writers such as Miguel Torga and Altino do Tojal, others disliked Beja's writing, describing the stories as 'dull' and in one case as being like 'torture' to read. If you proceeded on the basis that translation is about recreating the initial reading experience for another person at one language's remove – conveying the 'truest possible *feel* of the original', as Oliver Edwards puts it – it was clear that, had I asked each of my volunteers to translate the entire text, I would have been presented with nine different books, ranging from excruciating to magical. The reading experience that the translators worked from was not some immutable, Platonic reality but a deeply personal, subjective thing. When I opened a translation, I was not merely consuming a text that had gone through an extra stage of editorial treatment. Instead, I was inhabiting someone else's experience of a literary work; I was reading with another person's eyes.

Viewing translation in this way reveals several things. First of all, it explains the slipperiness of the concept and the difficulty most people have in articulating what's going on when someone converts a story from one language to another. As no two readings will ever be identical, taking another individual into the heart of so personal and subjective an experience as your own encounter with a text will feel different to each person engaged in it. Translation simply doesn't mean quite the same thing from one translator to the next, just as stories produce slightly – or sometimes drastically – different responses in those who read them.

Realising the intimacy of the process also sheds light on both the indignation of translators when critics ignore them and the fury that often trite, meaningless or wrong-headed comments evoke if the trans-lator does get a mention. In some ways, those who provide the framework for new language audiences to imagine stories risk more and go deeper than writers do when they produce a text. Rather than simply ushering readers into a world they have created (whether *ex nihilo* or out of whatever mental and emotional flotsam and jetsam come to hand), translators welcome us inside their own personal interaction with a book. When we comment on the words they have produced in response to a work they have read in another language, we are not merely critiquing the use of technical skills – though there is certainly much of this involved too – but also venturing to assess the way they read, how they imagine and, fundamentally, what the world looks like to them. To reject this casually, to write it off without sufficient thought or reason, is to strike at a deeply personal, cherished process: the way of seeing and, yes, interpreting that makes every reader unique, and the vast toolkit of words sharpened, calibrated and polished over a lifetime that each of us carries around.

The fact that translators are prepared to make themselves vulnerable in this way is testament to their generosity. It reveals the selflessness that underlies what they do – a selflessness that became all too clear to me when eight strangers and someone I had not seen in years volunteered to give up their time for the sake of nothing more than helping me reach my goal. Such enthusiasm and fearlessness shows up the process as an act of love. Indeed, Edith Grossman, for all her formidable fury, shows her true colours when she comes to write about her most impressive work to date, her translation of Miguel de Cervantes' *Don Quixote*, which she accepted after double-checking with the publishers that they hadn't called the wrong Grossman by mistake:

> I wanted English-language readers to savor its humor, its melancholy, its originality, its intellectual and esthetic complexity; I wanted them to know why the entire world thinks this is a great masterwork by an incomparable novelist. In the end, my primary consideration was this: *Don Quixote* is not essentially a puzzle for academics, a repository of Renaissance usage, a historical monument, or a text for the classroom. It is a work of literature, and

my concern as a literary translator was to create a piece of writing in English that perhaps could be called literature too.

Faced with such passion and generosity, we as readers need to approach translations with respect. We should encounter them with an awareness of what has been ventured and repay that personal investment with honesty, openness and self-awareness rather than arrogance, suspicion or false cleverness. And we must work hard to find fitting ways of framing our responses, building a vocabulary capable of doing the subject justice grapheme by grapheme and rejecting laziness and inanity as we go. For their part, translators will have to bear with us and allow us the space to do this. Painful and infuriating though it must be to watch your rendering of a work that may have spent months inhabiting your imagination handled roughly, pulled around and shaken to see if anything drops out, this sort of clumsy engagement has to be the first step for many readers in creating not just a critical tradition more suited to discussing translated literature but a reading culture in which stories written in other languages are more widely accepted and sought after. To do otherwise risks perpetuating a status quo in which the majority of critics – and by extension readers – feel uncomfortable with or unequal to tackling English versions of foreign-language works and consequently favour anglophone books to the exclusion of almost all else. It won't be easy and no doubt many stupid things will be said along the way. But it is important that we attempt it, even knowing that we are likely to make many mistakes. As Grossman writes, drawing on Samuel Beckett to sum up her feelings about her critically acclaimed translation of *Don Quixote*: '"Next time I'll have to fail better." That is all any of us can do.' Given what is at stake – from the pages of Cervantes to the battlefields of Iraq – it behoves us all to try.

12

Surveying the road ahead

technology and the internet

Reading the world in a single language would have been almost impossible thirty years ago. You certainly couldn't have assembled the material to do it in a matter of months. Even if you'd dedicated a decade or two to posting off hopeful inquiry letters to booksellers, academics, writers and literary reviewers in far-flung corners of the globe – or spent your life savings travelling to the parts English-language publishers don't reach – you'd have needed a pretty impressive network of bilingual friends to help you convert texts into something you could read. Given the way things were going in the final decades of the twentieth century, it's likely you'd have found new countries emerging faster than you could source titles from them. The project, should anyone have been mad enough to attempt it in the pre-internet era, would have been a nightmare; a labour of love; a life's work tinkered away at over the decades to the joshing, eye-rolling and exasperation of family and friends.

That it is possible to do such a thing in just a year these days is testament to the extraordinary times we live in. The 2.5 billion or so of us around the planet who use the internet have a level of access to information and each other that would have been inconceivable a handful of decades ago. We are able to find, send messages to and share information with people living very different lives in very different places and even – in the case of nations such as Ethiopia, where, according to the Ge'ez calendar, it is 2007 – different times. The World Wide Web represents, in the words of its inventor, Tim Berners-Lee, 'humanity connected', at least for those of us able to get online. And this ease of communication makes all sorts of things possible that would have been unimaginable prior to the beginning of widespread internet access in the early/mid-nineties. It allows us to form friendships with people we may never meet and talk to them for free. It enables us to seek out and follow news in an unprecedented way and verify facts that we would previously have been obliged to take on trust. And it makes it possible to find more narratives from more places than ever before. These days, as happened to me during my quest, a lament on Twitter about the lack of contemporary Montenegrin fiction in English can, in a matter of minutes, turn into a conversation with a novelist in the process of proofreading a translation of her first book (a month later, I was reading a copy of the work, *A Lullaby for No Man's Wolf* by Xenia Popovich, hot off the e-press). If, as veteran bookseller Lewis Buzbee claims in his memoir *The Yellow-Lighted Bookshop*, 'reading is a solitary act, but one that demands connection to the world,' the internet, like no other previous invention, has the power to transform our relationship to stories.

One of the consequences of the enhanced communication many of us now enjoy has been that individuals and small groups have more power than ever before to share their stories, influence others and effect change. From the earth-shattering revelations of National Security Agency whistleblower Edward Snowden, who kick-started a worldwide debate about surveillance in 2013, to the avalanche of tweets from protesters in North Africa and the Middle East that proved so instrumental in driving the Arab Spring, the internet has granted huge numbers of people the opportunity to be heard around the planet. It is, as journalist Tom Standage, has called it, a 'global megaphone'; or, in the words of Andrew O'Hagan, ghostwriter of *Julian Assange: The Unauthorised Autobiography*, a tool that has created 'a new kind of history, where military lies on a global scale [can be] revealed by a bunch of sleepy amateurs two foot from an Aga'.

This has proved to be the case for bibliophiles just as much as for anyone else. Voracious readers who have a flair for turning sentences of their own have found an international following through blogs, with people like Devonshire-based former community nurse Lynne Hatwell garnering many millions of views from some 125 countries since she launched her review site 'dovegreyreader scribbles' in 2006. In my own case, I found that the internet provided not merely an exceptional resource and a means of contacting experts, authors and enthusiasts who helped me read more widely than I ever could have done on my own, but also a spur. Many were the mornings when, stumbling bleary-eyed to the computer in the grey half-light of dawn, I was galvanised by an enthusiastic comment, an offer of help, or news that a stranger thousands of miles away had turned up a lead on a story or manuscript for me out of no other impulse than the desire to see me succeed in my endeavour. This sense that other people had invested in what I was doing urged me on, keeping me going when I started to flag and encouraging me to push the boundaries. Because of the interest and enthusiasm of people I'd never met, I refused to settle for a memoir about the Kuwaiti invasion written by a British woman who had lived in the country for several decades and instead spent the final weeks of 2012 trawling through Kuwait-based blogs until someone tipped me off about Danderma's self-published *The Chronicles of Dathra*. Out of a sense of responsibility and gratitude to all those who helped me, I spent ages tracking down a Harlem-based musician online in an effort to get his mum, poet Rashidah Ismaili Abubakr, to send me the manuscript of her short-story collection – the only book in English by a Beninois writer that seemed to be in existence at the time. And through sheer determination to honour the faith so many people had in me, I entered into an involved Twitter correspondence with, of all things, the Panama Canal, whose favourite writer, Juan David Morgan, was luckily able to send me an unpublished translation of one of his novels.

As a result of its extraordinary powers of amplification, the Web has provided a platform for numerous estimable personal projects that might have remained locked away in the back bedroom in previous decades. Sites such as themodernnovel.com – one reader's ongoing survey of literary fiction since 1900 published around the world in English, French, German, Italian, Portuguese and Spanish – provide an invaluable resource, bringing together scattered information so that a visitor can have an overview of a huge amount of book-related data in a handful of clicks. Meanwhile online ventures such as Steve Wasserman's 'Read Me Something You Love' – for which its creator records people reading an extract from one of their favourite books and talking about why they like it – have facilitated many wonderful conversations about literature. (When he interviewed me during my year of reading the world, Wasserman jokingly dubbed me Sisyphus, but there was certainly more than an element of the pot calling the kettle black about this, given the long hours he spends collecting and editing audio footage alongside his work as a counsellor and psychotherapist.) The status, location and financial situation of the person behind a cultural or artistic project are no longer quite as central to success as they once were; so long as you pitch your venture correctly, execute it well and put in the time to get it noticed, you stand a good chance of developing a following. On the internet, ideas have more scope to speak for themselves.

Some of them can be quite outlandish. From the cell-phone novels (written on and downloadable to mobiles) that caused a sensation in Japan, topping the bestseller charts in 2007, to cut-and-paste technology that makes it possible for readers to assemble their own texts out of snippets of others; from vooks (books combining video and text) and interactive choose-your-own-adventure stories, to Beatrix Potter ebooks where you can shake a tablet to make the leaves fall and splat blackberries on the page, digital technology and the Web have enabled publishers' and readers' imaginations to run riot when it comes to the things we can do with and to stories. As Martyn Lyons writes in *Books: A Living History*, 'as far as book-reading is concerned, there are no rules any more'.

Inevitably not all experiments in and around text succeed. When Arizona's Tucson-Pima Public Library system, as it was then known, opened a bookless branch stocked entirely with Web-based materials in

2002, users obliged the management to bring physical books in. It took another twelve years for anyone to attempt the same thing again in the US: the nation's next all-digital public library didn't open until 2014. By the same token, the wikinovel, *A Million Penguins* – to which UK publisher Penguin Books, in collaboration with De Montfort University's Institute of Creative Technologies, invited website visitors to contribute as they saw fit in 2007 – was an unqualified failure after hundreds of web users set out to hijack and sabotage it. The university's final report on the project, however, is upbeat in tone:

> Certainly, some of the participants in the project did attempt to 'write a novel' but it remains unclear as to whether they succeeded. What today appears not to be a novel as we know it may in time come to be seen as one, just as work once judged not to be poetry is often later brought into the critical fold. But for the moment at least the answer to whether or not a community can write a novel appears to be 'not like this'.

Yet for all the hiccups along the way, there's no question that the potential amplifying effects of the 'global megaphone' have enabled writers and translators to share work that might otherwise never have made it off the desk. While online communities such as authonomy.com and youwriteon.com have made it possible for aspiring authors to get feedback on their manuscripts – and led to book deals for people like Douglas Jackson and Miranda Dickinson – the ease and affordability of making work available on the internet have prompted many wordsmiths to go it alone, uploading their texts for anyone to dip into as they wish. Probably the first ever novel written in English by a Mauritanian national, *Angels of Mauritania and the Curse of the Language*, saw the light of day this way when its author, Mohamed Bouya Bamba, decided to self-publish and disseminate it virtually while he was studying for a PhD in the US in 2011. In the same way, numerous English translations are undertaken purely for personal interest or out of a desire to share a much-loved work free of charge online with those able to put together the right combination of search terms to find them. Often, they may be some of the few, if not only, pieces of literature available in English from places unrepresented on commercial publishers' lists – Mary Mintz' version of Uladzimir Karatkievich's Belarusian Gothic classic *King Stakh's Wild Hunt* and Fareesha Abdullah and Michael O'Shea's rendering of Abdullah Sadiq's *Dhon Hiyala and Ali Fulhu* from the Maldives being two good examples.

In addition, the interaction of readers online can have a significant impact on the story of what happens to a book after it is released into the world. While reviews on Goodreads and Amazon can dramatically affect a book's sales and profile, the interest a book generates online can determine whether or not it is translated into other languages or even other forms (indeed, the influence of online discussion on an author's popularity can be negative as well as positive, as crime novelist Lynn Shepherd found when hundreds of J.K. Rowling fans rushed to pepper her books with one-star reviews after she wrote a piece suggesting that the Harry Potter author should stop writing in 2014). I saw this first-hand when I was contacted by a film producer who had bought the rights to Tété-Michel Kpomassie's *An African in Greenland*, having heard about it through my project. She was meeting Kpomassie, now in his seventies, in Paris and said I should get in touch if I was passing through so that we could all have dinner together (a cause of great excitement for me, as Kpomassie is the author from my year of reading the world that I would most like to meet because of the infectious enthusiasm for adventure and discovery in his writing). At the time of writing, she is getting ready to go and scout for locations in Greenland and has hired a screenwriter to prepare the story of Kpomassie's remarkable odyssey from rural Togo to the Inuit communities for the big screen. With the help of the internet, reading, it seems, can be a transformative process even for narratives themselves.

*

Since Google announced its intention to digitise 15 million books from the collections of five of the world's most well-stocked libraries in 2004 as part of its mission 'to organise the world's information and make it universally accessible and useful' – a sort of virtual Notre-Dame construction project it estimates could take 300 years – a considerable proportion of the world's published works (with odd pages excised to get round copyright legislation) have become available gratis on the internet. The offering is such that when I contacted one academic to ask for suggestions of literature from some of the under-published and under-translated African nations on my list, he suggested rather gruffly that I could find everything I was looking for on Google Books. He's not right – at least, not yet. Although the total of 20 million books in more than 480 languages (including several written in Klingon) that the firm had digitised by November 2013 is impressive, it falls well short of the 129,864,880 published titles Google engineer Leonid Taycher claimed to be in existence in August 2010 – a figure that would no doubt be much larger now if anyone had the time or wherewithal to do the maths. Even given Google's prediction that it will have every book in existence converted into virtual form by the end of this decade, the publishing and translation barriers facing writers in many parts of the planet mean that we are probably some way off from being able to get hold of a commercially published book in English from every nation in the world.

If and when that day comes, it will no doubt be thanks to activity taking place elsewhere on the Web. Because, from many readers' perspectives, the most valuable thing that the internet provides is not free access to texts – about which many of us have mixed feelings where authors' interests are concerned – but the opportunity to share information and opinions about what we read. Pooling our resources through blogs, comment sections and recommendations sites, we are able to build interest-based communities in order to share passions, dislikes and knowledge. It is as though something of the intimate insight that Lewis Buzbee describes in *The Yellow-Lighted Bookshop* transfers to us when we exchange our thoughts and feelings about books online. Just as the dedicated vendor in the quirky independent wordmonger's leans companionably on the counter while a customer stutters out an awkward request and feels, in so doing, that his or her occupation is, in Buzbee's words, 'a little like looking into another person's heart', we put on a bit of that privilege when we advise each other about stories online. Shielded by the anonymity of the screen, freed from the responsibility of answering for our comments face to face (much in the same way as when we engage with fictional people in stories), we often seem able to be more forthcoming and to receive ideas more openly than we might do in real life. If the bookshop is, to Buzbee, a space where individuals can 'become part of a river of creation and imagination that has flowed without interruption for thousands of years', then the online reading community is, in some respects, its descendant. Indeed, by virtue of the faceless nature of much online interaction, which means that – at least until recently – ideas have been able to stand or fall on their own merits rather than simply by virtue of the influence of whoever articulated them, the internet provides a basis for the sort of global conversation Goethe envisaged when he first discussed the concept of *Weltliteratur*. In the face of the impossibly vast and burgeoning quantities of literature that so dismayed and bewildered academics in previous decades, it points towards a way of establishing the 'new critical method' that Italian literary scholar Franco Moretti calls for in response to 'the sheer enormity of the task' of trying to engage with, define and understand world literature. Freed from the responsibility of comprehending it all – of being the sort of world-literature expert that can never exist, at least not in human form – netizens are at liberty to pool what they know without fear of having their right to express such opinions attacked.

Such people can make valuable additions to the international bank of knowledge and opinion stored in cyberspace precisely because they are free to be wrong. Their strength lies in the fact that, as former CBS news executive Jonathan Klein said in an attempt to undermine the credibility of blogging back in 2004, many of them are little more than 'a guy sitting in his living room in his pyjamas writing what he thinks'. They can upload details of the obscure text they read at school or the little-known translation passed down from their grandmother's library because they have no obligation to be final arbiters of these things.

The value of this licence to be wrong becomes clear when you look at the working practices of the Web's most successful commercial venture, Google. Far from championing perfection in all things, the firm that as of February 2014 is the second-largest in the world in terms of market value, after Apple, builds freedom to fail into its most ambitious research and development as a matter of policy. Staff working in its 'Google X' laboratory are given resources to work on mind-boggling problems, or 'moonshots', such as how to create cars that don't crash. With the odds of success stacked against them, most of these projects are expected to lead to dead ends. In fact, failure is rewarded because, according to department head Astro Teller – the grandson of hydrogen-bomb developer Edward Teller – the ethos of celebrating abortive efforts encourages risk-taking and avoids the stagnation that can set in when people hold on to doomed ideas for fear of attempting anything else. As he told the BBC in January 2014, he sees the moonshot process as being akin to sending a team of scouts out to explore uncharted terrain for new mountains to climb: 'If you shame them when they come back, if you tell them that they've failed you because they didn't find a mountain, no matter how diligently they looked for [sic] or how cleverly they looked for it, those scouts will quit your company.' Instead, the idea is to celebrate the effort with the understanding that, once in a blue moonshot, an ambitious venture will turn up something significant.

In many ways, such thinking is a return to the ethos of previous centuries when moneyed, and usually male, European amateurs ventured out to see what they could find, unhampered by the fear of getting it wrong. The same impulse that inspired the Victorian tea magnate Frederick John Horniman, who founded the museum down my road – complete with its centrepiece walrus stuffed to twice the size of any of its living relatives because no one displaying it knew any better – drives these virtual explorers. Though the demographic of those involved may have changed somewhat, the spirit of the enterprise is similar. And for every ten bulbous walruses there's always the chance that someone will turn up the Rosetta Stone.

The majority of us sharing thoughts and information about books online can't boast the resources of either Frederick Horniman or Google X, but many of us share something of their spirit of adventure and experimentation. We participate in discussions and launch projects for our own ends and are therefore answerable first and foremost to ourselves. Protected by our amateur status, we have the freedom to fail that Google goes to such lengths to foster and can venture ideas and opinions that may often be flawed, wacky or weird, but are sometimes inspired. Instead of slaving away at the hopeless task of establishing an immutable world-literature canon that will do for the whole planet – something that could, in the words of University of California Santa Cruz associate professor Vilashini Cooppan, 'from some central location, cover everything, contain all the texts, represent the globe, hold firm in the face of dizzying difference' – those of us who talk about books in the virtual world are free to construct our own partial accounts of the planet's narratives, accounts that we have the ability to expand or reshape at any time, adding titles, authors and even countries as we go. We can add to one another's insights and we can 'correct each other' – 'the greatest use of World Literature', according to Goethe; indeed, to this day I receive messages from people bolstering, querying or challenging things I wrote during my year of reading the world. Through the 'pluri-subjectivity of interaction' which, as critic and academic Michael Cronin claims, the online arena provides, we can build our own personal world libraries or idioliteratures, influenced and enriched by the comments and insights of those with whom we exchange ideas, but unique and distinct to us. As the UK's first professor of international communications Philip M. Taylor observed towards the end of the nineties in his essay on 'Third Wave Info-Propaganda: Psychological

Operations in the Post-Cold War Era', 'the public increasingly have the capacity to map the world out for themselves'. These days, we have the tools to do the same with books too.

*

Given the democratisation and international connections the internet has made possible, it's no surprise that hundreds of millions of us have embraced the technology. One in four of the world's population now carries a smartphone, enabling them to log on wherever they go. According to a Global Internet User Survey conducted by the Internet Society in 2012, 80 per cent of those with internet access feel that the World Wide Web has a positive role for people and society, two-thirds see it as having a role in solving international problems and 83 per cent would argue that the ability to go online should be a basic human right. Even allowing for the organisation's interest in showing the innovation it campaigns to promote in a positive light, it seems safe to say that the majority of us appear to share the sentiments that Tim Berners-Lee expressed in the *Independent* newspaper some ten years after he first sent his proposal for the World Wide Web to the management at CERN: 'The Web is a tremendous grass roots revolution. All these people coming from very different directions achieved a change. There's a tremendous message of hope for humanity in that.'

Yet, for all the hope the Web inspires in many, recent years have seen clouds start to gather on the virtual horizon. As I write this, news is breaking that the Turkish government has blocked the social network-ing site Twitter so that anyone who attempts to access the platform inside its borders is redirected to a statement by the nation's telecoms regulator. 'I don't care what the international community says at all. Everyone will see the power of the Turkish Republic,' said prime minis-ter Recep Tayyip Erdogan, having vowed to wipe out the site after it carried allegations of corruption against some of his close associates. The move is the latest in a long line of governmental attempts to curb free communication online. From the stealth tactics of China's 'Fifty

Cent Party' (as discussed in chapter seven) to the blanket internet shut-downs in Egypt, Libya and Syria during the Arab Spring, the desire to control the sharing of politically sensitive material and ideas has prompted many in power to reach for the delete button, jeopardising everyone's connection to and therefore ability to read the world.

Yet the limitation of information exchange is only part of the story. At the other end of the spectrum, the gathering of data by some of the world's most powerful private companies could present every bit as much of a threat – particularly where books are concerned. Because what David Vise, author of *The Google Story*, has dubbed 'the brand that has become an extension of [our] brains' (and certainly the brand that has become near-synonymous with the internet for many of us) works by mining and storing details about the millions of individuals who use it in more than 100 languages every day, Google has amassed a huge amount of information about the world's online community. Indeed, its founders Sergey Brin and Larry Page have made no secret of the fact that they will not be satisfied until they have stored '100 per cent of user data' – an achievable goal, given the centrality of its search engine to most online activity. Building a data monopoly, the extent of which Winston Churchill could probably never have begun to imagine when he declared that 'the empires of the future are the empires of the mind' in the 1940s, Google has already made itself indispensable to most of us and it has done so by knowing us and the world we live in almost better than we know ourselves.

Looked at in this light, projects such as Google Books are not gener-ous, philanthropic gestures to open up knowledge to all mankind so much as money-spinning ventures. They make business sense. By driving traffic through Google's virtual domains, they further the company's opportunities to observe its customers' habits and plait the brand ever more tightly into our lives. According to American cultural historian and academic librarian Robert Darnton, 'When businesses like Google look at libraries, they do not merely see temples of learning. They see potential assets or what they call "content," ready to be mined.' Nicholas Carr agrees, as he argues in his Pulitzer

Prize-nominated book *The Shallows: What the Internet is Doing to Our Brains*: 'The great library that Google is rushing to create shouldn't be confused with the libraries we've known up until now. It's not a library of books. It's a library of snippets.'

Given Google's approach to words in other areas of its work, Carr may well have a point – 'You have to try and make the words less human and more a piece of the machinery,' former vice president Marissa Mayer told the *New York Times* when discussing the firm's style guide in 2009. Indeed, what Carr has called the company's 'steady colonization of additional types of content' suggests that the machinery may have more in common with the approach of previous ages than just the spirit of adventure: it smacks of the imperialism found in the writing of such eras too. This has proved a concern for commentators from other cultural backgrounds. Writing in *Le Monde*, former head of the Bibliothèque nationale de France Jean-Noël Jeanneney claimed that Google Books presents 'a risk of crushing domination by America in defining the idea that future generations have of the world'. 'I don't want the French Revolution retold just by books chosen by the United States,' he protested. Therein lies the rub: though Google may claim to be digitising all the published texts in existence – and may believe it is doing so – no one has a way of double-checking. Without an independent, approved catalogue of everything published ever, we cannot verify that all books will be fairly represented in a commercially controlled global library. By building a monopoly of what there is to know, Google is becoming a law unto itself, landscaping cyberspace as it sees fit while legislators fumble and flail in its wake. If Google says there are 129,864,880 books in the world, we have to take its word for it. And should a time come when some of this published content proves to be not to the management's taste, it's hard to see what would stop these texts disappearing quietly from the virtual shelves. It's conceivable that the sort of extreme censorship that many of us regard as the preserve of totalitarian regimes could one day pervade the entire virtual world, not at the hands of governments or supranational political organisations, but through the corporate decisions of some of the world's wealthiest private companies. And without any way of keeping independent track of what's out there, most of us would probably never know.

*

The potential or otherwise for information distortion and deletion by the big companies in control of vast swathes of virtual real estate is worrying, but for some it's the least of readers' concerns on the Web. Numerous commentators, many of them working with books, have reported alarming changes in reading habits in recent years – developments which some ascribe to the hours people spend online. University lecturers have reported that they have to teach from extracts because literature students no longer read entire texts (there's a sad parallel with higher-education institutions in some African nations, where professors sometimes use excerpts because their departments cannot afford the books); reading surveys have revealed a steady decline in the hours devoted to off-screen reading, with the US Bureau of Labor Statistics showing that the average American over the age of fourteen spent only 143 minutes a week reading printed material in 2008; and research by organisations such as the UK charity Booktrust has uncovered a cultural divide in Britain that sees those from deprived backgrounds forsaking written stories for TV and film. Perhaps most striking of all are the difficulties that previously dedicated readers have reported in focusing on narratives. Here's historian David Bell writing in *The New Republic* about his encounter with an ebook back in 2005:

> I start reading, but while the book is well written and informative, I find it remarkably hard to concentrate. I scroll back and forth, search for key words, and interrupt myself even more often than usual to refill my coffee cup, check my e-mail, check the news, rearrange files in my desk drawer. Eventually I get through

the book and am glad to have done so. But a week later I find it remarkably hard to remember what I have read.

For Nicholas Carr, such struggles to maintain concentration go hand in hand with engagement with non-printed text and have a troubling explanation. Because of the plasticity of our brains – the same adaptability that makes it possible for our grey matter to rewire itself to make us more empathetic in response to stories – Carr maintains that the way we interact with text online is fundamentally changing how we read. 'Calm, focused, undistracted, the linear mind is being pushed aside by a new kind of mind that wants and needs to take in and dole out information in short, disjointed, often overlapping bursts – the faster, the better,' he writes. With clicks equating to revenue for many of the big players on the internet, Carr argues, the companies with the power to shape the architecture of the Web actively promote distraction over the kind of concentration that deep, rewarding reading requires, with the result that, in the words of blogger and science-fiction writer Cory Doctorow, whenever we log on we inhabit an 'ecosystem of interruption technologies'. The upshot is that those of us who spend a lot of time online are fundamentally altering our brain chemistry, becoming ever more like 'lab rats constantly pressing levers to get tiny pellets of social or intellectual nourishment' and finding it harder and harder to give lengthy, linear narratives the attention they deserve. Unable to focus on a subject long enough to gain anything other than a superficial grasp of it, we risk turning into what Richard Foreman has called '"pancake people" – spread wide and thin as we connect with that vast network of information accessed by the mere touch of a button'. Looking ahead, some commentators fear that this state of affairs could affect not only the way we read but the way we write. In an article for the *Wall Street Journal* in 2009, Steven Johnson foresaw a sinister future for a publishing industry beholden to the tyrannies of Search Engine Optimisation:

Writers and publishers will begin to think about how individual pages or chapters might rank in Google's results, crafting sections explicitly in the hopes that they will draw in that steady stream of search visitors. Individual paragraphs will be accompanied by descriptive tags to orient potential searchers; chapter titles will be tested to determine how well they rank.

It's a compelling argument, and one that will no doubt strike a chord with anyone who has lamented the ease with which the internet facilitates procrastination. Despite its noble beginnings, the World Wide Web is unquestionably host to a huge amount of vacuous, spurious and irrelevant material and is a great drain on time and attention. A comment by a Reddit user (which itself went viral on social media) captured the issue perfectly: in response to a discussion about what would be the hardest thing to explain to a time traveller from the 1950s about our lives, 'nuseramed' observed that it would be the fact that we carry a machine that gives us access to the entirety of data available to human beings – and that we use it to view photographs of pets and pick fights with people we've never met.

Before we all rush to unplug and banish ourselves from cyberspace in an effort to preserve our autonomy, identities and concentration spans, however, it is worth reflecting that, unprecedented though the time we're living through seems, we have, to some extent, been here before. As Tom Standage points out in *Writing on the Wall: Social Media – The First 2,000 Years*, many of the elements of the brave new digital age played a part in the societies of previous eras. From the gossipy graffiti on the walls of Pompeii and the poems copied and circulated in the Tudor court, to the banter of the telegraph operators (arguably the world's first 'online' community) and the DIY broadcasts so popular in the early days of radio until the US Government's 1912 Radio Act gave it the power to shut stations down 'in time of war or public peril or disaster', human beings have always sought means to exchange messages – both silly and serious – in the way we do today.

Indeed, as Standage puts it, the one-way media most of us grew up with was 'a temporary state of affairs, rather than the natural order of things'. And just as there have been numerous means of circulating information throughout history that offer parallels with the internet today, so there have always been those concerned about the effects of the new. Here's journalist and critic W.J. Stillman writing about the pernicious influence of the telegraph in the *Atlantic Monthly* in 1891:

> The effect is disastrous, and affects the whole range of our mental activities. We develop hurry into a deliberate system, skimming of surfaces into a science, the pursuit of novelties and sensations into the normal business of our lives . . . The frantic haste with which we bolt everything we take, seconded by the eager wish of the journalist not to be a day behind his competitor, abolishes deliberation from judgement and sound digestion from our mental constitutions. We have no time to go below surfaces, and as a general thing no disposition.

Going even further back, here's Erasmus heaping scorn upon the rash of printers springing up during the early sixteenth century, who, he was convinced, would:

> fill the world with pamphlets and books that are foolish, ignorant, malignant, libellous, mad, impious and subversive; and such is the flood that even things that might have done some good lose all their goodness.

And here's Plato's Socrates giving his view on that newfangled business you and I know as writing:

> If men learn this, it will implant forgetfulness in their souls; they will cease to exercise memory because they rely on that which is written, calling things to remembrance no longer from within

themselves, but by means of external marks. What you have discovered is a recipe not for memory, but for reminder. And it is no true wisdom that you offer your disciples, but only its semblance, for by telling them of many things without teaching them you will make them seem to know much, while for the most part they know nothing, and as men filled, not with wisdom but with the conceit of wisdom, they will be a burden to their fellows.

Taking the long view, it could be that many of the reservations expressed about the effects of the digital era prove groundless in the decades to come. Perhaps, as Standage argues, the concerns of the internet's critics amount to little more than 'the modern incarnation of the timeless complaint of the intellectual elite, every time technology makes publishing easier, that the wrong sort of people will use it to publish the wrong sort of things'.

What we do know is that it's too early to tell. While Standage is right that 'the technology that is demonized today may end up being regarded as wholesome and traditional tomorrow', as has been the case in the past, it's also true that the rapidity and reach of the internet is unmatched. Unlike poor W.J. Stillman, twenty-first-century journalists don't worry about being beaten by a day but by seconds – an anxiety that has seen many a respected individual release erroneous information in recent years in the scramble to be first with the news. With some 500 million tweets, more than two million blog posts and well over 100 billion emails pouring into cyberspace every day, we are bombarded with an unprecedented number of words.

In the absence of much concrete evidence either way as yet and the perspective that distance gives us, we are left to build arguments based on our own experience and feelings about the issues involved. For my part, I did not find that distraction was a major obstacle in my year of reading 197 books, but then I was urged on by the thought of all the people who had gone out of their way to help me. By the same token, despite Carr's concern about the prevalence and effects of clicking, I have not seen proof of this first-hand: every thousand views of my blog garners only a handful of clicks away from the site, despite three or four hyperlinks being embedded in nearly every post. It may be that the average visitor to my blog is more bookish, and hence traditional and linear in their style of perusing texts than most (or perhaps people simply don't read the articles at all), but the small sample of online behaviour I've had the opportunity to observe doesn't corroborate the dizzying, down-the-rabbit-hole clicking of links that Carr describes. But it's early days and so much has happened since the World Wide Web first flickered into existence that it will take years to unpack the implications. As Carr himself points out, 'the way the Web has progressed as a medium replays, with the velocity of a time-lapse film, the entire history of modern media. Hundreds of years have been compressed into a couple of decades.' At this stage, we are ill-equipped to take stock.

Predicting what lies ahead is always risky and nowhere more so than in the arena of the internet, which makes quaint nonsense of most attempts to sketch out the future in a matter of years if not months. Nevertheless, if I had to come down on one side of the argument or the other, I would venture that long, complex, linear narratives will continue to be read and valued in some form and that stories will remain central to who we are in the decades to come. But then I suppose I would say that: I love books. It will be for future generations to judge whether the time we are living through, a moment in history that sees us consuming more text per head than ever before, will prove favourable or fatal to the linear narrative. The possibility exists that someone will find this volume stuffed in a box in an attic in a hundred years' time and marvel – not at the concept of working through a sample of literature from every country in a year, but at the idea of reading books itself.

*

Fairly early on in my blogging career – a mere month into my year of reading the world – I had a salutary experience. Having read Oonya Kempadoo's relatively graphic coming-of-age novel *Buxton Spice*, I wrote a post praising the writer's descriptions of physical intimacy in the novel, titled it 'Guyana: Sex and how to do it' and pressed 'Publish'.

I was utterly unprepared for what happened next. No sooner was the post live than it became a magnet for large numbers of people looking for sex in Guyana – so much so in fact that, after 'a year of reading the world', 'guyana sex' became the second most popular search term bringing people to the blog for the life of the project, with numerous variations on the theme featuring further down the list. It was as though, with my tongue-in-cheek title, I had unwittingly opened a portal through which hordes of faceless people in search of erotic acts in South America's only English-speaking country stepped, looked around for a moment, decided my offering wasn't for them and went back the way they'd come. It was unsettling and perplexing – I couldn't help wondering what (if anything) they made of my thoughts on litera-ture before they disappeared off into the virtual shadows once more.

These days, I get very few sex tourists visiting my blog (or at least those who do stop by don't make their other interests obvious). The search term 'guyana sex' hardly ever features on the list of routes that people have taken to find the site. Much as I might like to believe this has to do with a culture change in the country that has long been recognised as a hot spot for human trafficking, the likeliest explanation has very little to do with the people involved. The reality is that in the three years or so that my blog has existed – surely a good century in Web terms – Google's PageRank algorithm has had ample opportunity to log the habits of both the people who hang out on ayearofreadingth-eworld.com and those who click away as fast as they arrive. Training what David Vise has called its 'laserlike focus on serving the best inter-ests of [its] users' on the little glitch that my non-search-engine-optimised title caused, Google has ironed out the problem. It has, as Vise puts it, made an art of 'reaching into the minds of searchers to divine not what keywords they actually typed, but what they *meant* to type'. Increasingly, what we see reflected back at us when we look for something online is not *the* world but a reading of *our* world – a mathematically calculated reflection of the insides of our own heads.

The advantages are obvious, but to those of us for whom efficiency isn't the sole reason for trying to find things out, there are negative aspects too. Privacy and surveillance issues aside, streamlined search means that we are less and less likely to unearth things by chance. The sort of lucky finds that punctuated my project – the CV of an academic in Vermont who had translated a novel by the Cormoros' first published novelist for fun, for example, or the Facebook page of the band of one of the only citizens of Luxembourg ever to publish a novel in English – are getting less and less likely. The joy of stumbling upon something when we were in the process of looking for something else entirely and thereby making a connection we might never have otherwise managed is being expunged, click by click. It seems somehow sad that these days you can't search for a prostitute in Georgetown and end up on a book blog by mistake.

In many ways, this is a continuation of what University of Chicago sociologist James Evans lamented when he observed a marked decline in the number of citations in scholarly articles from 1945 to 2005. The reason, Evans posited, was that working online was saving academics time by taking them only to directly relevant material rather than obliging them to read around the subject, as they would have done in library research. The result, he claimed, was 'a narrowing of science and scholarship'. Each researcher was locked into his or her particular niche of expertise and spending less and less time digesting the tangential material that would have placed many findings in context, 'facilitated broader comparisons and led researchers into the past'.

The truth is that some of the mind-expanding aspects of library research were present in the early days of the internet. Before search algorithms became so precise, there was a lot more scope to happen upon something by surprise – so much so that, in the course of my project I even nicknamed making such serendipitous connections 'stoogling' (a conflation of stumbling and googling). In the last year or so this has happened less and less. It's been a while since I stoogled on anything.

Google search isn't the only area in which our horizons are narrowing online. Since my project finished, Facebook has implemented charges for sending messages to people who are not 'friends' and provided users with the opportunity to pay to boost posts, giving prominence to paid-for content and reducing the screen time for everything else. A similar system pertains on Twitter, where companies can pay for promoted tweets, ensuring their messages stay at the top of results and get in front of the eyes of users who fit their target demographic. Elsewhere, newspapers like the *Guardian* have segregated their websites into country editions, allowing them to tailor what they present according to each audience. In addition, legislators originally caught off guard by the rapidity of the Web's development are beginning to catch up, mooting laws that, while often appearing to protect the vulnerable, may frequently have the effect of limiting access to information and silencing dissent online.

Although many of these changes may seem relatively minor in isolation and no doubt make good business sense for the organisations concerned, their cumulative effect is worrying. Slowly but surely, the global network that enabled unprecedented free communication between individuals around the world in the first years of this century – making it possible for people to collaborate across cultural, geographical and economic barriers and to read as never before – is separating out into national, financial, political and social compartments, with those who are able to pay most likely to be able to ensure that their voices are heard. The words of Joe Bloggs, Fulano de Tal, Wanjiku and Aam Aadmi are getting drowned out by the silken tones of those with the savvy and resources to hire the 'global megaphone' and make it work for them. For those of us lucky enough to have enjoyed the exhilarating freedom of the early days of the World Wide Web, it's hard not to feel that a portal to something precious is shimmering shut, or to shake the mournful sense that legislation and monetisation are at last coming puffing up behind us, bringing playtime to an end.

Some are determined not to go gentle into that good night. In an effort to combat damaging censorship and other threats to the Web's democratic ethos, Tim Berners-Lee seized the opportunity of the twenty-fifth anniversary of his invention to call for an 'Internet Users Bill of Rights' through his 'Web We Want' campaign in 2014. Organisations such as English PEN are monitoring and challenging decisions that threaten freedom of speech in cyberspace. Similarly, watchdogs like Article 19 are calling for 'net neutrality' that would require internet service providers and governments to 'treat all traffic and data on the internet equally' and pushing for online access to be enshrined as a human right in international law. Whether or not they and others like them succeed in influencing decision-makers will have a huge impact on the geography of the virtual landscape.

Looking up at my year of reading the world books, which still sit on Steve's bowed but-not-yet-broken shelf, I can't help but hope that these campaigns prevail. There they are: my companions for that extraordinary year, the books that conspired to stretch the boundaries of my thinking. There's the colourful spine of Dany Laferrière's *I am a Japanese Writer* and the dog-eared manuscript of Julia Duany's short story. Over on the right, I see Srđan Valjarević's witty *Lake Como*, Tahar Ben Jelloun's mind-boggling *The Sand Child* and Abdulrazak Gurnah's *Desertion* with its eloquent appeal against resigning yourself to living in a racialised world, while on the Kindle lying on the desk next to me, the manuscripts of *Ualalapi*, *The Tale of Aypi*, *The Golden Horse* and the crowd-sourced translation of *A casa do pastor* still lurk.

Behind these books stands another rank of stories: those of the people who helped me find and understand the things I read along the way. Marie-Thérèse Toyi smiles out from the battered spine of *Weep Not Refugee*, Guillermo Yuscarán twinkles in the bright cover design of *Points of Light*, and Alejandro Cao de Benós seems to stare warily at me from his Pyongyang office through the autobiography of Ri In Mo. I picture Jens Nielsen about to hand over Aglaja Veteranyi's estate to the Swiss National Archive when I catch sight of the black jacket of *Why the Child is Cooking in the Polenta* and hear the peals of laughter coming down the line from the Sammarinese ministry of culture every time the faded cover of *The Republic of San Marino* catches my eye. And for me *Cloudstreet* and *Ripples and Other Stories* will always be synonymous with Jason and Rafidah, those wonderful strangers and unwitting task-masters who between them set me off on the whole adventure, sending me wading through more than 50,000 pages – a good 1,000 kilometres of reading matter if I were to lay it end to end.

These texts are souvenirs of the longest year of my life; a time so packed with incident, thought, new encounters and discovery that, looking back, it seems more like a decade than a single twelve-month span. They are proof that here and now – in what may turn out to be a brief moment in history – extraordinary things are possible.

How much longer this continues to be the case remains to be seen. As we press ahead with defining the rules that will control who can reach what online, we are constructing the reality we will inhabit. These issues will affect our access not just to information, but to each other. They will determine whether or not the strangers of the future are able to exchange ideas and narratives freely across the globe; they will shape how we look at places and cultures far removed from our direct experience; and they will dictate whether it remains possible for a woman in Kuala Lumpur to stumble upon an obscure blog and decide to send someone on the other side of the planet a book. The choices we make in the next few years will control not just the stories that come into our orbit, but how we read them too. Ultimately, they will decide whether the technology we live through opens our minds or locks us ever more tightly into our own little worlds.

The 196 (. . . and Kurdistan)

AFGHANISTAN

The Patience Stone (*Syngué sabour: Pierre de patience*) by Atiq Rahimi,
translated from the French by Polly McLean (Vintage Digital, 2010)

ALBANIA

Broken April (*Prilli i thyer*) by Ismail Kadare,
translation © New Amsterdam Books and Saqi Books Publisher (Vintage Digital, 2003)

ALGERIA

The Sexual Life of an Islamist in Paris (*La Vie sexuelle d'un islamiste à Paris*) by Leila Marouane,
translated from the French by Alison Anderson (Europa Editions, 2010)

ANDORRA

The Teacher of Cheops (*El mestre de Kheops*) by Albert Salvadó,
translated from the Catalan/Spanish by Marc Brian Duckett (Albert Salvadó, 2011)

ANGOLA

The Whistler (*O assobiador*) by Ondjaki,
translated from the Portuguese by Richard Bartlett (Aflame Books, 2008)

ANTIGUA AND BARBUDA

Lucy by Jamaica Kincaid (Plume, 1991)

ARGENTINA

Seconds Out (*Segundos afuera*) by Martín Kohan,
translated from the Spanish by Nick Caistor (Serpent's Tail, 2010)

ARMENIA

Armenian Golgotha by Grigoris Balakian,
translated from the Armenian by Peter Balakian with Aris Sevag (Vintage, 2010)

AUSTRALIA

Cloudstreet by Tim Winton (Picador, 2011)

AUSTRIA

Frozen Time (*Die gefrorene Zeit*) by Anna Kim,
translated from the German by Michael Mitchell (Ariadne Press, 2010)

AZERBAIJAN

Ali and Nino (*Ali und Nino*) by Kurban Said,
translated from the German by Jenia Graman (Vintage, 2000)

BAHAMAS, THE

Thine is the Kingdom by Garth Buckner (Ravenna Press, 2008)

BAHRAIN

QuixotiQ by Ali Al Saeed (iUniverse, 2004)

BANGLADESH

The Good Muslim by Tahmima Anam (Canongate Books, 2011)

BARBADOS

Song of Night by Glenville Lovell (Soho Press, 1998)

BELARUS

King Stakh's Wild Hunt (*Дзікае паляванне караля Стаха*) by Uladzimir Karatkievich,
translated from the Belarusian by Mary Mintz (Belarusian Literature in English Translations, 2006)

BELGIUM

Invitation to a Voyage (*L'Invitation au voyage*) by François Emmanuel,
translated from the French by Justin Vicari (Dalkey Archive Press, 2011)

BELIZE

On Heroes, Lizards and Passion by Zoila Ellis (Cubola Productions, 1997)

BENIN

Stories We Tell Each Other by Rashidah Ismaili Abubakr (forthcoming)

BHUTAN

The Circle of Karma by Kunzang Choden (Zubaan/Penguin India, 2005)

BOLIVIA

Sangre dulce/Sweet Blood by Giovanna Rivero Santa Cruz, translated from the Spanish by Kathy S. Leonard (Editorial La Hoguera, 2006)

BOSNIA AND HERZEGOVINA

How the Soldier Repairs the Gramophone (*Wie der Soldat das Grammofon repariert*) by Saša Stanišić, translated from the German by Anthea Bell (Grove Press, 2008)

BOTSWANA

A Question of Power by Bessie Head (Heinemann, 1974)

BRAZIL

House of the Fortunate Buddhas (*A casa dos Budas ditosos*) by João Ubaldo Ribeiro, translated from the Portuguese by Clifford E. Landers (Dalkey Archive Press, 2011)

BRUNEI

Four Kings by Christopher Sun and Jimmy Chan (CreateSpace, 2011)

BULGARIA

Natural Novel (*Естествен роман*) by Georgi Gospodinov, translated from the Bulgarian by Zornitsa Hristova (Dalkey Archive Press, 2005)

BURKINA FASO

The Parachute Drop (*Le parachutage*) by Norbert Zongo, translated from the French by Christopher Wise (Africa World Press, Inc., 2004)

BURUNDI

Weep Not, Refugee by Marie-Thérèse Toyi (Emhai Printing & Publishing Company, 2007)

CAMBODIA

In the Shadow of the Banyan by Vaddey Ratner (Simon & Schuster, 2012)

CAMEROON

Mission to Kala (*Mission terminée*) by Mongo Beti, translated from the French by Peter Green (Mallory Publishing, 2008)

CANADA

Mauve Desert (*Le Désert mauve*) by Nicole Brossard, translated from the French by Susanne de Lotbinière-Harwood (Coach House Books, 1990, 2010)

CAPE VERDE

The Last Will & Testament of Senhor da Silva Araújo (*O testamento do Sr Napumoceno da Silva Araújo*) by Germano Almeida, translated from the Portuguese by Sheila Faria Glaser (New Directions, 2004)

CENTRAL AFRICAN REPUBLIC

Daba's Travels from Ouadda to Bangui (*Les Randonnées de Daba*) by Pierre Makombo Bamboté, translated from the French by John Buchanan-Brown (Pantheon, 1970)

CHAD

Told by Starlight in Chad (*Au Tchad sous les étoiles*) by Joseph Brahim Seid, translated from the French by Karen Haire Hoenig (Africa World Press, Inc., 2007)

CHILE

The Private Lives of Trees (*La vida privada de los arboles*) by
Alejandro Zambra,

translated from the Spanish by Megan McDowell (Open letter, 2010)

CHINA

Banished! (《扎根》)by Han Dong,

translated from the Mandarin by Nicky Harman (University of Hawaii
Press, 2009)

COLOMBIA

Delirium (*Delirio*) by Laura Restrepo,

translated from the Spanish by Natasha Wimmer (Vintage, 2008)

COMOROS

The Kaffir of Karthala (*Le Kafir du Karthala*) by Mohamed
Toihiri,

translated from the French by Anis Memon (unpublished)

CONGO, DEMOCRATIC REPUBLIC OF
Full Circle by Frederick Yamusangie (iUniverse, 2003)

CONGO, REPUBLIC OF

Johnny Mad Dog (*Johnny chien méchant*) by Emmanuel Dongala,
translated from the French by Maria Louise Ascher (Picador, 2005)

COSTA RICA

Cadence of the Moon (*En clave de luna*) by Óscar Núñez Olivas,
translated from the Spanish by Joanna Griffin (Aflame Books, 2007)

CÔTE D'IVOIRE

Allah is Not Obliged (*Allah n'est pas obligé*) by Ahmadou
Kourouma,

translated from the French by Frank Wynne (Vintage, 2007)

CROATIA

Our Man in Iraq (*Naš čovjek na terenu*) by Robert Perišič,
translated from the Croatian by Will Firth (Istros Books, 2012)

CUBA

Afro-Cuban Tales (*Cuentos negros de Cuba*) by Lydia Cabrera, translated from the Spanish by Alberto Hernandez-Chiroldes and Lauren Yoder (University of Nebraska Press, 2004)

CYPRUS

Ledra Street (*Οδός Λήδρας*) by Nora Nadjarian (Armida Publications, 2006)

CZECH REPUBLIC

Too Loud a Solitude (*Příliš hlučná samota*) by Bohumil Hrabal, translated from the Czech by Michael Henry Heim (Abacus, 2011)

DENMARK

The Exception (*Undtagelsen*) by Christian Jungersen, translated from the Danish by Anna Paterson (Phoenix, 2007)

DJIBOUTI

In the United States of Africa (*Aux Etats-Unis d'Afrique*) by Abdourahman A. Waberi, translated from the French by David and Nicole Ball (University of Nebraska Press, 2009)

DOMINICA

The Snake King of the Kalinago by Grade 6 of Atkinson School, Bataka, Dominica (Papillote Press, 2010)

DOMINICAN REPUBLIC

The Brief Wondrous Life of Oscar Wao by Junot Diaz (Faber, 2009)

EAST TIMOR

The Crossing: A Story of East Timor (*Cronica de uma travessia: A epoca do ai-dik-funam*) by Luis Cardoso, translated from the Portuguese by Margaret Jull Costa (Granta, 2000)

ECUADOR

The Villagers (Huasipungo) by Jorge Icaza, translated from the Spanish by Bernard Dulsey (Arcturus Paperbacks, 1974)

EGYPT

Spectres (أطفايا) by Radwa Ashour,
translated from the Arabic by Barbara Romaine (Arabia Books, 2010)

EL SALVADOR

Senselessness (*Insensatez*) by Horacio Castellanos Moya,
translated from the Spanish by Katherine Silver (New Directions, 2008)

EQUATORIAL GUINEA

Shadows of Your Black Memory (*Las Tinieblas de tu memoria negra*)
by Donato Ndongo,
translated from the Spanish by Michael Ugarte (Swan Isle Press, 2007)

ERITREA

The Consequences of Love by Sulaiman Addonia (Vintage Digital,
2008)

ESTONIA

The Beauty of History (*Ajaloo ilu*) by Viivi Luik,
translated from the Estonian by Hildi Hawkins (Norvil Press, 2007)

ETHIOPIA

Beneath the Lion's Gaze by Maaza Mengiste (Vintage Digital,
2010)

FIJI

Kava in the Blood by Peter Thomson (Booksurge, 2008)

FINLAND

The Year of the Hare (*Jäniksen vuosi*) by Arto Paasilinna,
translated from the Finnish by Herbert Lomas (Peter Owen Publishers,
2009)

FRANCE

Just Like Tomorrow (*Kiffe kiffe demain*) by Faïza Guène,
translated from the French by Sarah Ardizzone (Definitions, 2006)

GABON

Mema by Daniel Mengara (Heinemann Educational Publishers,
2003)

THE GAMBIA

Folk Tales and Fables from The Gambia (volume 1) by Dembo Fanta Bojang and Sukai Mbye Bojang (Educational Services, Gambia, 2011)

GEORGIA

Contemporary Georgian Fiction,
edited and translated from the Georgian by Elizabeth Heighway (Dalkey Archive Press, 2012)

GERMANY

All the Lights (*Die Nacht, die Lichter*) by Clemens Meyer,
translated from the German by Katy Derbyshire (And Other Stories, 2011)

GHANA

Journey by Gheysika Adombire Agambila (Sub-Saharan Publishers, 2006)

GREECE

Kassandra and the Wolf (*Η Κασσάνδρα και ο Λύκος*) by Margarita Karapanou,
translated from the Greek by N.C. Germanacos (Clockroot Books, 2009)

GRENADA

The Ladies are Upstairs by Merle Collins (Peepal Tree Press, 2011)

GUATEMALA

The President (*El señor president*) by Miguel Angel Asturias,
translated from the Spanish by Frances Partridge (Waveland Press, 1997)

GUINEA

The Guardian of the Word (*Le Maître de la parole*) by Camara Laye,
translated from the French by James Kirkup (Fontana, 1980)

GUINEA BISSAU

Unity and Struggle: speeches and writings of Amilcar (*Unidade e luta*) by Amílcar Cabral,
translated from the Portuguese by Michael Wolfers (Monthly Review Press, 1982)

GUYANA

Buxton Spice by Oonya Kempadoo (Phoenix, 1998)

HAITI

I am a Japanese Writer (*Je suis un écrivain japonais*) by Dany Laferrière,

translated from the French by David Homel (Douglas & McIntyre, 2011)

HONDURAS

Points of Light by Guillermo Yuscarán (Nuevo Sol Publicaciones, post-1989)

HUNGARY

Metropole (*Epepe*) by Ferenc Karinthy,

translated from the Hungarian by George Szirtes (Telegram Books, 2012)

ICELAND

Stone Tree (*Steintré*) by Gyrðir Elíasson,

translated from the Icelandic by Victoria Cribb (Comma Press, 2008)

INDIA

Kaalam (*Kaalam*) by M.T. Vasudevan Nair,

translated from the Malayalam by Gita Krishnankutty (Orient Blackswan, 2012)

INDONESIA

Durga/Umayi by Y.B. Mangunwijaya,

translated from the Indonesian by Ward Keeler (University of Washington Press, 2004)

IRAN

Touba and the Meaning of Night (*Tuba va ma'na-ye shab*) by Shahrnush Parsipur,

translated from the Persian by Havva Houshmand and Kamran Talattof (The Feminist Press at the City University of New York, 2006)

IRAQ

The Madman of Freedom Square (مجنون ساحة الحرية) by Hassan Blasim,

translated from the Arabic by Jonathan Wright (Comma Press, 2011)

IRELAND

Ulysses by James Joyce, read by Jim Norton with Marcella Riordan, directed by Roger Marsh, produced by Nicolas Soames (Naxos, 2004)

ISRAEL

Blooms of Darkness (פרחי האפלה) by Aharon Appelfeld,

translated from the Hebrew by Jeffrey M. Green (Alma Books, 2012)

ITALY

Gomorrah (*Gomorra*) by Roberto Saviano,

translated from the Italian by Virginia Jewiss (Pan Books, 2008)

JAMAICA

John Crow's Devil by Marlon James (Macmillan Caribbean, 2008)

JAPAN

Manazuru (真鶴) by Hiromi Kawakami,

translated from the Japanese by Michael Emmerich (Counterpoint, 2010)

JORDAN

Cities of Salt (مدن الملح) by Abdelrahman Munif,

translated from the Arabic by Peter Theroux (Vintage International, 1989)

KAZAKHSTAN

The Nomads («Кочевники») by Ilyas Yesenberlin,

translated by Anon (Ilyas Yesenberlin Foundation, 1998)

KENYA

Kenya, Will You Marry Me? by Philo Ikonya (Langaa Research & Publishing Common Initiative Group, 2011)

KIRIBATI

Waa in Storms by Teweiariki Teaero (Institute of Pacific Studies, University of the South Pacific, 2004)

KURDISTAN

The Man in Blue Pyjamas: A prison memoir (*Pyawiky bijama shin*) by Jalal Barzanji,
based on a translation from the Kurdish by Sabah Salih (University of Alberta Press, 2012)

KUWAIT

The Chronicles of Dathra, a Dowdy Girl from Kuwait (volume 1), by Danderma, illustrated by Fatima F. Al-Othman (danderma.net, 2011)

KYRGYZSTAN

Jamilia (*Djamilia*) by Chingiz Aitmatov,
translated from the Russian by James Riordan (Telegram, 2007)

LAOS

Mother's Beloved: Stories from Laos (ccແງccມ) by Outhine Bounyavong,
translated from the Lao by Anon (University of Washington Press, 1999)

LATVIA

With Dance Shoes in Siberian Snows (*Ar balles kurpēm Sibīrijas sniegos*) by Sandra Kalniete,
translated from the Latvian by Margita Gailītis (Dalkey Archive Press, 2009)

LEBANON

One Thousand and One Nights by Hanan Al-Shaykh (Bloomsbury, 2011)

LESOTHO

Basali!: Stories by and about women in Lesotho edited by K. Limakatso Kendall (University of Natal Press, 1995)

LIBERIA

Konkai: Living Between Two Worlds by Mardia Stone (Cotton Tree Press, 2011)

LIBYA

The Bleeding of the Stone (نزيف الحجر) by Ibrahim Al-Koni, translated from the Arabic by May Jayyusi and Christopher Tingley (Interlink Books, 2002)

LIECHTENSTEIN

Seven Years in Tibet (*Sieben Jahre in Tibet*) by Heinrich Harrer, translated from the German by Richard Graves (Flamingo, 1994)

LITHUANIA

No Men, No Cry ('Collective' series) (International Cultural Programme Centre, 2011)

LUXEMBOURG

Minute Stories by Robi Gottlieb-Cahen (Éditions Phi, 2014)

MACEDONIA

Conversation with Spinoza (*Razgovor so Spinoza*) by Goce Smilevski,
translated from the Macedonian by Filip Korzenski (Northwestern University Press, 2006)

MADAGASCAR

Voices from Madagascar edited by Jacques Bourgeacq and Liliane Ramarosoa (Ohio University Press, 2002)

MALAWI

The Jive Talker: Or, How to Get a British Passport by Samson Kambalu (Vintage Digital, 2008)

MALAYSIA

Ripples and Other Stories by Shih-Li Kow (Silverfish Books, 2008)

MALDIVES

Dhon Hiyala and Ali Fulhu by Abdullah Sadiq,
translated from the Dhivehi by Fareesha Abdullah and Michael O'Shea (© F. Abdullah and M. O'Shea, 2004)

MALI

The Fortunes of Wangrin (*L'Etrange destin de Wangrin*) by Amadou Hampâté Bâ,
translated from the French by Aina Pavolini Taylor (Indiana University Press, 1999)

MALTA

Happy Weekend by Immanuel Mifsud,
translated from the Maltese by Rose Marie Caruana, Mary Darmanin, Albert Gatt and Maria Grech Ganado (Midsea Books, 2006)

MARSHALL ISLANDS

Marshall Islands Legends and Stories told by Tonke Aisea et al.,
collected, edited and translated by Daniel A. Kelin II, illustrated by Nashton T. Nashon (Bess Press Inc., 2003)

MAURITANIA

Angels of Mauritania and the Curse of the Language by Mohamed Bouya Bamba (Mohamed Bouya Bamba, 2011)

MAURITIUS

Benares by Barlen Pyamootoo,
translated from the French by Will Hobson (Canongate, 2004)

MEXICO

Like Water for Chocolate: A Novel in Monthly Installments with Recipes, Romances and Home Remedies (*Como agua para chocolate*) by Laura Esquivel,
translated from the Spanish by Carol and Thomas Christensen (Anchor, 2002)

MICRONESIA, FEDERATED STATES OF

The Book of Luelen by Luelen Bernart,
translated from the Pohnpeian dialect and edited by John Fischer, Saul Riesenberg and Marjorie Whiting (Australian National University Press, 1977)

MOLDOVA

The Story of An Ant (Сказка про муравья) by Ion Drutse,

translated from the Moldovan by Iraida Kotrutse, illustrated by Nina Danilenko (Kishinev Literatura Artistika, 1988)

MONACO

Grace Kelly: Princesse du Cinéma edited by Richard and Danae Projetti (Stanislas Choko, 2007)

MONGOLIA

The Blue Sky (*Der blaue Himmel*) by Galsan Tschinag, translated from the German by Katharina Rout (Milkweed Editions, 2006)

MONTENEGRO

A Lullaby for No Man's Wolf (*Uspavanka za Vuka Ničijeg*) by Xenia Popovich, translated from the Montenegrin by Xenia Popovich (Xenia Popovich, 2012)

MOROCCO

The Sand Child (*L'Enfant du sable*) by Tahar Ben Jelloun, translated from the French by Alan Sheridan (Quartet Books, 1988)

MOZAMBIQUE

Ualalapi by Ungulani Ba Ka Khosa, translated from the Portuguese by Isaura de Oliveira and Richard Bartlett (translation unpublished)

MYANMAR

Smile as they Bow by Nu Nu Yi, translated from the Burmese by Alfred Birnbaum and Thi Thi Aye (Hyperion, 2008)

NAMIBIA

The Purple Violet of Oshaantu by Neshani Andreas (Heinemann, 2001)

NAURU

Stories from Nauru by Ben Bam Solomon et al. (The University of the South Pacific Nauru Centre & Institute of Pacific Studies, 1996)

NEPAL

The Lazy Conman and Other Stories by Ajit Baral, illustrated by Durga Baral (Penguin India, 2009)

NETHERLANDS

The Twin (Boven is het stil) by Gerbrand Bakker,

translated from the Dutch by David Colmer (Vintage, 2009)

NEW ZEALAND

Once Were Warriors by Alan Duff (Vintage, 1995)

NICARAGUA

Infinity in the Palm of her Hand (El infinito en la palma de la mano) by Gioconda Belli,

translated from the Spanish by Margaret Sayers Peden (Harper, 2010)

NIGER

The Epic of Askia Mohammed recounted by Nouhou Malio,

translated from the Songhay by Thomas A. Hale et al. (Indiana University Press, 1996)

NIGERIA

The Secret Lives of Baba Segi's Wives by Lola Shoneyin (Serpent's Tail, 2011)

NORTH KOREA

My Life and Faith by Ri In Mo,

translated from the Korean by Anon (Foreign Languages Publishing House, Pyongyang, Juche 86 (1997))

NORWAY

Hunger (Sult) by Knut Hamsun,

translated from the Norwegian by George Egerton (Dover, 2003)

OMAN

My Grandmother's Stories: folk tales from Dhofar collected and transcribed by Khadija bint Alawi Al-Dhahab,

translated by W. Scott Chahanovich, Munira Al-Ojaili, Fatima Al-Mashani, Muna Al-Mashani, Muna Saffrar, illustrated by Fatima bint Alawi Muqaybil (Sultan Qaboos Cultural Center, 2012)

PAKISTAN

The Wandering Falcon by Jamil Ahmad (Penguin, 2011)

PALAU

Spirits' Tides by Susan Kloulechad (unpublished)

PALESTINE

Mordechai's Moustache and his Wife's Cats (شارب مخدريا وقطط زوجتـ)
by Mahmoud Shukair,
translated from the Arabic by Issa J. Boullata, Elizabeth Whitehouse,
Elizabeth Winslow and Christina Phillips (Banipal Books, 2007)

PANAMA

The Golden Horse (*El caballo de oro*) by Juan David Morgan,
translated from the Spanish by John Cullen (translation unpublished)

PAPUA NEW GUINEA

Mata Sara by Regis Tove Stella (University of Papua New Guinea
Press and Bookshop, 2010)

PARAGUAY

I the Supreme (*Yo el Supremo*) by Augusto Roa Bastos,
translated from the Spanish by Helen R. Lane (Faber & Faber, 1988)

PERU

Death in the Andes (*Lituma en los Andes*) by Mario Vargas
Llosa,
translated from the Spanish by Edith Grossman (Faber & Faber,
1996)

PHILIPPINES

Ilustrado by Miguel Syjuco (Picador, 2010)

POLAND

Illegal Liaisons (*Nielegalne związki*) by Grażyna Plebanek,
translated from the Polish by Danusia Stok (Stork Press, 2012)

PORTUGAL

The Mandarin and Other Stories (*O Mandarim*) by José Maria Eça
de Queiroz,
translated from the Portuguese by Margaret Jull Costa (Dedalus,
2009)

QATAR

The Corsair (القرصان) by Abdulaziz Al Mahmoud,
translated from the Arabic by Amira Nowaira (Bloomsbury Qatar
Foundation Publishing, 2012)

ROMANIA

The Băiuț Alley Lads (*Băiuțeii*) by Filip & Matei Florian,
translated from the Romanian by Alistair Ian Blyth (University of
Plymouth Press, 2010)

RUSSIA

One Day in the Life of Ivan Denisovich (Один день Ивана
Денисовича) by Aleksandr Solzhenitsyn,
translated from the Russian by Ralph Parker (Penguin Classics, 2000)

RWANDA

Teta: a story of a young girl by Barassa (Real Africa Books, 2010)

SAINT KITTS AND NEVIS

Only God Can Make a Tree by Bertram Roach (Athena Press,
2008)

SAINT LUCIA

Neg Maron: Freedom Fighter by Michael Aubertin (Caribbean
Diaspora Press, 2000)

SAINT VINCENT AND THE GRENADINES

The Moon is Following Me by Cecil Browne (Matador, 2010)

SAMOA

Telesa: The Covenant Keeper by Lani Wendt Young (Lani Wendt
Young, 2011)

SAN MARINO

The Republic of San Marino by Giuseppe Rossi (The Governmental
Tourist Body Sport and Spectacle of the Republic of San Marino,
1976)

SÃO TOMÉ AND PRINCIPE

The Shepherd's House (*A casa do pastor*) by Olinda Beja,

translated from the Portuguese by Yema Ferreira, Ana Fletcher, Tamsin
Harrison, Margaret Jull Costa, Clare Keates, Ana Cristina Morais,
Robin Patterson, Ana Silva and Sandra Tavares (translation
unpublished)

SAUDI ARABIA

Girls of Riyadh (بنات الرياض) by Rajaa Alsanea,
translated from the Arabic by Rajaa Alsanea and Marilyn Booth (Penguin,
2008)

SENEGAL

So Long a Letter (Une si longue lettre) by Mariama Bâ,
translated from the French by Modupé Bodé-Thomas (Heinemann
International Literature & Textbooks, 1989)

SERBIA

Lake Como (Komo) by Srđan Valjarević,
translated from the Serbian by Alice Copple-Tošić (Geopoetika Publishing, Belgrade, 2009)

SEYCHELLES

Voices: Seychelles Short Stories by Glynn Burridge (Nighthue
Publications, 2000)

SIERRA LEONE

A Long Way Gone by Ishmael Beah (Fourth Estate, 2007)

SINGAPORE

Fistful of Colours by Suchen Christine Lim (SNP Editions,
2003)

SLOVAKIA

Rivers of Babylon (Rivers of Babylon) by Peter Pišťánek,
translated from the Slovak by Peter Petro (Garnett Press, 2007)

SLOVENIA

*The Golden Shower or What Men Want (Zlati Dez ali Kaj Hoce
Moski)* by Luka Novak,
translated from the Slovenian by Urska Charney (Guernica Editions,
2012)

SOLOMON ISLANDS

The Alternative by John Saunana (University of the South Pacific, 1980)

SOMALIA

Secrets by Nuruddin Farah (Penguin, 1999)

SOUTH AFRICA

African Delights by Siphiwo Mahala (Jacana Media, 2011)

SOUTH KOREA

The Guest (손님) by Hwang Sok-Yong,
translated from the Korean by Kyung-Ja Chun and Maya West (Seven Stories Press, 2011)

SOUTH SUDAN

'To Forgive is Divine Not Human' by Julia Duany (ayearofreadingtheworld.com, 2012)

SPAIN

Exiled from Almost Everywhere (*El exiliado de aqui y alla*) by Juan Goytisolo,
translated from the Spanish by Peter Bush (Dalkey Archive Press, 2011)

SRI LANKA

Metta (*Podu Purushaya*) by Sunethra Rajakarunanayake,
translated from the Sinhala by Carmen Wickramagamage (The Three Wheeler Press, 2011)

SUDAN

Season of Migration to the North (موسم الهجرة إلى الشمال) by Tayeb Salih,
translated from the Arabic by Denys Johnson-Davies (Penguin, 2003)

SURINAME

The Cost of Sugar (*Hoe duur was de suiker?*) by Cynthia McLeod,
translated from the Dutch by Gerald R. Mettam (HopeRoad, 2011)

SWAZILAND

Weeding the Flowerbeds by Sarah Mkhonza (Sarah Mkhonza, Xlibris, 2009)

SWEDEN

Montecore (*Montecore: en unik tiger*) by Jonas Hassen Khemiri, translated from the Swedish by Rachel Willson-Broyles (Knopf, 2011)

SWITZERLAND

Why the Child is Cooking in the Polenta (*Warum das Kind in der Polenta kocht*) by Aglaja Veteranyi, translated from the German by Vincent Kling (Dalkey Archive Press, 2012)

SYRIA

Damascus Nights (*Erzähler der Nacht*) by Rafik Schami, translated from the German by Philip Boehm Publisher (Arabia Books, 2011)

TAIWAN

Crystal Boys (孽子) by Pai Hsien-yung, translated from the Chinese by Howard Goldblatt (Gay Sunshine Press, 1995)

TAJIKISTAN

Hurramabad (*Хуррамабадскую трилогию*) by Andrei Volos, translated from the Russian by Arch Tait (GLAS, 2001)

TANZANIA

Desertion by Abdulrazak Gurnah (Bloomsbury, 2005)

THAILAND

Time: a Thai Novel (เวลา) by Chart Korbjitti, translated from the Thai by Marcel Barang (Thai Fiction Publishing, 2010)

TOGO

An African in Greenland (*L'Africain du Groenland*) by Tété-Michel Kpomassie, translated from the French by James Kirkup (New York Review Books, 2001)

TONGA

A Providence of War by Joshua Taumoefolau (Lulu, 2009)

TRINIDAD AND TOBAGO

One Scattered Skeleton by Vahni Capildeo (unpublished, extracts published in *London: City of Disappearances* edited by Iain Sinclair, Penguin, 2006)

TUNISIA

Talismano (*Talismano*) by Abdelwahab Meddeb,
translated from the French by Jane Kuntz (Dalkey Archive Press, 2011)

TURKEY

The Forty Rules of Love by Elif Shafak (Penguin, 2011)

TURKMENISTAN

The Tale of Aypi by Ak Welsapar,
translated from the Turkmen by W.M. Coulson (translation unpublished)

TUVALU

Tuvalu: A History by Simati Faaniu, Vinaka Ielemia, Taulu Isako, Tito Isala, Laumua Kofe (Rev.), Nofoaiga Lafita, Pusineli Lafai, Kalaaki Laupepa (Dr), Nalu Nia, Talakatoa O'Brien, Sotaga Pape, Laloniu Samuelu, Enele Sapoaga, Pasoni Taafaki, Melei Telavi, Noatia Penitala Teo, Vaieli Tinilau, edited by Hugh Laracy (Institute of Pacific Studies, 1983)

UGANDA

Abyssinian Chronicles by Moses Isegawa (Picador, 2011)

UKRAINE

Death and the Penguin (*Smert' postoronnego*) by Andrey Kurkov, translated from the Russian by George Bird (Melville International Crime, 2011)

UNITED ARAB EMIRATES

The Wink of the Mona Lisa and Other Stories from the Gulf (غمزة الموناليزا) by Mohammad Al Murr,
translated from the Arabic by Jack Briggs (Motivate Publishing, 1998)

UNITED KINGDOM

Martha, Jack and Shanco (*Martha Jac a Sianco*) by Caryl Lewis,
translated from the Welsh by Gwen Davies (Parthian, 2007)

UNITED STATES OF AMERICA

American Gods by Neil Gaiman (Headline, 2001)

URUGUAY

The Decapitated Chicken and Other Stories (*La gallina degollada*)
by Horacio Quiroga,
translated from the Spanish by Margaret Sayers Peden (University of
Wisconsin Press, 2004)

UZBEKISTAN

The Railway (ЖЕЛЕЗНАЯ ДОРОГА) by Hamid Ismailov,
translated from the Russian by Robert Chandler (Vintage, 2007)

VANUATU

Laef Blong Mi: From village to nation by Sethy John Regenvanu
(Institute of Pacific Studies and Emalus Campus, University of the
South Pacific, 2004)

VATICAN CITY

Shroud of Secrecy: The story of corruption within the Vatican (*Via col
vento in Vaticano*) by The Millenari,
translated from the Italian by Ian Martin (Key Porter Books, 2000)

VENEZUELA

The Sickness (*La Enfermedad*) by Alberto Barrera Tyszka,
translated from the Spanish by Margaret Jull Costa (MacLehose Press, 2011)

VIETNAM

The Sorrow of War (*Nỗi buồn chiến tranh*) by Bao Ninh,
English version by Frank Palmos from translation by Phan Thanh Hao
(Minerva, 1994)

YEMEN

The Hostage (الرهينة) by Zayd Mutee' Dammaj,
translated from the Arabic by May Jayyusi and Christopher Tingley
(Interlink Books, 1994)

ZAMBIA

A Cowrie of Hope by Binwell Sinyangwe (Heinemann, 2000)

ZIMBABWE

The Hairdresser of Harare by Tendai Huchu (Weaver Press, 2010)

Select Bibliography

In many ways, everything I've ever read has informed this book. However, as it wouldn't be practical to list this – even if it were possible – I've limited this list to titles, publications, articles, websites and organisations (in addition to the 197 texts read for my year of reading the world) that are cited in detail or that had a particular bearing on my thinking during the project and writing process. Any omissions or errors are mine.

BOOKS

Ackroyd, Peter, *Dickens* (London: Sinclair-Stevenson, 1990)

Akbari, Suzanne Conklin, Wiebke Denecke, Vinay Dharwadker, Barbara Fuchs, Caroline Levine, Pericles Lewis, Emily Wilson, Martin Puchner (eds.), *Norton Anthology of World Literature, The, Third Edition* (New York: W.W. Norton & Company, 2012)

Alden, J.B., *Alden's Cyclopedia of Universal Literature, Presenting Biographical and Critical Notices and Specimens from the Writings of Eminent Authors of All Age* (1889; Stockbridge: Hardpress, 2013)

Appignanesi, Lisa (ed.), *Free Expression is No Offence* (London: Penguin, 2005)

Armstrong, Paul B., *How Literature Plays with the Brain: The Neuroscience of Reading and Art* (Baltimore and London: John Hopkins University Press, 2013)

Bailey, Sydney D., *The United Nations: A Short Political Guide* (London: Macmillan, 1989)

Barker, William, *The Adages of Erasmus* (Toronto: University of Toronto Press, 2001)

Barnet, Richard, *Roots of War* (1972; New York: Viking, 1973)

Boswell, James, *The Life of Samuel Johnson* (1791; London: Penguin, 2008)

Bowring, John, *A Visit to the Philippine Islands* (London: 1859)

Boxall, Peter (ed.), *1001 Books You Must Read Before You Die* (2006; London: Cassell Illustrated, 2008)

Brotton, Jerry, *A History of the World in Twelve Maps* (London: Penguin, 2013)

Broun, Heywood and Margaret Leech, *Anthony Comstock: Roundsman of the Lord* (New York: Boni, 1927)

Buzbee, Lewis, *The Yellow-Lighted Bookshop* (Minnesota: Graywolf Press, 2006)

Callil, Carmen, Nicholas Carr, Jane Davis, Mark Haddon, Blake Morrison, Tim Parks, Michael Rosen, Zadie Smith, Jeanette Winterson, Maryanne Wolf and Mirit Barzillai, *Stop What You're Doing and Read This!* (London: Vintage, 2011)

Carey, John, *The Intellectuals and the Masses: Pride and Prejudice Among the Literary Intelligentsia, 1880–1939* (London: Faber & Faber, 1992)

Carr, Nicholas, *The Shallows: How the Internet is Changing the Way We Think* (London: Atlantic Books, 2011)

Cheshire, Jenny and Dieter Stein (eds.), *Taming the Vernacular: From Dialect to Written Standard Language* (London: Longman, 1997)

Churchill, Winston, *War Speeches: From June 25, 1941 to September 6, 1943* (Boston: Houghton Mifflin, 1953)

Collier, Paul, *The Bottom Billion* (Oxford: Oxford University Press, 2008)

Conrad, Joseph, *Nostromo* (1904; Hertfordshire: Wordsworth Editions, 1996)

Curtin, Philip, *The Image of Africa: British Ideas and Action, 1780–1850* (Wisconsin: University of Wisconsin Press, 1964)

Dames, Nicholas, *The Physiology of the Novel: Reading, Neural Science, and the Form of Victorian Fiction* (Oxford: Oxford University Press, 2007)

Damrosch, David, *How to Read World Literature* (West Sussex: Wiley-Blackwell, 2008)

Damrosch, David, *What is World Literature?* (Princeton: Princeton University Press, 2003)

Davidson, Basil, *The African Past: Chronicles from Antiquity to Modern Times* (London: Longmans, 1964)

Demick, Barbara, *Nothing to Envy: Real Lives in North Korea* (London: Granta 2010)

Desai, Kiran, *The Inheritance of Loss* (2006; London: Penguin 2007)

D'haen, Theo, César Domínguez and Mads Rosendahl Thomsen (eds.), *World Literature: A Reader* (Abingdon: Routledge, 2013)

Edwards, Oliver, *Talking of Books* (London: Heinemann, 1957)

Evans, Nicholas, *Dying Words: Endangered Languages and What They Have to Tell Us* (West Sussex: Wiley-Blackwell, 2010)

Evatt, Herbert Vere, *The United Nations* (Oxford: Oxford University Press, 1948)

Fanon, Frantz, and Constance Farrington (tr.), *The Wretched of the Earth* (*Les damnés de la terre*) (1965; 1967; 1983; 1990; London: Penguin, 2001)

Finnegan, Ruth, *Oral Literature in Africa* (Oxford: Clarendon Press, 1970)

Fischer, Steven Roger, *A History of Reading* (2003; London: Reaktion Books, 2005)

Furnham, Adrian and Stephen Bochner, *Culture Shock: Psychological Reactions to Unfamiliar Environments* (York: Methuen, 1986)

Gibbs, James and Jack Mapanje, *The African Writers' Handbook* (Oxford: African Books Collective, 1999)

Goethe, Johann von Wolfgang and Johann Peter Eckermann, John Oxenford (tr.) and J.K. Moorhead, *Conversations of Goethe with Johann Peter Eckermann* (*Gespräche mit Goethe*) (1836; 1848; Boston: Da Capo Press, 1998)

Greenberger, Allen J., *The British Image of India: A Study in the Literature of Imperialism 1800–1960* (Oxford: Oxford University Press, 1969)

Grenoble, Lenore A., and Lindsay J. Whaley (eds.), *Endangered Languages: Language Loss and Community and Response* (Cambridge: Cambridge University Press, 1998)

Grossman, Edith, *Why Translation Matters* (Yale: Yale University Press, 2010)

Guibernau, Montserrat, *The Identity of Nations* (Cambridge: Polity, 2007)

Hakemulder, Jèmeljan, *The Moral Laboratory: Experiments Examining the Effects of Reading Literature on Social Perception and Moral Self-concept* (Amsterdam: John Benjamins Publishing, 2000)

Hale, Thomas A., *Griots and Griottes* (Indiana: Indiana University Press, 2007)

Haley, Alex, *Roots* (1976; 1977; London: Vintage, 1991)

Hanne, Michael, *The Power of the Story* (Oxford: Berghahn, 1994)

Haraszti, Miklós, and K. Landesmann and S. Landesmann (trs.), *The Velvet Prison: Artists Under State Socialism* (*A Cenzura Esztetikaja*) (1987; London: I.B. Tauris, 1988)

Harden, Blaine, *Escape from Camp 14: One Man's Remarkable Odyssey from North Korea to Freedom in the West* (London: Pan, 2013)

Ingersoll, Earl G. and Mary C. Ingersoll (eds.), *Conversations with Anthony Burgess* (Jackson: University Press of Mississippi, 2008)

Iser, Wolfgang, *The Act of Reading: A Theory of Aesthetic Response* (Baltimore & London: John Hopkins University Press, 1978)

Keen, Suzanne, *Empathy and the Novel* (New York: Oxford University Press, USA, 2007)

King James Bible, The (London: 1611)

Kirkpatrick, David, *The Facebook Effect: The Inside Story of the Company That Is Connecting the World* (London: Simon & Schuster, 2010)

Larson, Charles R., *The Ordeal of the African Writer* (London: Zed Books, 2001)

Lemon, Lee T. and Marion J. Rees (eds. and trs.), *Russian Formalist Criticism: Four Essays* (Lincoln: University of Nebraska Press, 1965)

Luard, Evan, *The United Nations: How it Works and What it Does* (1979; London: Palgrave Macmillan, 1994)

Lyons, Martyn, *Books: A Living History* (2011; London: Thames & Hudson, 2013)

Magill, Frank N., *Masterpieces of World Literature in Digest Form* (New York: Harper & Row, 1952)

Manguel, Alberto, *A History of Reading* (1996; London: Flamingo, 1997)

Mason, Alane, Dedi Felman and Samantha Schnee (eds.), *Literature from the Axis of Evil: Writing from Iran, Iraq, North Korea, and Other Enemy Nations* (2006; New York: The New Press, 2007)

Mendelson, Charlotte, *Almost English* (London: Mantle, 2013)

Mill, John Stuart, *A System of Logic, Ratiocinative and Inductive* (London: 1843)

Mill, John Stuart, *On Liberty* (London: 1859)

Milton, John, *Aeropagitica: A Speech for the Liberty of Unlicensed Printing to the Parliament of England* (London: 1644)

Ní Chuilleanáin, Eiléan, Cormac Ó Cuilleanáin and David Parris (eds.), *Translation and Censorship: Patterns of Communication and Interference* (Dublin: Four Courts Press, 2009)

Orwell, George, *The Road to Wigan Pier* (1937; London: Penguin, 2001)

Parker, Mike, *Map Addict: A Tale of Obsession, Fudge & the Ordnance Survey* (London: Collins, 2009)

Pecora, Vincent P., *Nations and Identities: Classic Readings* (West Sussex: Wiley-Blackwell, 2001)

Plato and Reginald Hackforth (tr.), *Phaedrus* (Cambridge: Cambridge University Press, 1952)

Pollard, David E. (ed.), *Translation and Creation: Readings of Western Literature in Early Modern China* (Amsterdam: John Benjamins Publishing, 1998)

Post, Chad W., *The Three Percent Problem: Rants and Responses on Publishing, Translation and the Future of Reading* (Rochester: Open Letter, 2011)

Reinhardt, Éric and Sam Taylor (tr.), *The Victoria System* (*Le système Victoria*) (London: Hamish Hamilton, 2013)

Rundle, Christopher, and Kate Sturge (eds.), *Translation Under Facism* (London: Palgrave Macmillan, 2010)

Rushdie, Salman, *The Satanic Verses* (1988; London: Vintage, 1998)

Said, Edward W., *Culture & Imperialism* (1993; London: Vintage, 1994)

Said, Edward W., *Orientalism* (1978; 1995; Penguin, 2003)

Sale, George (tr.), *The Koran: Commonly Called the Alkoran of Mohammed* (London: 1734)

Schneider, Helga, *Let Me Go* (London: Heinemann, 2004)

Smith, Nigel (ed.), *Literature and Censorship* (Cambridge: D.S. Brewer, 1993)

Somerville, William, *The Poems of William Somerville* (London: The Press of C. Whittingham, 1822)

Spufford, Francis, *The Child That Books Built* (London: Faber & Faber, 2002)

Standage, Tom, *Writing on the Wall: Social Media – The First 2,000 Years* (London: Bloomsbury Publishing, 2013)

Sze, Arthur (ed.), *Chinese Writers on Writing* (Texas: Trinity Unity Press, 2010)

Taithe, Bertrand, and Tim Thornton, *Propaganda: Political Rhetoric and Identity, 1300–2000* (Stroud: Sutton Publishing, 1999)

Tedlock, Dennis, *The Spoken Word and the Work of Interpretation* (1983; Pennsylvania: University of Pennsylvania Press, 1991)

Thirlwell, Adam (ed.), *Multiples: 12 Stories in 18 Languages by 61 Authors* (London: Portobello Books, 2013)

Turville-Petre, Thorlac, *England the Nation: Language, Literature and National Identity 1290–1340* (Oxford: Oxford University Press, 1996)

Tutuola, Amos, *The Palm-Wine Drinkard* (1952; London: Faber & Faber, 1977)

319

Venuti, Lawrence (ed.), *The Translation Studies Reader* (Abingdon: Routledge, 2004)

Vise, David, *The Google Story* (2005; London: Macmillan, 2008)

Walcott, Derek, *The Poetry of Derek Walcott, 1948–2013* (London: Faber & Faber, 2014)

Wilkinson, Jane, *Talking with African Writers: Interviews with African Poets, Playwrights and Novelists* (London: James Currey, 1992)

ARTICLES AND PUBLICATIONS

Addison, Joseph, Column (*Spectator*, No. 383, 20 May 1712)

Allen, Esther (ed.), *To Be Translated or Not to Be: PEN/ IRL Report on the International Situation of Literary Translation* (Institut Ramon Llull, 2007)

Anon, 'Network Effects: How a new communications technology disrupted America's newspaper industry—in 1845' (*The Economist*, 17 December 2009)

Anon, Review of *Kinder than Solitude* (*Kirkus Reviews*, 1 February 2014)

Article 19, *Freedom of Expression and ICTs: Overview of International Standards* (Article 19, 2013)

Bell, David, 'The Bookless Future' (*New Republic*, 2 May 2005)

Berger, Joseph, 'German Students Confront the Holocaust' (*New York Times*, 10 February 2008)

Borger, Julian, 'New South African press law "more harmful than apartheid-era censorship"' (*Guardian*, 6 June 2012)

Boyle, Kevin, *Article 19 World Report 1988: Information, Freedom and Censorship* (London: Longman Group, 1988)

Brendon, Piers, 'A Moral Audit of the British Empire' (*History Today*, Vol. 57, No. 10, 2007)

Comer Kidd, David and Emanuele Castano, 'Reading Literary Fiction Improves Theory of Mind' (*Science*, 18 October 2013, Vol. 342, no. 6, 156, pp. 377–80)

Donahaye, Jasmine, *Three Percent? Publishing Data and Statistics on Translated Literature in the United Kingdom and Ireland* (Literature Across Frontiers, 2012)

Dumont, Léon, 'L'Habitude' (*Revue Philosophique*, 1876)

Engdahl, Horace, 'Canonization and World Literature: The Nobel Experience' in Karen-Margrethe Simonsen and Jakob Stougard-Nielsen (eds.),

World Literature, World Culture: History, Theory, Analysis (Aarhus: Aarhus University Press, 2008)

Evans, James, 'Electronic Journals and the Narrowing of Science and Scholarship' (*Science*, 321, 2008)

Farrington, Julia, *Taking the Offensive: Defending Artistic Freedom of Expression in the UK* (Index on Censorship, 2013)

Flood, Alison, 'Writers attack "overrated" Anglo-American literature at Jaipur festival' (*Guardian*, 20 January 2014)

Franzen, Jonathan, 'What's Wrong with the Modern World?' (*Guardian*, 13 September 2013)

Gleed, Alasdair, 'Booktrust Reading Habits Survey 2013: A national survey of reading habits and attitudes to books amongst adults in England' (DJS Research Ltd, 2013)

Goldenberg, Suzanne, 'Canadian scientists protest against government censorship' (*Guardian*, 16 September 2013)

Gordon, David, 'Big in Japan' (*New York Times*, 10 January 2014)

Holson, Laura M., 'Putting a Bolder Face on Google' (*New York Times*, 28 February 2009)

Hung, Eva, 'Giving Texts a Context: Chinese Translations of Classical English Detective Stories 1896–1916,' in David Pollard (ed.), *Translation and Creation*

Jauss, Hans Robert and Elizabeth Benzinger (tr.), 'Literary History as a Challenge to Literary Theory' (*New Literary History*, Vol. 2, No. 1, 1970)

Jivanda, Tomas, 'Twitter blocked in Turkey hours after PM Tayyip Erdogan vowed to "eradicate" website' (*Independent*, 21 March 2014)

Johnson, Steven, 'How the E-Book Will Change the Way We Read and Write' (*Wall Street Journal*, 20 April 2009)

Keller, Bill, 'Let's Ban Books, or At Least Stop Writing Them,' (*New York Times*, 13 July 2011)

Kundera, Milan, and Linda Asher (tr.), 'Die Weltliteratur' in *The Curtain: An Essay in Seven Parts* (London: Faber & Faber, 2007)

Larrabee, Eric, 'Palm-Wine Drinkard Searches for a Tapster' (*The Reporter*, 12 May 1953)

Levinson, Charles, 'Iraq's "terps" face suspicion from both sides' (*Christian Science Monitor*, 17 April 2006)

Lively, Penelope, 'Abroad' (London: Penguin, 2013)

Mason, Bruce and Sue Thomas, *A Million Penguins Research Report* (De Montfort University, April 2008)

Nabokov, Vladimir, 'Problems of Translation: *Onegin* in English' (*Partisan Review* 22, 1955)

Oberg, Kalervo, 'Cultural Shock: Adjustment to New Cultural Environments' (*Practical Anthropology 7*, 1960)

O'Hagan, Andrew, 'Ghosting' (*London Review of Books*, Vol. 36, No. 5, 6 March 2014)

Poulet, Georges, 'Phenomenology of Reading' (*New Literary History*, Vol. 1, No. 1, October 1969)

Russell, Bertrand, 'Logical Positivism' (*Revue Internationale de Philosophie*, IV (1950), 18)

Todd, Tamsin, 'Father of the Internet' (*Independent*, 17 May 1999)

Wilson, Edmund, 'The Strange Case of Pushkin and Nabokov' (*The New York Review of Books*, 15 July 1965)

WEB SOURCES AND SITES

Abrahamsen, Eric, '30 Years of. . . Literature?' (Paper Republic, 2008) (paper-republic.org/ericabrahamsen/30-years-of-literature/)

Adichie, Chimamanda Ngozi, 'The Danger of a Single Story' (TED, 2009) (ted.com/talks chimamanda_adichie_the_danger_of_a_single _story)

Arabic Literature (in English) (arablit.wordpress.com)

A Year of Reading the World (ayearofreadingtheworld.com)

Booking a Room with a View (bookingaroomwithaview.blogspot.co.uk)

Books LIVE, South Africa (bookslive.co.za)

Caribbean Literature Action Group (craiblit.org)

Caribbean Review of Books, The (caribbeanreviewofbooks.com)

Danderma's Weblog (danderma.co)

Dovegreyreader Scribbles (dovegreyreader.typepad.com)

Fox News, 'How the Blogosphere Took on CBS' Docs' (foxnews.com/story/2004/09/17/how-blogosphere-took-on-cbs-docs)

Kinna Reads (kinnareads.wordpress.com)

La Plume Burundaise (ikirundi.wordpress.com)

Me and My Big Mouth (meandmybigmouth.typepad.com)

Modern Novel, The (themodernnovel.com)

Peake-Tomkinson, Alex, 'Charlotte Mendelson: Invisible Alien' (bookanista.com/charlotte-mendelson)

Reading Around the World (uoguelph.ca/~pkron/World_Book_Project/ Welcome.html)

Reading the World (readingtheworld.co.uk)

Read Me Something You Love (readmesomethingyoulove.com)

Sleepless in Samoa (sleeplessinsamoa.blogspot.co.uk)

Taycher, Leonid, 'Books of the world, stand up and be counted! All 129,864,880 of you'(booksearch.blogspot.co.uk/2010/08/books-of-world-stand-up-and-be-counted.html)

Three Percent (rochester.edu/College/translation/threepercent)

Tony's Reading List (tonysreadinglist.blogspot.co.uk)

Tunisian Literature (in English) (tunisianlit.wordpress.com)

Världsbokbloggen (varldsbokbloggen.blogspot.se)

Winstonsdad's Blog (winstonsdad.wordpress.com)

Words Without Borders (wordswithoutborders.org)

ORGANISATIONS

The Africa Centre, London (africacentre.org.uk)

African Books Collective (africanbookscollective.com)

Anglo-Belarusian Society (absociety.org.uk)

Article 19 (article19.org)

Booktrust (booktrust.org.uk)

British Centre for Literary Translation (bclt.org.uk)

Centre for the Art of Translation (catranslation.org)

Commonwealth Writers (commonwealthwriters.org)

English PEN (englishpen.org)

Estonian Literature Centre (estlit.ee)

European Union Prize for Literature (euprizeliterature.eu)

Exiled Writers Ink! (exiledwriters.co.uk)

Free Word (freewordcentre.com)

Ingeborg Bachmann Centre for Austrian Literature, London (igrs.sas. ac.uk/ingeborg-bachmann-centre-austrian-literature)

Institut français de Mauritanie (institutfrancais-mauritanie.com)

International Writing Program, Iowa (iwp.uiowa.edu)

Literature Across Frontiers (lit-across-frontiers.org)

NGC Bocas Lit Fest, Trinidad and Tobago (bocaslitfest.com)

North Korea Books (north-korea-books.com)

Palabras Errantes (palabraserrantes.com)

Paper Republic: Chinese literature in translation (paper-republic.org)

PEN International (pen-international.org)
Poetry Translation Centre (poetrytranslation.org)
Scottish Poetry Library (scottishpoetrylibrary.org.uk)
Silverfish Books, Kuala Lumpur (silverfishbooks.com)
Sultan Qaboos Cultural Center, Washington, DC (sqcc.org)
Thai Fiction in Translation (thaifiction.com)
Translators Association (societyofauthors.org/translators-association)
University of Papua New Guinea Press and Bookshop (pngbuai.com)
Welsh Books Council (cllc.org.uk)
Words Without Borders (wordswithoutborders.org)
Writers Association of Bhutan (writersofbhutan.com)
Writers Association of The Gambia (gamwriters.com)

PERMISSIONS CREDITS

Acknowledgements

The list of people to whom I owe thanks for making this book and the project behind it possible runs into the thousands. Many of the key figures are mentioned in the foregoing pages, but there are plenty of others whom I haven't been able to include in this account, but whose contributions and support have been invaluable. Among them are colleagues who sent out links to the blog and undertook research on my behalf; friends who cheerfully agreed to root through English-language bookshops for me on trips abroad; journalists and bloggers around the globe who gave airtime and column inches to my venture, encouraging ever more people to get involved; experts who shared their knowledge in response to my sometimes frantic and often naïve questions; and of course the very many bibliophiles all over the planet who to this day visit the blog, make suggestions, share information, send me books and cheer me on.

It would be impossible to name them all. However, there are a few who deserve particularly warm thanks. Thinking back on my year of reading the world, I must mention Deng Gach Pal and Julia Duany who went to such lengths to help me get the project off to a memorable start and now face huge challenges and threats to their own safety as they try to work for lasting peace in South Sudan. And I have to take my hat off once more to the nine Portuguese speakers – all bar one of them people I had never met – who came to my rescue to translate Olinda Beja's *A casa do pastor*. Yema Ferreira, Ana Fletcher, Tamsin Harrison, Margaret Jull Costa, Clare Keates, Ana Cristina Morais, Robin Patterson, Ana Silva and Sandra Tavares, your generosity is inspiring.

I have written about the short shrift translators often get when it comes to receiving credit for their work. But the truth is that there is a host of people who rarely get much in the way of public acknowledgement behind almost every commercially published book. In my case, these people are my editors Michal Shavit and Gemma Wain in the UK and Canada, and Elisabeth Kerr in the US, whose faith in the project made it possible for my book to travel and find a home in the States; the teams at Harvill Secker and W. W. Norton & Company for their enthusiasm and expertise; and my agent Caroline Hardman, her partner Joanna Swainson and co-agent Sarah Levitt in New York, who have been unfailing sources of advice, support and encouragement. Thanks too to my friend, writer Rosie Fiore, for introducing us.

Away from the book and the blog, there are many people without whom I would never have been able to contemplate embarking on such a madcap adventure: the friends and family who not only put up with me being very dull as I tried to work my way through one book every 1.87 days for twelve months but who bore with me for years before that as I fashioned a precarious career working with words and made dubious attempts at writing. To all of you – and in particular to my mum Pat, dad Richard, and brothers David and George – I owe huge thanks (and numerous drinks).

Finally, grazie mille to the person who lived every moment of the project and writing process with me, and who built the shelf on which the books I read still sit. Steve, you have been there for me in so many ways that it would take another book to describe them. I am lucky to share my life with you. Here's to tickets and many more adventures to come.